Curriculum for Excellence

First Level
Book 1A

Written by the TeeJay Writing Group

Hachette UK's policy is to use papers that are natural, renewable and recyclable products and made from wood grown in well-managed forests and other controlled sources. The logging and manufacturing processes are expected to conform to the environmental regulations of the country of origin.

Orders

Please contact Hachette UK Distribution, Hely Hutchinson Centre, Milton Road, Didcot, Oxfordshire, OX11 7HH. Telephone: +44 (0)1235 827827. Email education@hachette.co.uk
Lines are open from 9 a.m. to 5 p.m., Monday to Friday. You can also order through our website: www.hoddereducation.co.uk.

If you have queries or questions that aren't about an order, you can contact us at hoddergibson@hodder.co.uk

The legal bit

First published in 2020 by
TeeJay Publishers, an imprint of Hodder Gibson, which is part of the Hodder Education Group.
An Hachette UK Company
211 St Vincent Street
Glasgow, G2 5QY

Impression number 5 4

Year 2023 2022 2021

Printed in the UK

A catalogue record for this title is available from the British Library.

ISBN: 978 1 9077 8942 7

First Level Book 1A

This book, along with Book 1B can be used in both Primary and Secondary with pupils who have successfully completed CfE Early Level.

- Most pupils will complete the contents of Books 1A and 1B throughout Primary 2 to 4, some earlier.
  As a guide, Book 1B might be started with the majority of pupils at the beginning of, or part way through P3.

- There are no A and B exercises. The two books cover the **entire First Level CfE course** without the teacher having to pick and choose which questions to leave out and which exercises are important. They all are!

- Pupils who cope well with the contents of First Level should commence work on Second Level during P5 or even late P4. Books 2A and 2B can then be used to work through CfE Second Level during the latter part of Primary.

- Book 1A contains a 9 page **Chapter Zero** which primarily revises every topic from CfE Early Level and can be used as a diagnostic tool. This could be followed by **TeeJay's** diagnostic assessments * of the work of Early Level.

- Non-calculator skills are emphasised and encouraged throughout the book.

- Each chapter has a **Revisit - Review - Revise** exercise as a summary. Answers for 'The 3Rs' are available at www.hoddergibson.co.uk/answers-teejay-maths-1A

- Homework is available as a photocopiable pack.*

- **TeeJay's Assessment Pack** for each Level, Early to Third, can be used topic by topic or combined to form a series of First Level cumulative Tests.

We make no apologies for the multiplicity of colours used throughout the book, both for text and in diagrams - we feel it helps brighten up the pages !!

T Strang, J Geddes, J Cairns

(January 2012)

* Available for purchase separately.

Contents

Revision of Early Level

1. Which one is **smaller** (**a** or **b**) ?

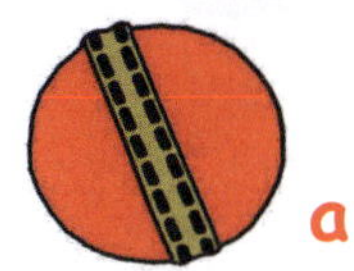

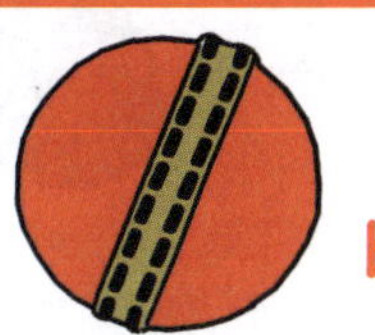

2. Which one is **bigger** ?

3. Which one is **heavier** ?

4. Which one is **lighter** ?

5. Who is **taller** - Lara or Tommy ?

6. Which is **shorter** - pen or pencil ?

7. Which holds **more** - kettle or basin ?

8. How many ?

a

b

c

d

9. a How many **more** to make **12** ?

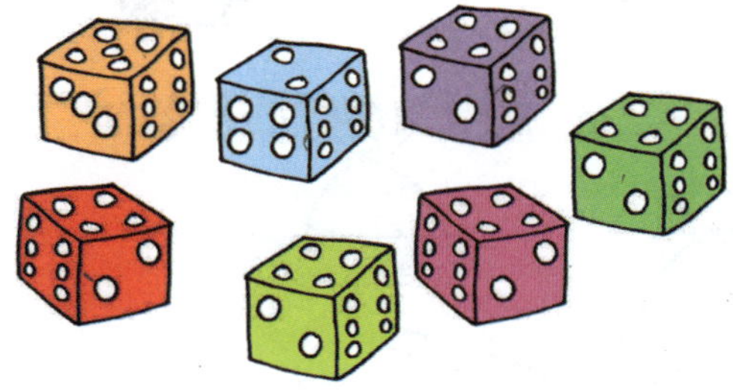

b How many **more** to make **17** ?

10. What are the **missing** numbers ?

a 12 13 14 ? 16

b 11 10 9 8 ? 6

11. Write these numbers **in order**. Start with the **smallest**.

12. a Write the number 1 less than 16.

b Write the number 2 more than 17.

13. Add :-

a 6 + 3	b 4 + 2	c 5 + 5
d 2 + 5	e 7 + 2	f 4 + 4.

14. Take away :-

a 4 - 3	b 6 - 1	c 9 - 5
d 8 - 4	e 6 - 3	f 3 - 3.

15. a How many sugar mice sweets ?

b Share them equally between 2 friends.

How many mice will each friend get ?

16. 

a How many coloured pencils ?

b Share them equally among 3 pupils.

How many pencils will each pupil get ?

17. Have any of these shapes been split into **2 equal** parts ? (**Yes** or **No**).

a

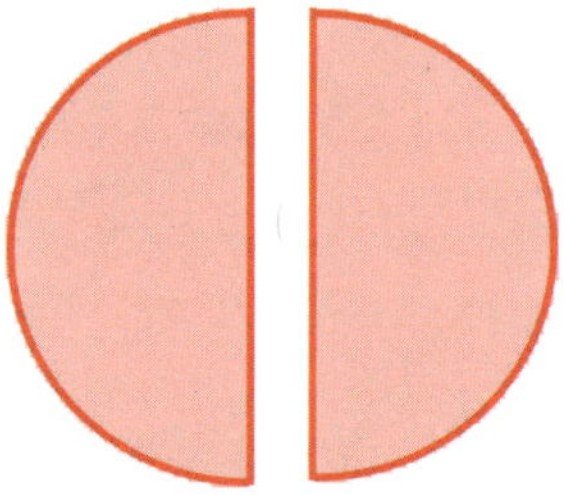

b

c

d

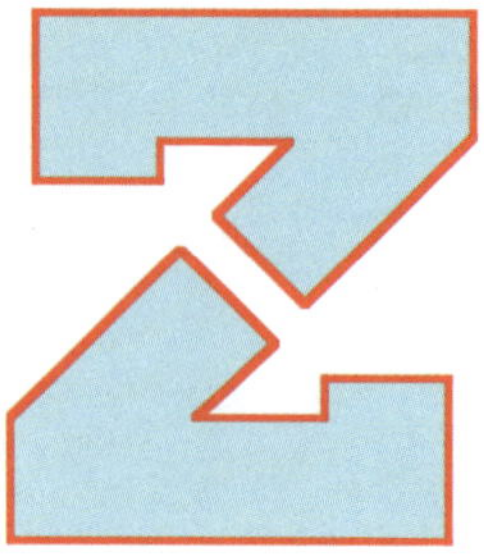

18. **How much** do each of these cost ?

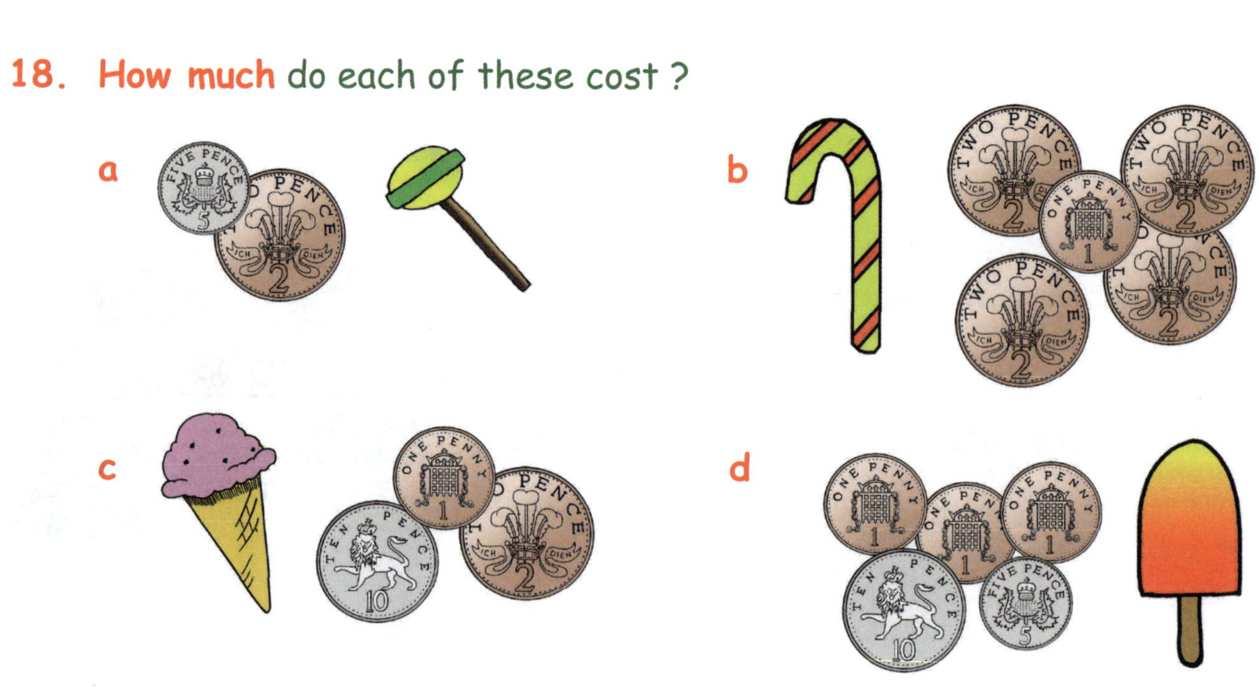

a

b

c

d

19. Which **coins** are needed to pay for these **exactly** ?

20. a How many  coins make  ?

b How many  coins make  ?

c How many  coins make  ?

21. How much **change** ?

a

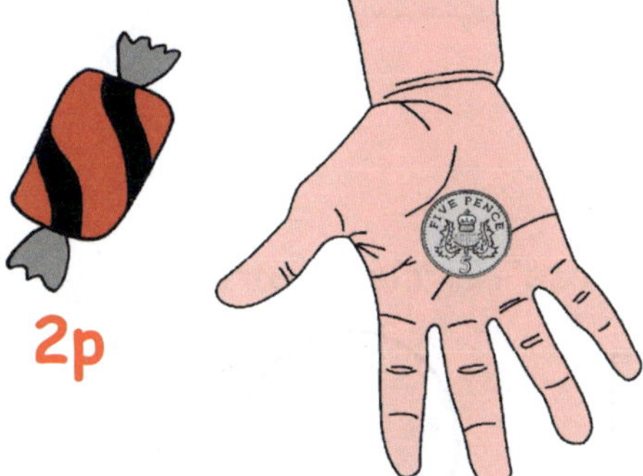

2p

b

6p

22. What **times** are shown ?

a

b

c

23. a What is the day just **before** Wednesday ?

b What day is **2** days **after** Friday ?

24. Write down the time shown on each clock :-

a

b

c

d

25. How many **pencils** can fit on this strip of wood ?

26. Draw the **next** shape in these patterns :-

a 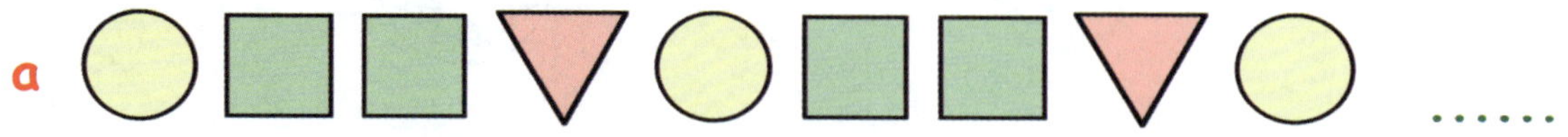 ......

b  ......

27. Write the name of each **shape**. (Choose - circle, square, triangle, rectangle).

a 
b 
c 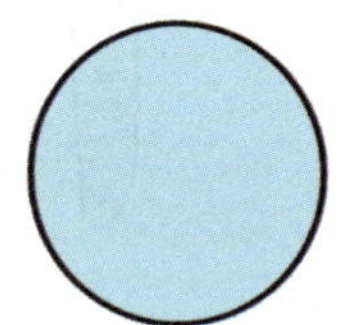
d 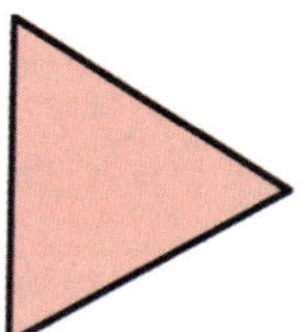

28. Write the name of each **object**. (Choose from cone, pyramid, cylinder, cube).

a 
b 
c 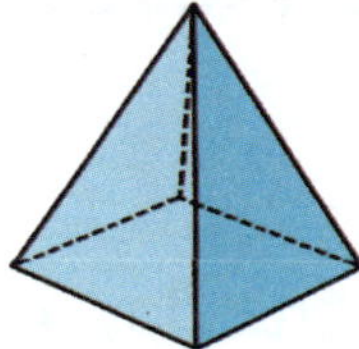
d 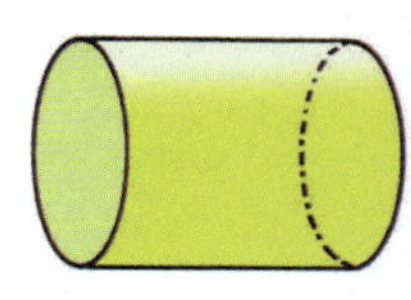

29. a Which fruit is **just** in **front** of the melon ?

b Which fruit is **just behind** the strawberry ?

c Which fruit is **at the back** ?

30. This shape has a cube, a cuboid, a cone and a cylinder.

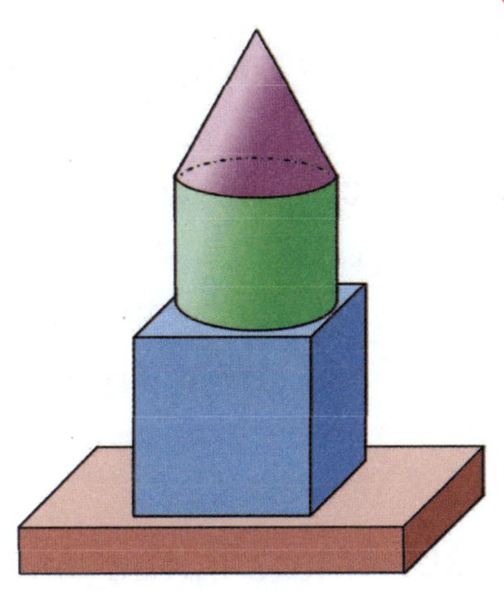

  a Which shape is **on top** ?

  b Which shape is **just above** the cube ?

  c Which shape is **just below** the cube ?

31. Look at the farm animals.

  a Which animal is **on the very left** ?

  b Which animal is **just to the right** of the pig ?

  c Which animal is **just to the left** of the cow ?

  d Which animal is **in the middle** ?

32. Do these shapes have **symmetry** ? (**Yes** or **No**).

a 

b 

c 

33. How many ?   a I I I   b I I I I I I

34. a How many **children** ?

b How many **girls** ?

c How many **boys** wearing **glasses** ?

35. Mugs in the dinner hall.

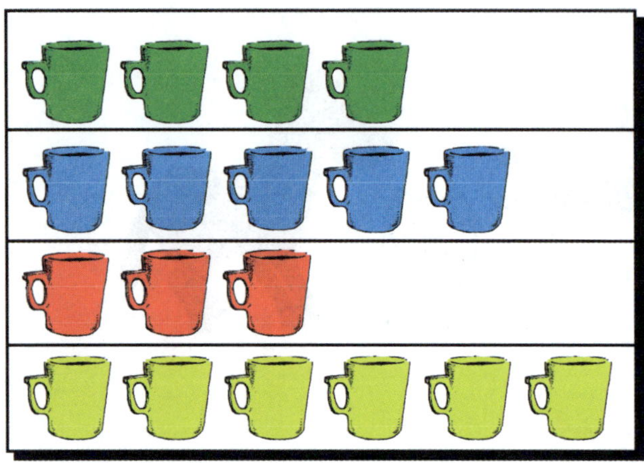

a How many **green** mugs ?

b How many **blue** mugs ?

c How many mugs **altogether** ?

d How many **more yellow** mugs than **red** mugs ?

36. Coins in Tim's pocket.

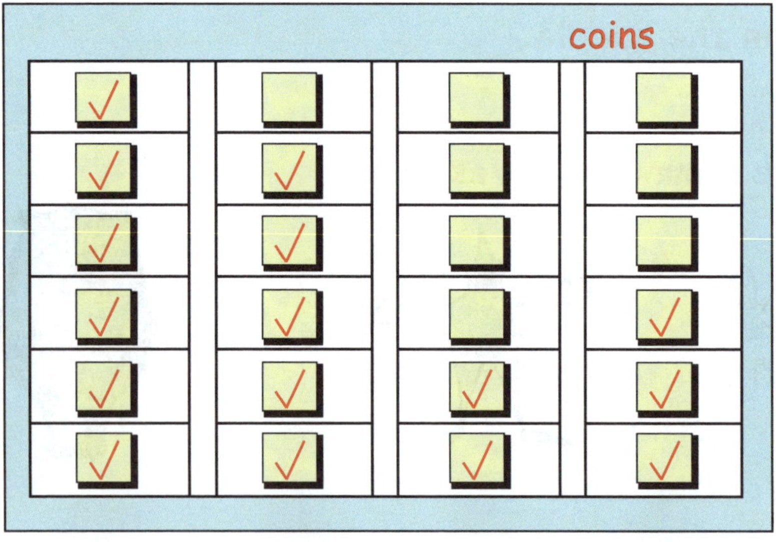

a How many  ?

b How many  ?

c How many **more**  than  ?

37. School Sports Day is on today.

a What event is on at 11.00 ?

b At what time are the **prizes** ?

c When is **lunch** ?

Time	Event
10.00	Long Jump
11.00	100 metres
Noon	Lunch
1.00	Team Relay
2.00	Prizes

38. Two shop prices are as shown.

Where is it **cheaper** to buy :-

a the bike

b the doll's house ?

	Toyshop	Superstore
Bike	£10	£8
Doll's House	£12	£14

39. Look at the TV times shown.

a What is on **BBC 1** at :-

(i) 4.00 (ii) 6.00 ?

b What is on **BBC 2** at :-

(i) 5.00 (ii) 6.00 ?

c On what channel **and** at what time is the News on ?

d I turn on the TV on BBC 2 at ten minutes **before** six o'clock.

What am I watching ?

TV Times

Time	BBC 1	BBC 2
4.00	Kid Zone	News
5.00	Jungle Fun	Quiz
6.00	Cartoons	Weather

Whole Numbers 1

Understand place value for numbers up to 20.

Numbers 1 - 20

Remember what the number 17 means.

17 means 1 7 (tens units) = 1 lot of ten and 7 units.

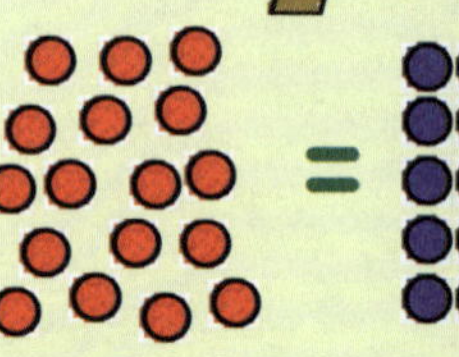

You should know all the numbers from 1 to 20.

Exercise 1

Worksheet 1·1

1. a 14 means 1 lot of ten and .... units.

   b 19 means .... lot of ten and .... units.

   c 12 means .... lot of .... and .... units.

2. Write down all the missing numbers :-

   a 1 2 3 .... 5 .... 7 8 9 ....

   b 11 .... 13 14 .... 16 17 20

   c 2 3 .... 6 .... 8 .... 11 ....

   d 8 9 .... 13 .... 15 ....

   e 10 9 .... 7 6 .... 3 2 1

   f 20 19 .... 17 .... 15 14 11

   g 9 .... 7 5

   h 15 11

   i 20 19 ....

   j .... 10 9 .... .

Numbers 20-30

Recognise and Order numbers from 20 to 30.

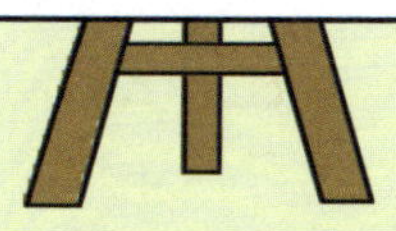

Each **full** jar holds 10 sweets. Count them.

Here, we have 1 full jar and 7 sweets.

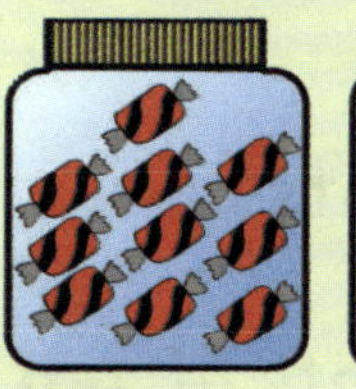

= 17 sweets.

Here, we have 2 full jars.

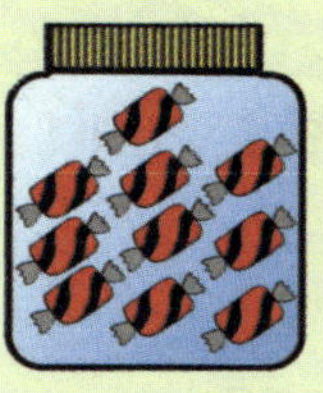

This is called 20 (twenty).

This time, we have 2 full jars and 4 sweets.

This is called 24 (twenty four).

24 means 2 (tens) 4 (units) = 2 lots of ten and 4 units.

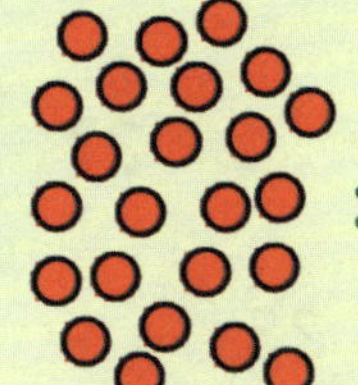

Exercise 2

Worksheet 1·2

1. How many sweets ?

a  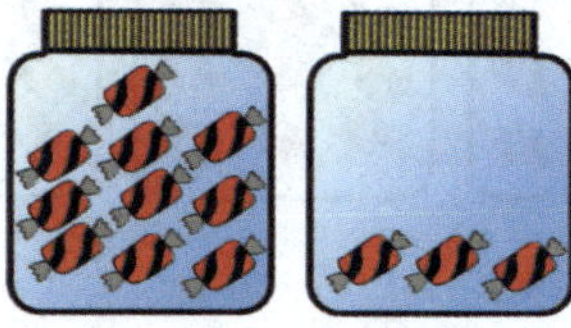

b 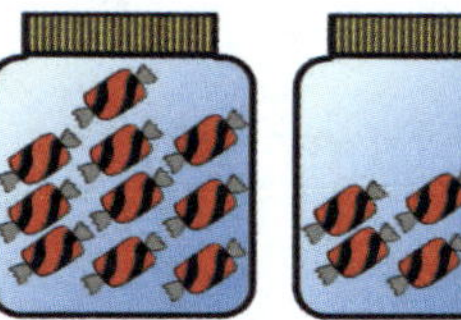

c 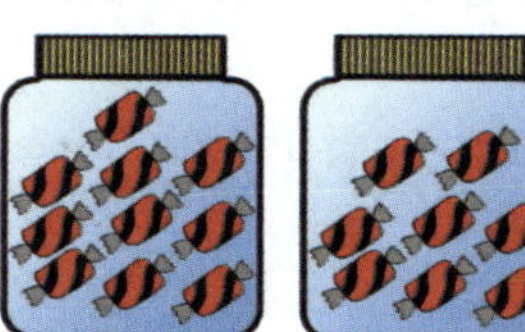

d 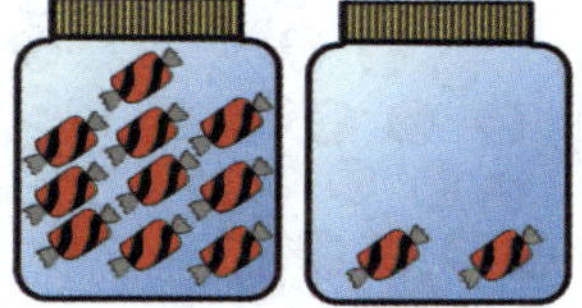

e 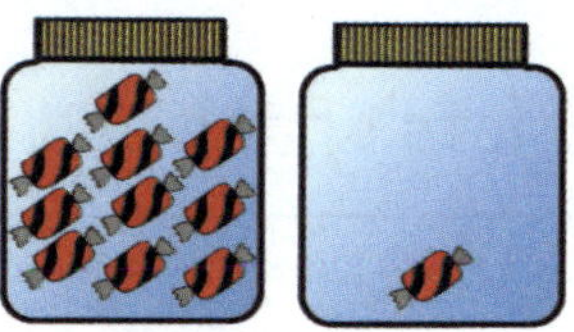

f  

Worksheet 1·3

2. Draw empty jars like this.

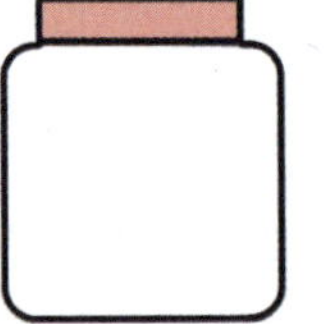

Fill them with sweets to show :-

a 21 b 24 c 27 d 29

e 20 f 23 g 25 h 28.

3. a 23 means 2 lots of ten and .... units.

b 26 means .... lots of ten and .... units.

c 24 means .... lots of .... and .... units.

4. Write down all the missing numbers :-

a 21 .... 23 24 .... 26 27 29

b 12 13 .... 16 .... 18 19 22

c 18 19 .... 24 .... 26 ....

d 29 .... 27 26 .... 23 22 21

e 24 23 .... 21 .... 19 18 15

f 16 .... 18 ....

The number just after 29 is called thirty.

It is written as 30. (Three lots of 10).

	tens	units	
30 means	3	0	= 3 lots of ten and 0 units.

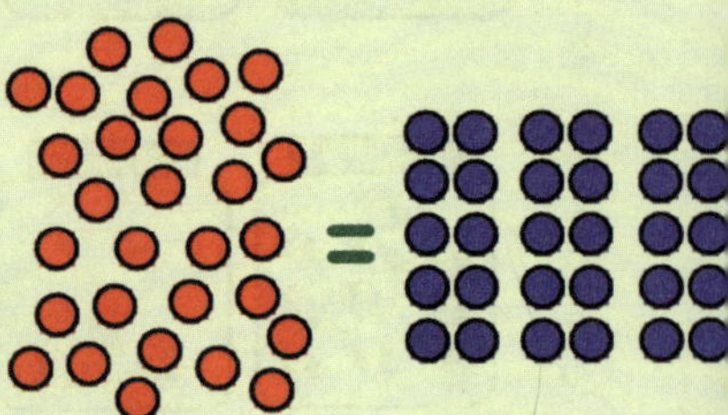

Numbers from 30 to 100

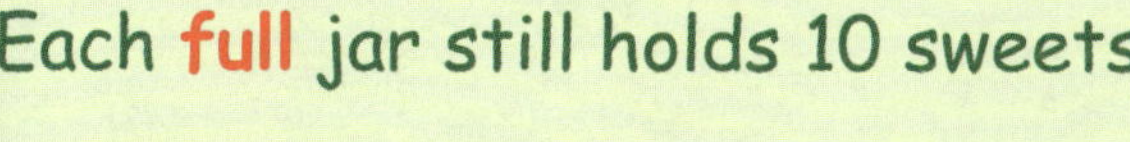

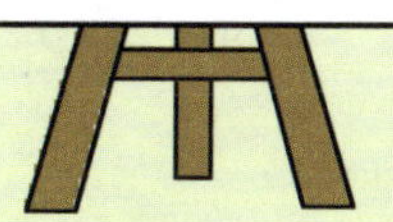

Recognise and Order numbers from 30 to 100.

Each **full** jar still holds 10 sweets.

3 full jars and **4 sweets**.

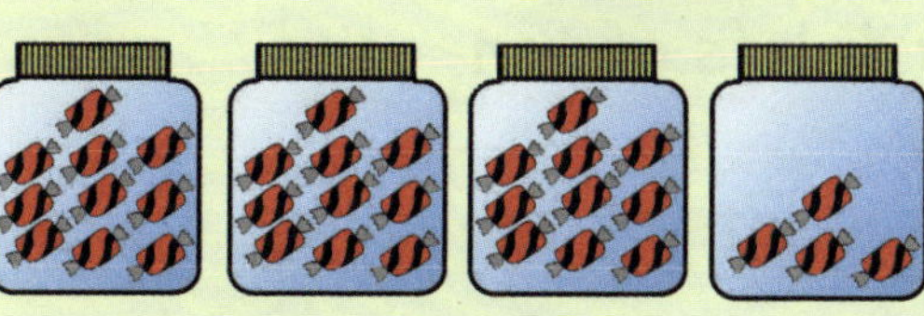

= **34 sweets**.

4 full jars and **7 sweets**.

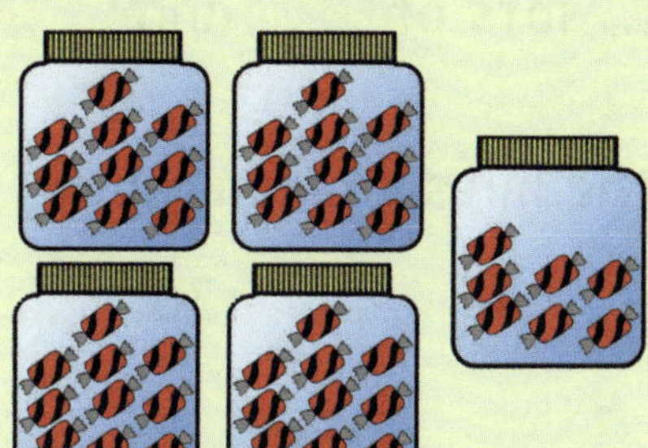

= **47 sweets**.

This time, we have **6 full jars**.

= **60 sweets**.

Exercise 3

Worksheet 1·4

1. How many sweets ?

a

 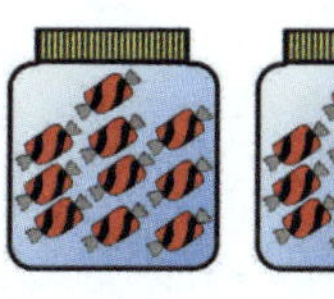 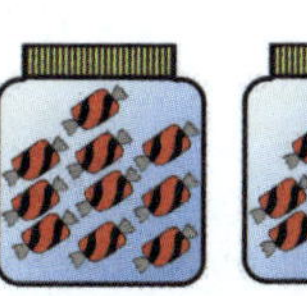 

b

  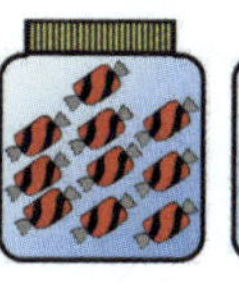 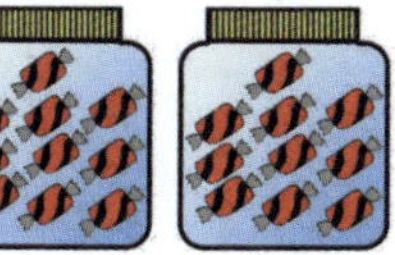

c

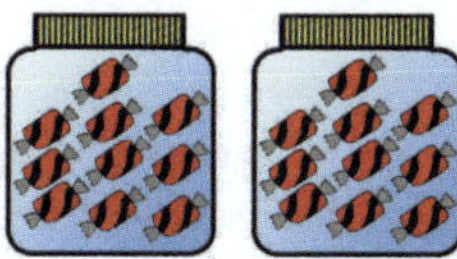  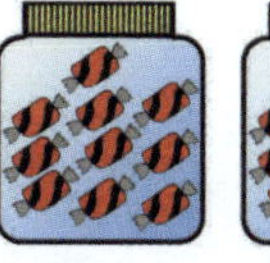  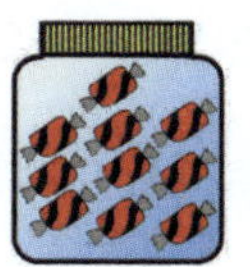 

d

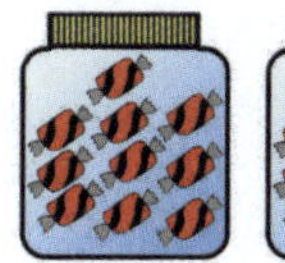      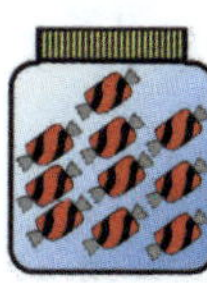  

Worksheet 1·5

2. Draw empty jars like this.
   Fill them with sweets to show :-

   a 32   b 46   c 54   d 69.

3. a **54** means **5** lots of **ten** and .... **units**.

   b **68** means .... lots of **ten** and .... **units**.

   c **91** means .... lots of .... and .... **units**.

4. Write down all the missing numbers.

   a 31 32 .... 34 .... 36 .... 39 ....

   b 60 61 .... 64 .... 67 ....

   c 83 84 85 .... 87 90

   d 47 48 .... 51 .... 53 .... 55 ....

   e 79 .... 81 83   f 38 .... 40 42

   g 57 .... 59 ....   h .... 97 .... 99 ....

5. Write down all the missing numbers.

   a 57 56 54   b 39 .... 37 36 ....

   c 90 .... 88 86   d .... 65 64 ....

6. What is the next number **up** from :-

   a 37   b 56   c 79   d 90 ?

7. What is the number just **down** from :-

   a 48   b 23   c 81   d 60 ?

8. **Copy** this grid of numbers.
Fill in all the missing numbers.

Worksheet 1·6

0	1	2	---	4	---	6	7	8	---
10	11	---	13	---	15	16	---	18	---
20	---	22	23	---	25	---	27	28	---
30	31	---	33	---	35	---	---	38	39
---	41	---	43	---	---	46	---	48	---
50	---	---	53	---	---	---	57	---	59
---	---	62	63	---	65	---	---	68	---
70	---	---	---	---	---	---	77	---	79
80	---	---	---	---	85	---	---	88	---
---	91	---	93	---	---	---	---	---	---

9. What is the number just up from **99** ?

10. Use your table of numbers here. What is the next number ?

a 2 4 6 8 10 12 .....
b 5 7 9 11 13 15 .....
c 14 16 18 20 22 .....
d 31 33 35 37 39 .....
e 10 20 30 40 50 .....
f 25 35 45 55 65 .....

11. What is the next number ?

a 16 14 12 10 8 .....
b 25 23 21 19 17 .....
c 55 45 35 25 .....
d 100 80 60 40 .....

Word Problems

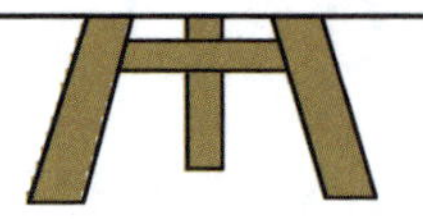

Be able to solve problems given in a word sentence.

Exercise 4

1. John is 62 years old. Alex is 2 years **older**.

   How old is Alex ?

2. Billy has 59p. Joe has 3p **more** than Billy.

   How much does Joe have ?

3. Jana is 87 cm tall. Kayley is 2 cm **taller**.

   How tall is Kayley ?

4. Zac weighs 39 kilograms. John is 4 kilograms **heavier**.

   What weight is John ?

5. Lisa has £28.

   Jameela has £5 **more** than Lisa.

   How much money has Jameela ?

6. Troy is 50 years old. Dave is 3 years **younger**.

   How old is Dave ?

7. Gill has 31 T-shirts.

   Lynn has 2 fewer T-shirts than Gill.

   How many T-shirts does Lynn have?

8. The dog is 46 centimetres tall.

   The cat is 4 centimetres **smaller**.

   How tall is the cat ?

Worksheet 1·7

Reading Scales

Exercise 5

Worksheet 1·8

Recognise where numbers should be placed on a scale.

1. What number is the arrow pointing to ?

39 40 41 42 43 44 45 50

2. What numbers are the arrows pointing to ?

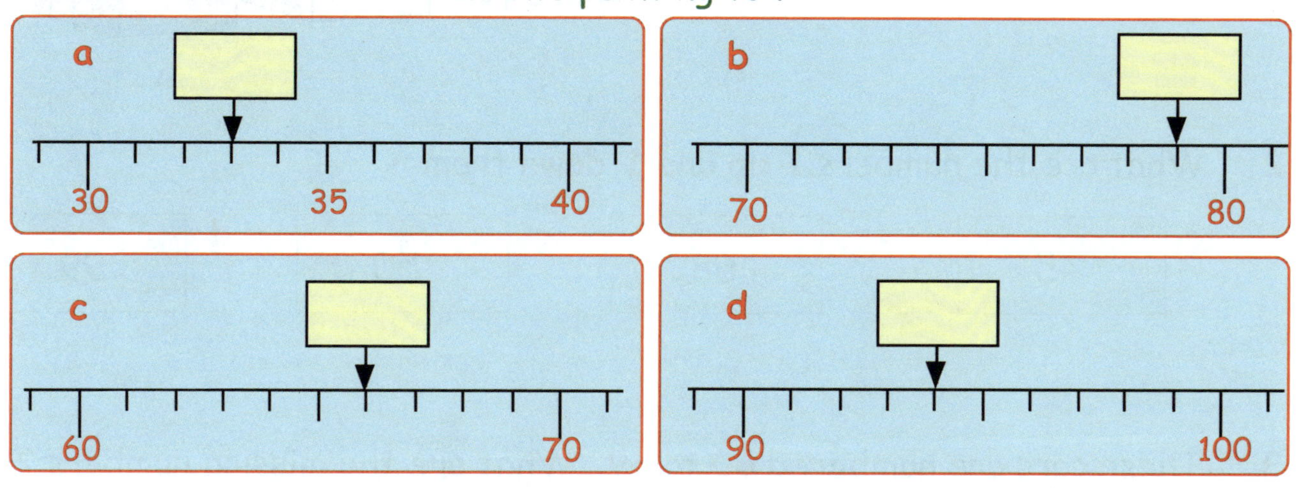

3. Write the missing numbers.

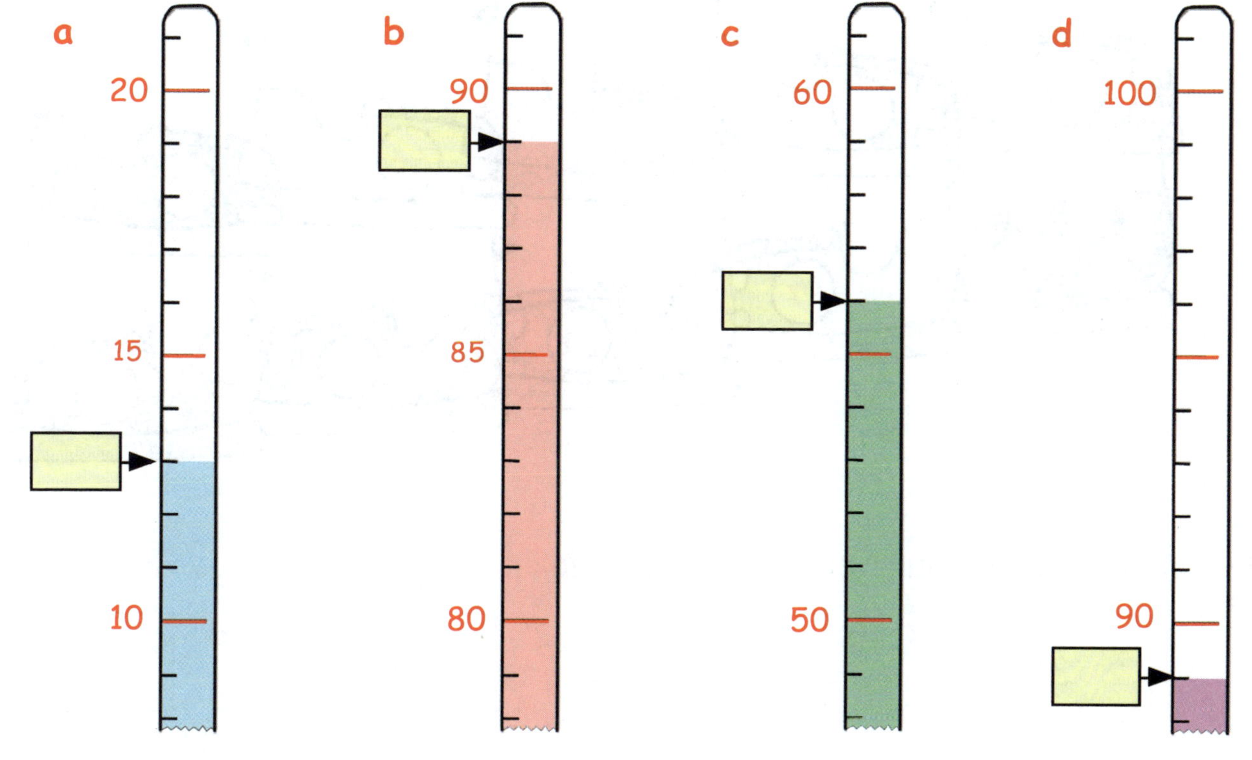

Missing Numbers

Exercise 6

Be able to recognise patterns and insert missing numbers.

Worksheet 1·9

1. What are the missing house numbers ?

2. What are the numbers **1 up** and **1 down** from :-

a ... 45 ... b ... 68 ... c ... 50 ... d ... 99 ...

3. These cars are numbered **60** to **69**. What are the missing numbers ?

4. What are the numbers **2 up** and **2 down** from :-

a ... 36 ... b ... 84 ... c ... 22 ... d ... 91 ...

Worksheet 1·10

5. The boats are numbered **91** to **100**.

What are the **3** missing numbers ?

6. These cards are numbered **in order**.

75 is the **smallest** numbered card.

What number is on the **bottom** card ?

7.

end
start
70
40
42
44
46
50
54
60
62

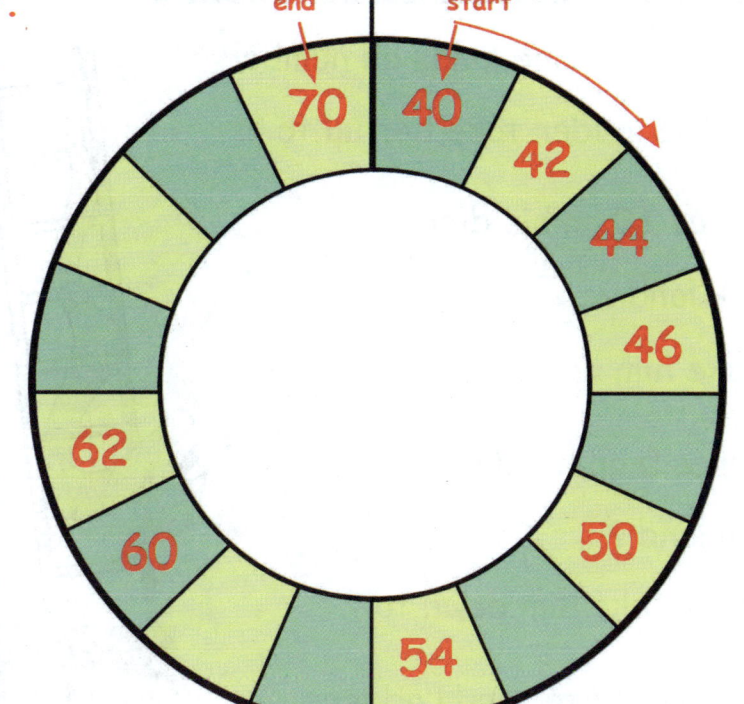

The numbers on this wheel go from **40** to **70**.

They go up in **2's**.

Copy or **trace** the wheel and fill in the missing numbers.

Snakes and Ladders

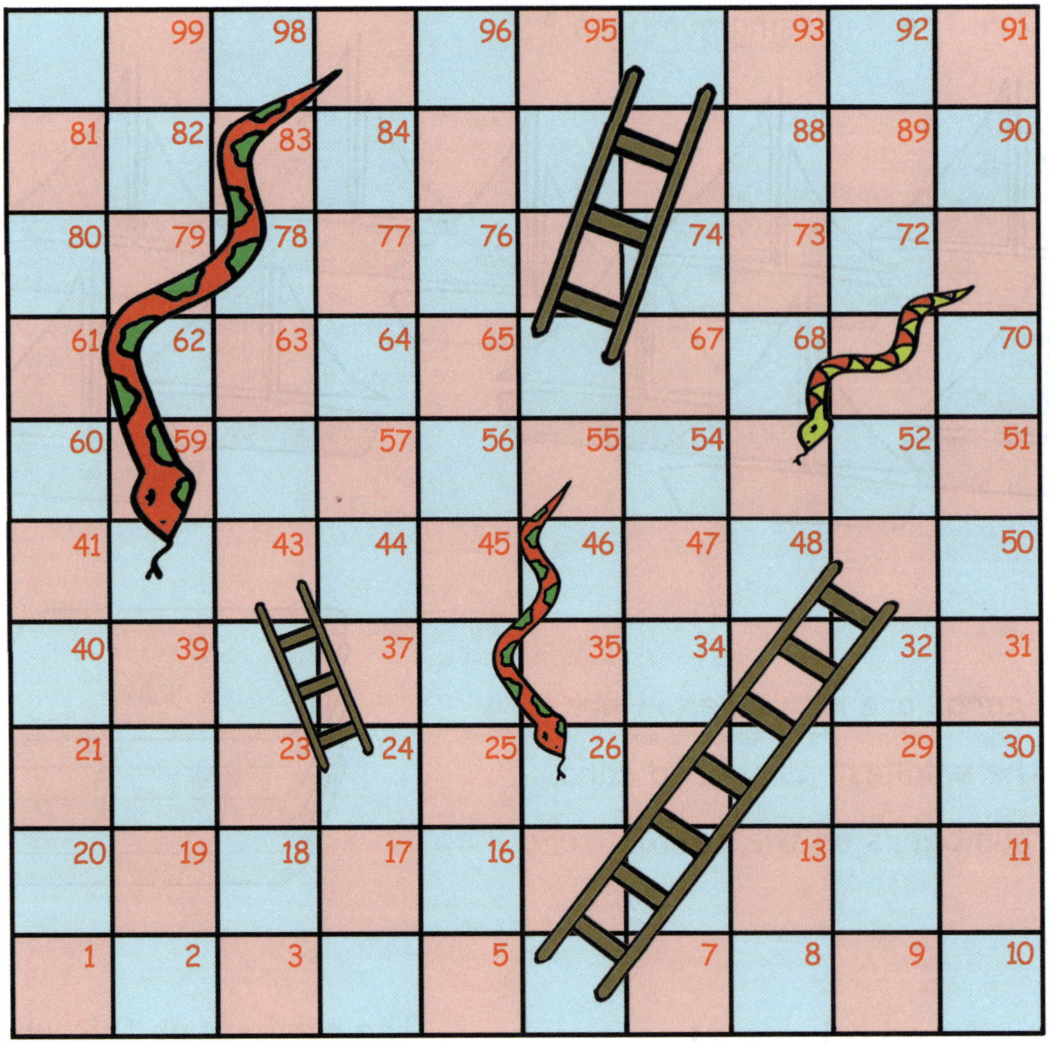

	99	98		96	95		93	92	91
81	82	83	84				88	89	90
80	79	78	77	76		74	73	72	
61	62	63	64	65		67	68		70
60	59		57	56	55	54		52	51
41		43	44	45	46	47	48		50
40	39		37		35	34		32	31
21		23	24	25	26			29	30
20	19	18	17	16			13		11
1	2	3		5		7	8	9	10

8. Laura is playing Snakes and Ladders. She lands on number **6**.

   What numbered square does the ladder take her **up** to ?

9. Rick is on square **61**. He scores **10** on his dice.

   a On what square does Rick land ?

   b Where does the snake take him **down** to ?

10. Ian is on square **92**. He scores **5** on his dice.

    a On what square does Ian land ?

    b Where does the long snake take him **down** to ?

11. Ask your teacher if you can play Snakes and Ladders.

Worksheet 1·11

The 3 Я's

Revisit - Review - Revise

1. How many sweets are in these jars ?

a  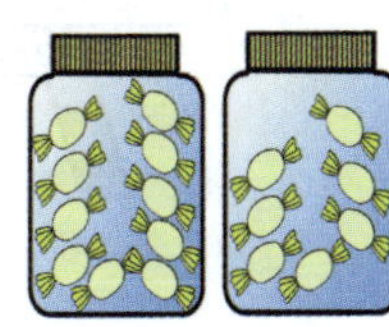

b 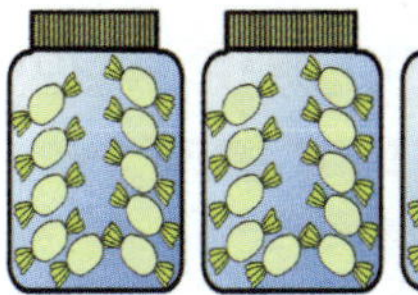

c   

2. Write down all the missing numbers :-

   a 4 5 .... 7 8 9 .... 11 ....

   b 26 25 24 .... 21 ....

   c 5 7 9 11 .... 19 ....

   d 75 65 55 .... 15 ....

   e 80 70 .... 40 .... 10 ....

3. What is the number just **up** from :-

   a 27 b 46 c 59 d 90 ?

4. What is the number **two down** from :-

   a 12 b 25 c 50 d 81 ?

5. What numbers do arrows A, B and C point to ?

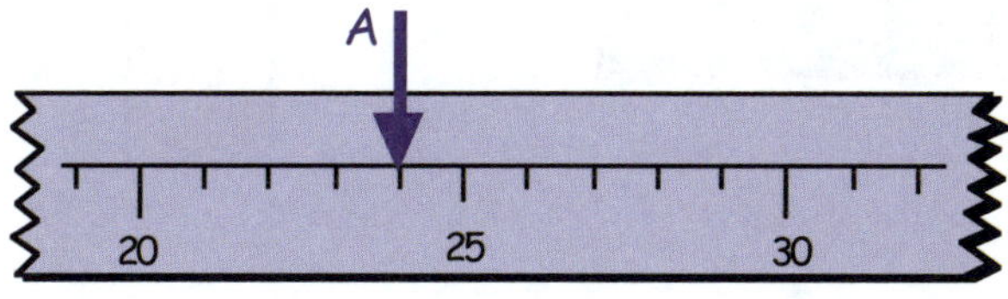

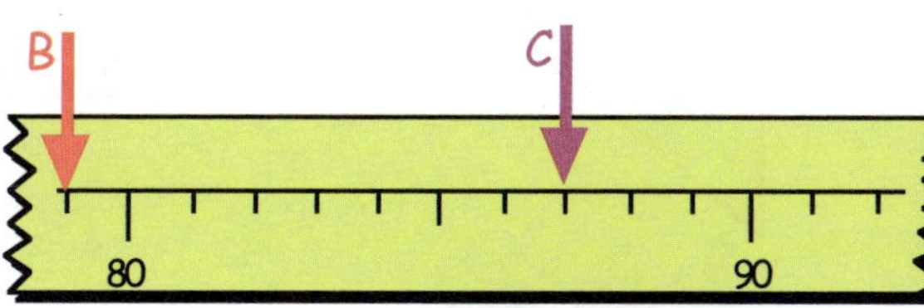

6. There are 27 pastries on a plate.

   If Harry eats 5 of them, how many are left ?

7. A vending machine has 36 packets of sandwiches in it.

   If 4 more are put in, how many will there be now ?

Symmetry

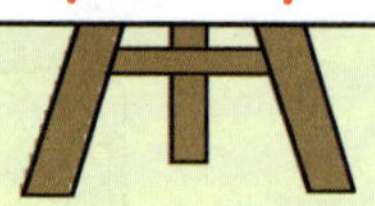

When a shape is folded along a line and the 2 parts fit exactly, the shape is said to have **symmetry** (or be **symmetrical**).

Can you see that each shape below has symmetry ? (They can be folded over a line and fit exactly).

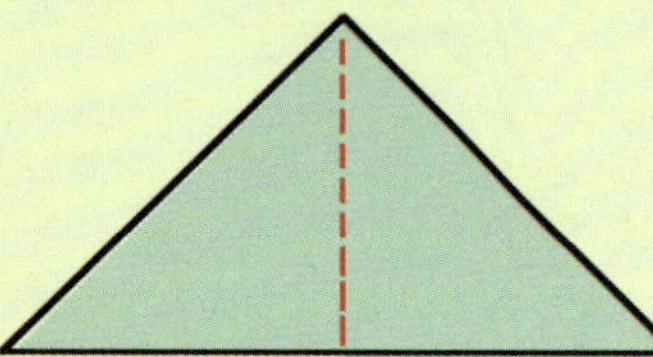

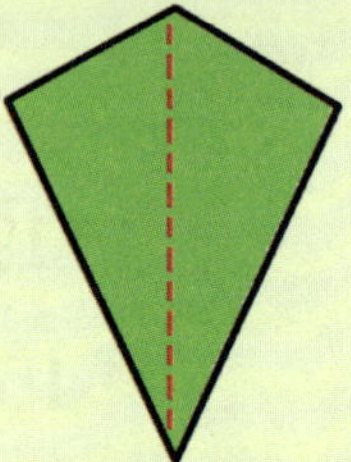

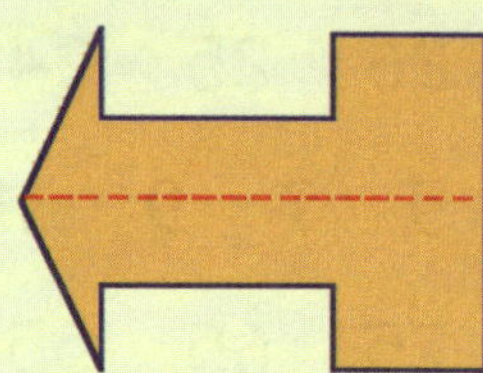

These shapes are **symmetrical**.

Exercise 1

Worksheet 2·1 Worksheet 2·2

1. Do these shapes have symmetry ? (Write Yes or No).

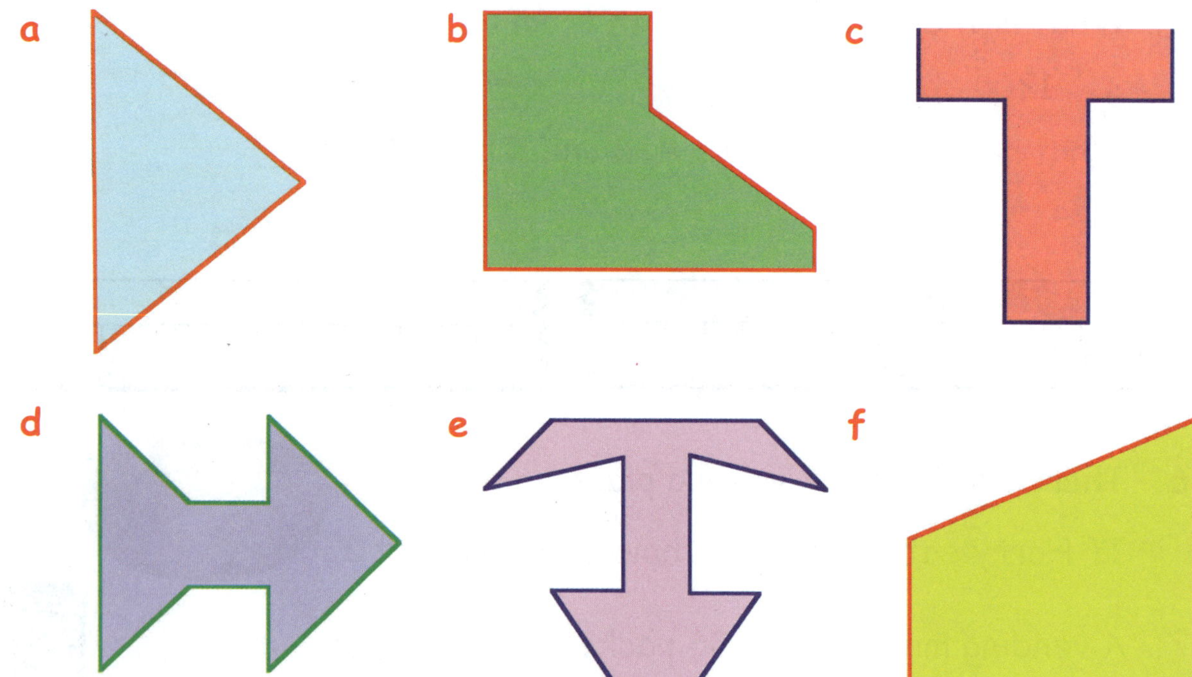

2. Do these shapes have symmetry ? (Write Yes or No).

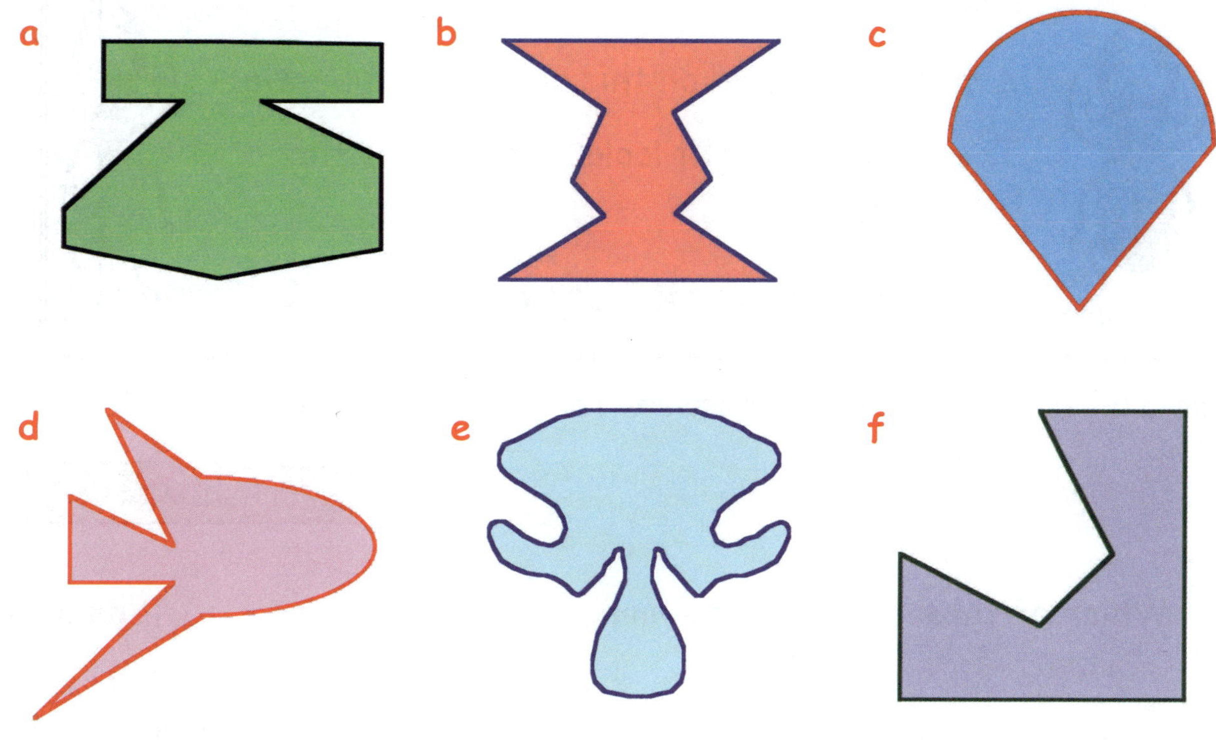

3. The shapes below are ALL symmetrical.

How many ways can each shape be folded to show symmetry ?

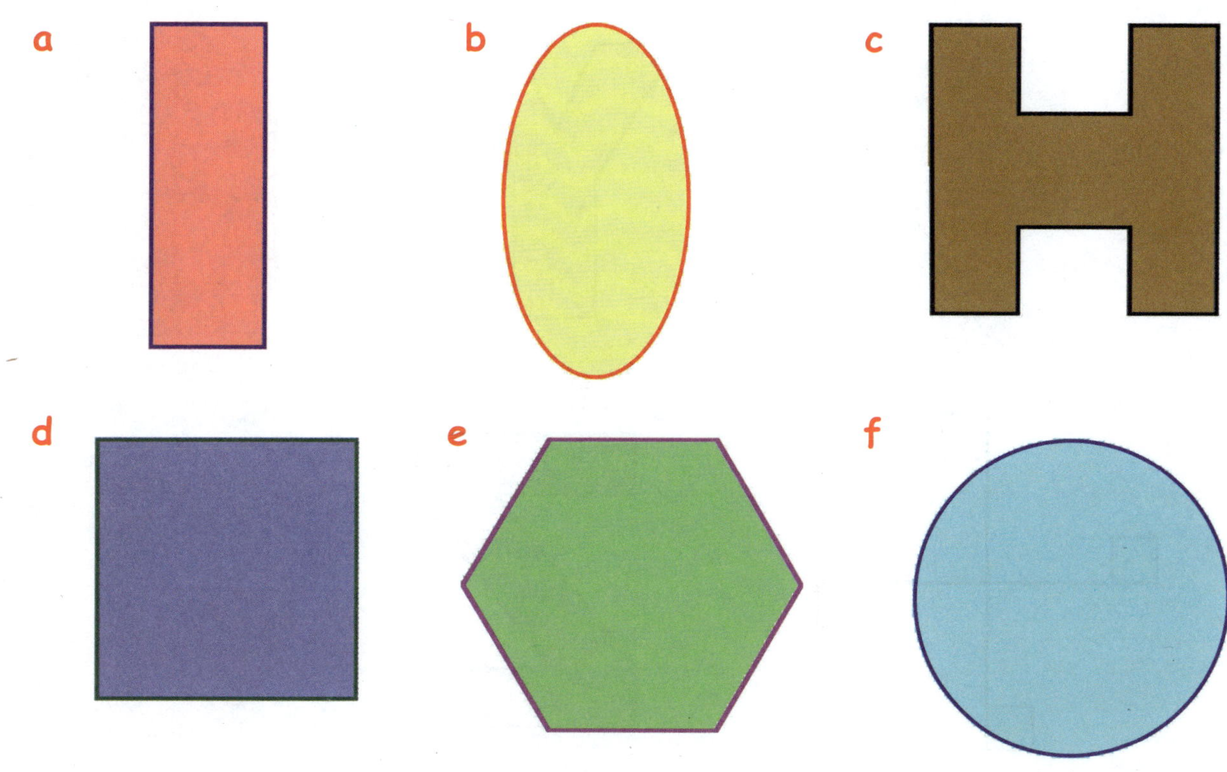

Symmetry can be found using a **mirror**.

A mirror is placed on this picture of a beetle.

The **bit** on the right looks the same as the **bit** on the left.

The mirror shows the picture is **symmetrical**.

Use a **mirror** to check your answers for the last two pages.

Worksheet 2·4

4. Which of these shapes are **symmetrical** ? **(Use a mirror)**. (**Yes** or **No**).

a

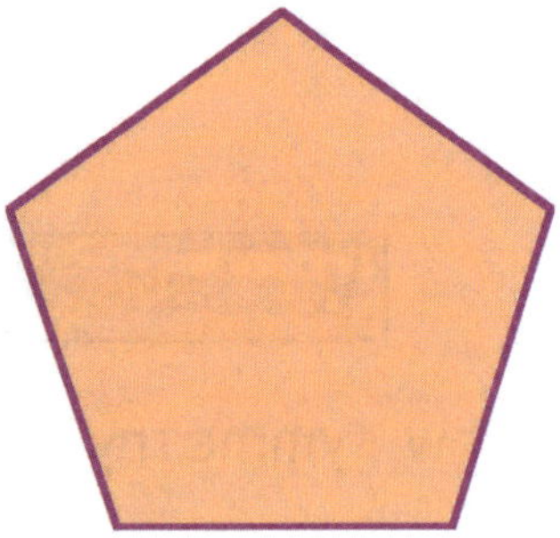

b

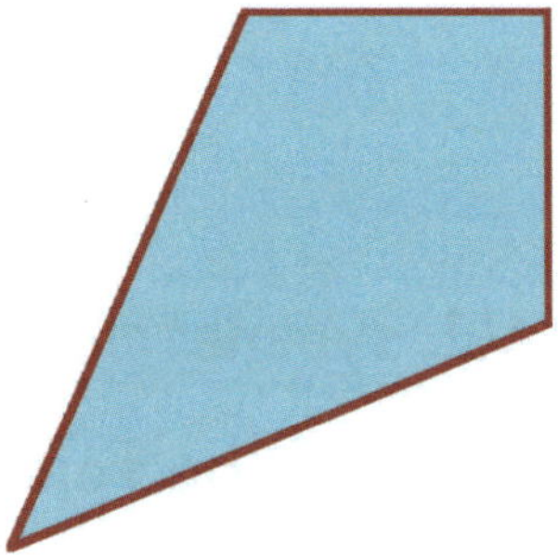

c

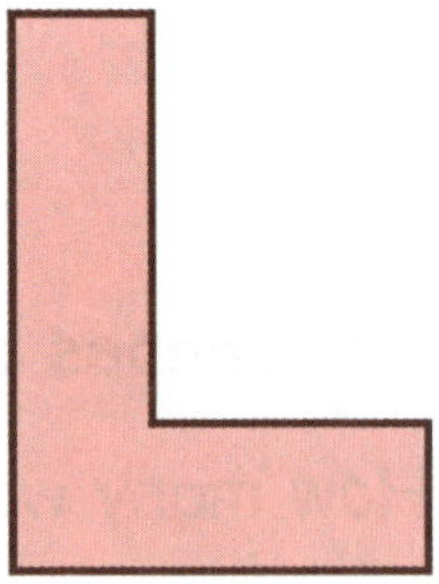

d

e

f

g

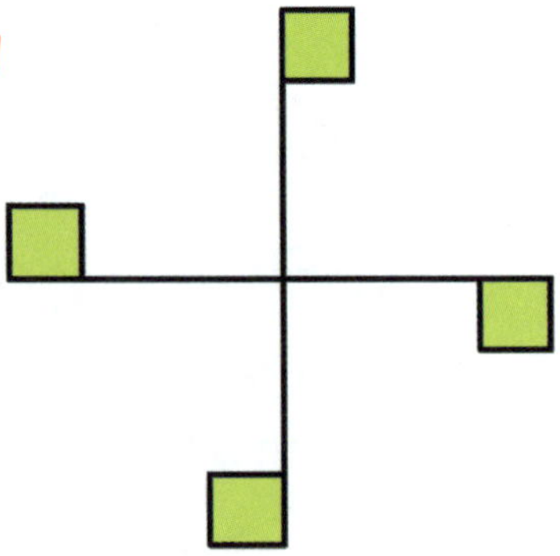

h

i

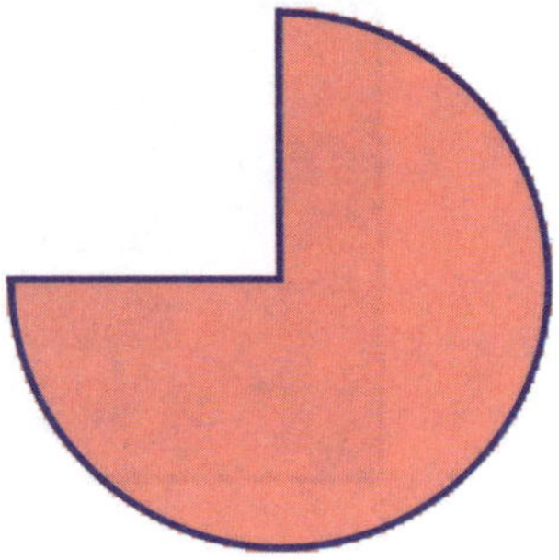

Symmetry in the Real World

Identify symmetry in the real world.

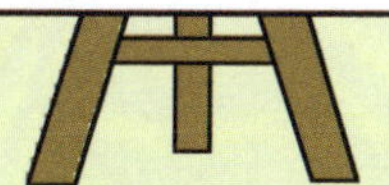

Symmetry can also be found in the real world.

Exercise 2

1. Use a mirror to check that the pictures above are **symmetrical**.

2. Which of these pictures are **symmetrical** ? **(Use a mirror)**.

a

b

c

d

e

f

g

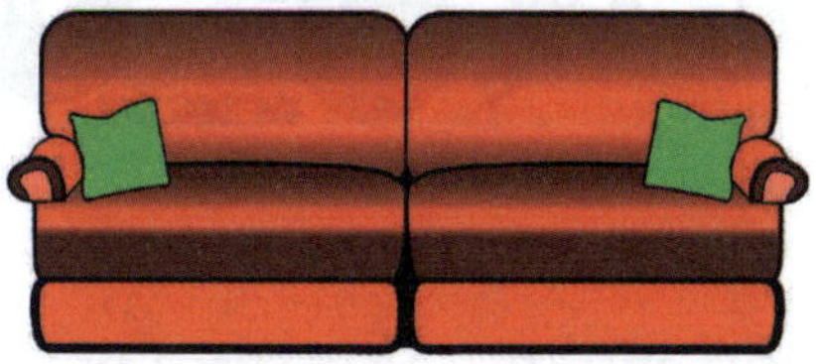

h

i

2. j

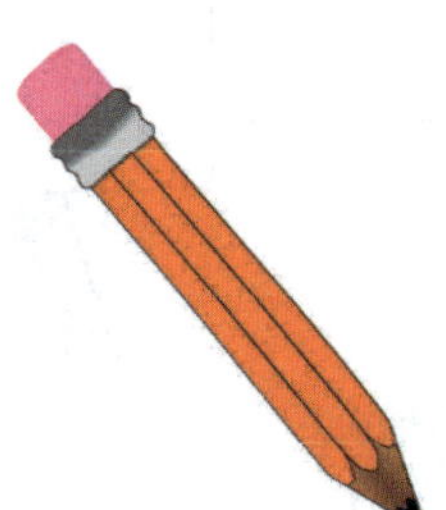

k

l

3. Which of these road signs are **symmetrical** ? (Yes or No).

a

b

c

d

e

f

4. Write down a list of things that have symmetry in :-

a the classroom b your house.

5. Look at the road signs above.

a Find out the meaning of each sign.

b Find other road signs that are symmetrical. (Find out what they mean).

6. Collect some pictures that are symmetrical and make a poster for your classroom wall.

7. Which of the four shapes, (A, B, C or D), should be added to the pink shape to make it symmetrical ?

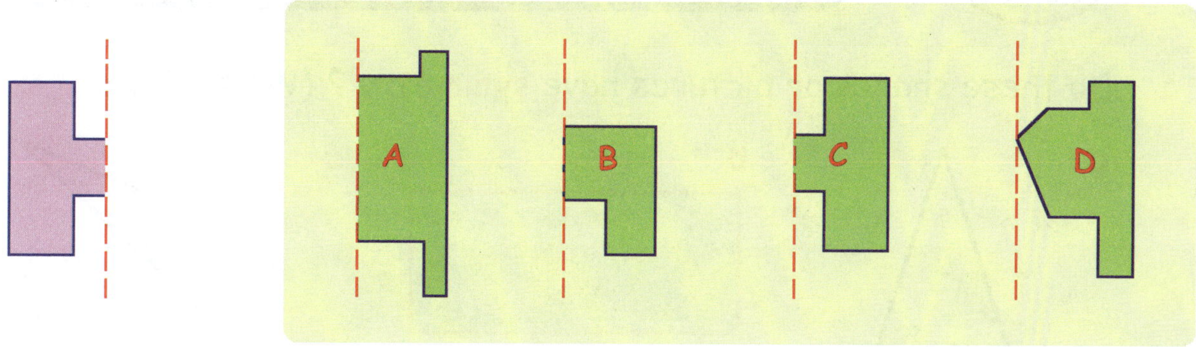

8. Which of the four shapes, (E, F, G or H), should be added to the orange shape to make it symmetrical ?

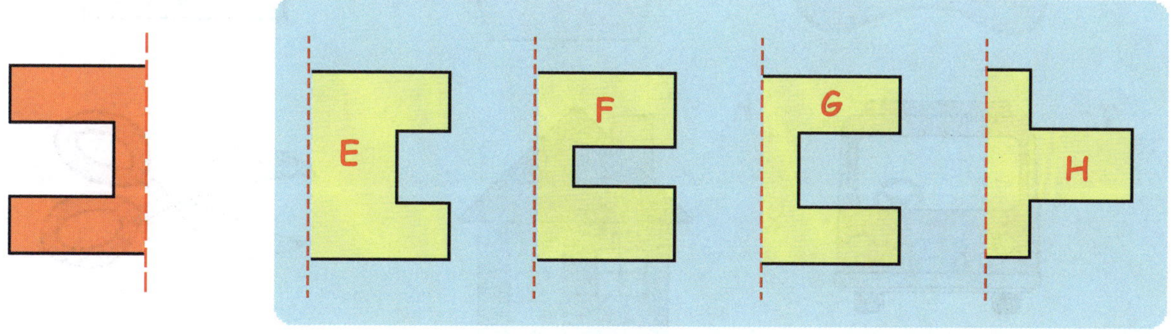

9. Which of the four shapes, (P, Q, R or S), should be added to the purple shape to make it symmetrical ?

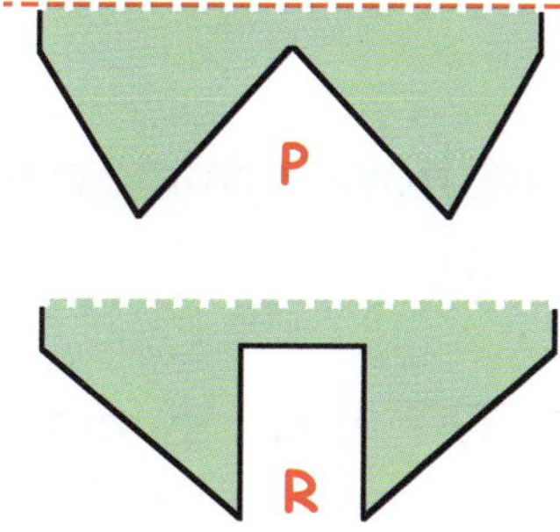

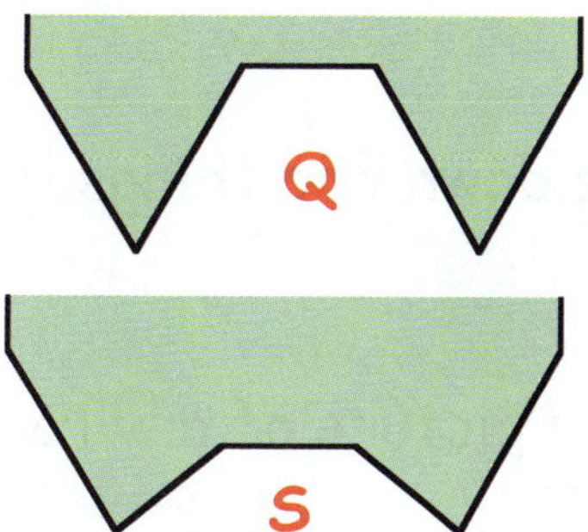

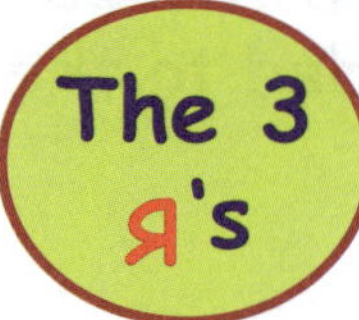

Revisit - Review - Revise

1. Do these shapes or pictures have **symmetry** ? (Write **Yes** or **No**).

a

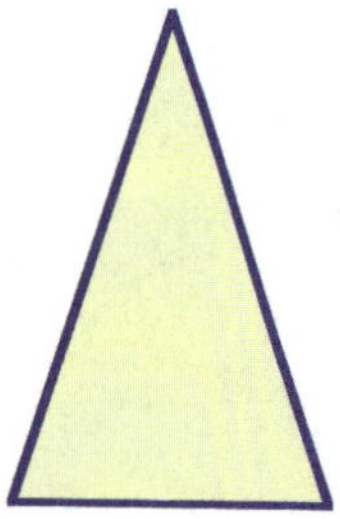

b

c

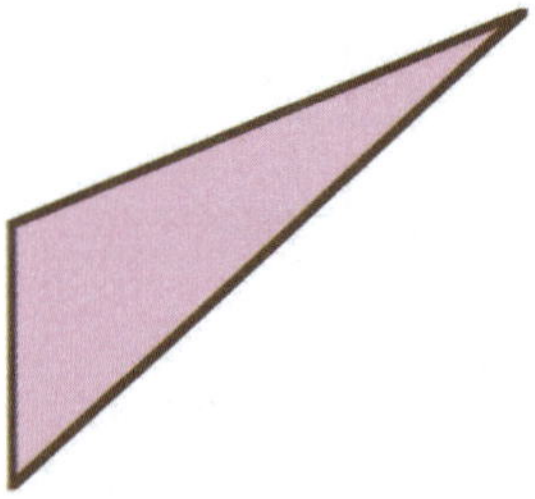

d

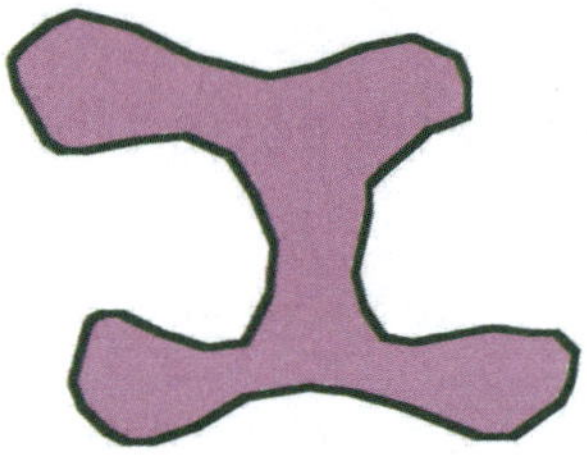

e

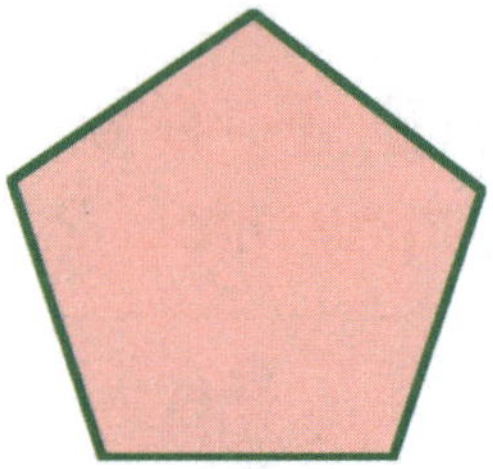

f

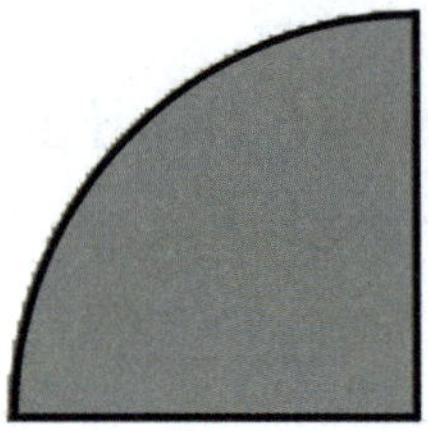

g

h

i

j

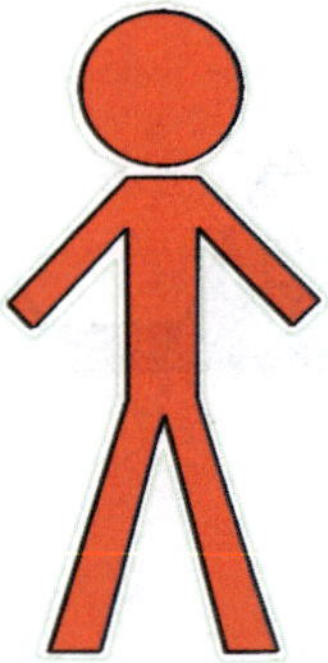

k

l

2. Write down five things in the real world that have symmetry.

3. Draw a picture of any road sign that does **NOT** have symmetry.

Whole Numbers 2

Hundreds, Tens and Units

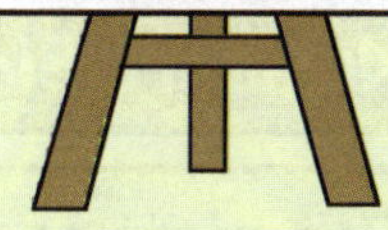

Remember :- 54 is 5 tens and 4 units.

	tens	units	
54 means	5	4	= 5 lots of ten and 4 units.

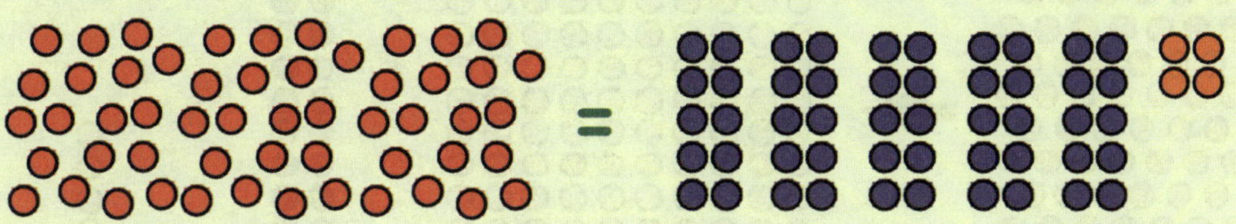

Exercise 1

1. **Copy** the picture and put in numbers and counters to finish it.

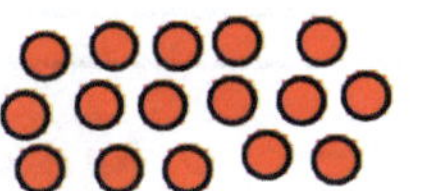

=

16 = ... ten and ..... units

2. **Copy** and **fill in** the boxes to make the correct number :-

a	13 = [1] ten and [ ] units	b	27 = [ ] tens and [7] units
c	34 = [ ] tens and [ ] units	d	41 = [ ] tens and [ ] unit
e	68 = [ ] tens and [ ] units	f	70 = [ ] tens and [ ] units
g	9 = [ ] tens and [ ] units	h	99 = [ ] tens and [ ] units.

3. I have 57 one pence coins. I want to put them in bundles of 10.

   a How many **full** bundles of 10 can I make ?

   b How many one pence coins will I have left over ?

4. Angus bought **83** tropical fish. He wants to put them in tanks with 10 fish in each tank.

   a How many **full** tanks of 10 will he get ?

   b How many fish will be left to go in the spare tank ?

Worksheet
3·2

Numbers Bigger than 100

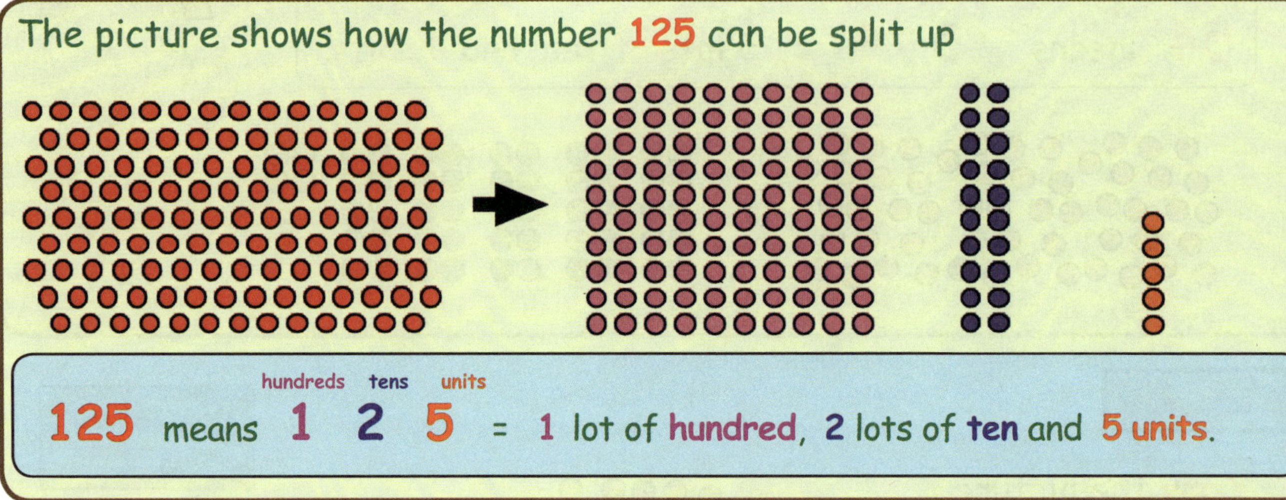
The picture shows how the number 125 can be split up
hundreds tens units
125 means 1 2 5 = 1 lot of hundred, 2 lots of ten and 5 units.

5. **Copy** and **Complete** :- **237** = ... **hundreds**, ... **tens** and ... **units**.

6. Write these numbers in **hundreds**, **tens** and **units** :-

   a **418** = ... hundreds, **1** ten and ... units.

   b **657** = ... hundreds, ... tens and ... units.

   c **902** = ... hundreds, ... tens and ... units.

   d **892** = ... hundreds, ... tens and ... units.

   e **760** = ... hundreds, ... tens and ... units.

418

7. Do the same with these numbers :-

a	300	b	727	c	602	d	930
e	275	f	384	g	717	h	989
i	172	j	658	k	284	l	547.

8. How many **£1** coins and **10p** coins will you get for :-

a	340p	**b**	630p	**c**	960p
d	450p	**e**	880p	**f**	570p
g	500p	**h**	700p	**i**	1000 ?

9. Seven friends have some money.

How many **1p** coins would each of them get ?

a Anna - £1 and 74p. **b** Beryl - £2 and 48p.

c Carol - £6 and 20p. **d** Daria - £5 and 82p.

e Evelyn - **Four** 10p coins and **one** 5p coin.

f Fatima - **One** £1 coin and **eight** 10p coins.

g Gina - **Nine** £1 coins, **seven** 10p coins and **four** 2p coins.

10. George goes to the newsagent and pays for his magazine.

He hands over the exact amount :-

four £1 coins

three 10p coins and

nine 1p coins.

How much did the magazine cost ?

11. Sarah's mum gives her **six** £1 coins, **seven** 10p coins and **five** 1p coins to pay for a cinema ticket and popcorn.

How much does Sarah have ?

Place Value

Understand
place value for
numbers
up to 1000.

A number can be written in **words** and in **digits**.

(**digits** means numbers like 1, 2, 3, 4, ...)

You should be able to change a number from one to the other.

Seven hundred and eighty nine written using digits is **789**.

354 written in words is "three hundred and fifty four"

Seven hundred
and eighty nine
789✓

Exercise 2

Worksheet 3·3

1. Write the following numbers using **digits** :-

a twenty three	**b** thirty eight	**c** forty one
d seventy five	**e** sixty two	**f** ninety
g twelve	**h** eighty	**i** fifty nine.

2. Write the following numbers using **digits** :-

a one hundred and seventeen	**b** two hundred and forty three
c five hundred and sixty four	**d** three hundred and twenty seven
e eight hundred and fifty five	**f** seven hundred and fourteen
g nine hundred and seventy	**h** six hundred and sixty six
i eight hundred and eight	**j** nine hundred and ninety nine.

3. Write these numbers using **words** :-

a 58	**b** 32	**c** 46	**d** 19
e 70	**f** 88	**g** 178	**h** 319
i 919	**j** 504	**k** 800	**l** 1000.

4. There are **137** penguins in a zoo.

Write this number in **words**.

5. 

In the same zoo there are **two hundred and nine** lizards.

Write this number using **digits**.

6. Write the number that comes **just before** :-

a 47	b 65	c 82	d 91
e 77	f 60	g 345	h 628
i 951	j 640	k 790	l 800.

7. Write the number that comes **just after** :-

a 27	b 77	c 19	d 39
e 98	f 102	g 368	h 109
i 876	j 698	k 620	l 999.

8. In a marathon race, Marius did well to finish in position **419**.

Joe finished the race **just after** Marius.

What was Joe's position ?

9. Put each of these groups of numbers in the correct order.

Start with the **highest**.

a 23, 58, 46, 19

b 75, 46, 81, 55, 49

c 70, 88, 72, 79, 81

d 158, 168, 173, 179, 161

contd.

9. e 302, 297, 453, 511, 388 f 452, 175, 234, 428, 301

g 703, 578, 857, 519, 800 h 265, 256, 526, 625, 562

10. Put each of these groups of numbers in the correct order.

Start with the **smallest**.

a 19, 21, 33, 12 b 55, 62, 57, 41, 50

c 106, 165, 172, 140, 114 d 581, 295, 259, 499, 501

e 357, 430, 330, 389, 403 f 576, 657, 756, 567, 675.

11. Aunt Hazel is aged **89**. Uncle Frank is **91**. Auntie Ida is **94**.

Grannie Marshall is **72**. Uncle David is **87**. Grandpa Sim is **70**.

a Who is the **youngest** ? b Who is the **oldest** ?

c Who is the **second youngest** ? d Who is the **oldest man** ?

Worksheet 3·5

12. What numbers are the arrows pointing to ?

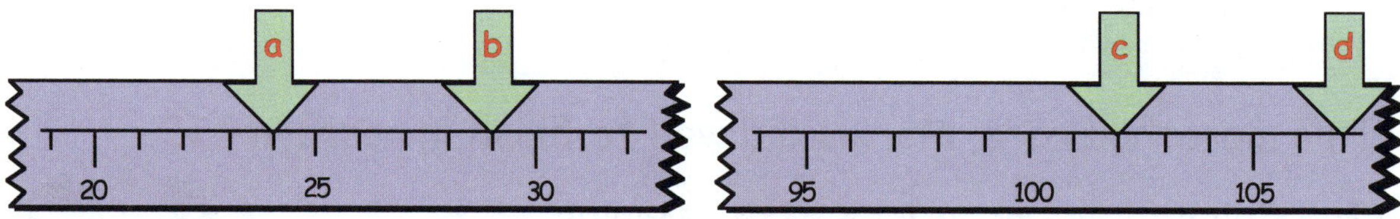

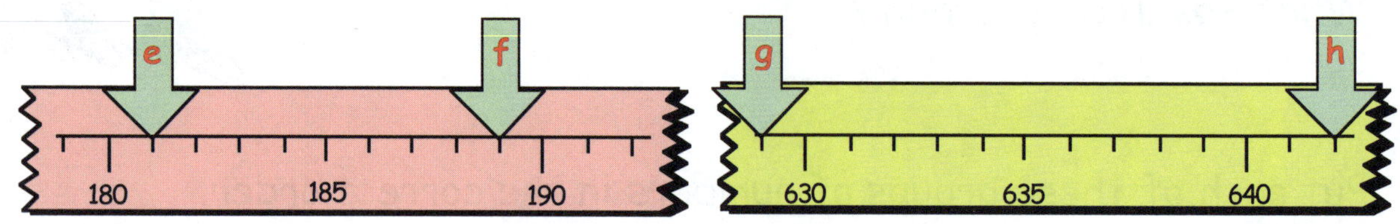

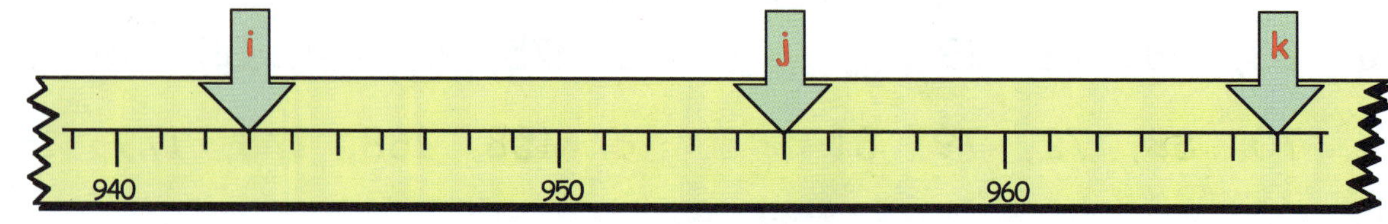

13. What numbers are shown on these meters ?

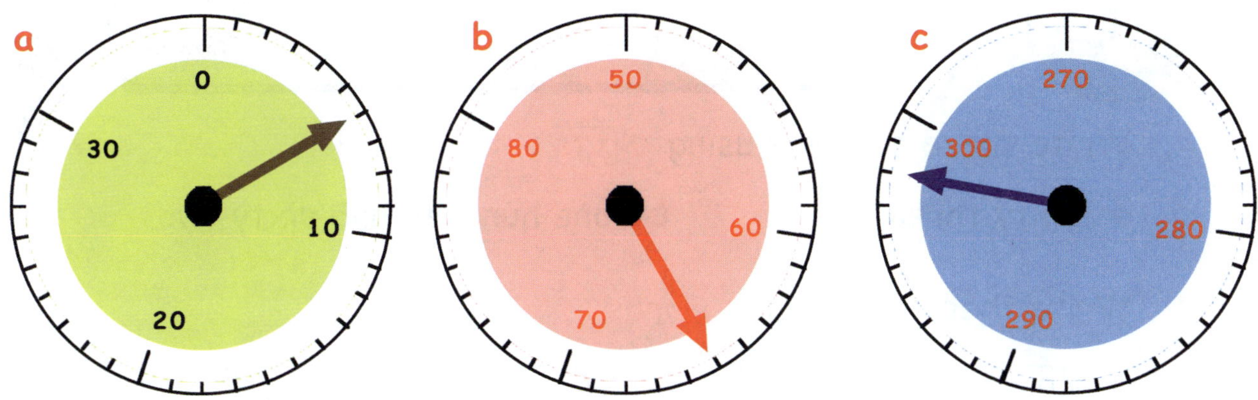

14. **Seven hundred and twenty six** people attended a gig starring Paul McCourtney at the SECC in Glasgow.

Write this number using **digits**.

15. A housing estate has **607** houses in it.

Write this number in **words**.

16. Write the answers to these **in words** :-

a Derek tried the long jump.

How far did he jump ?

b How heavy is the TV ?

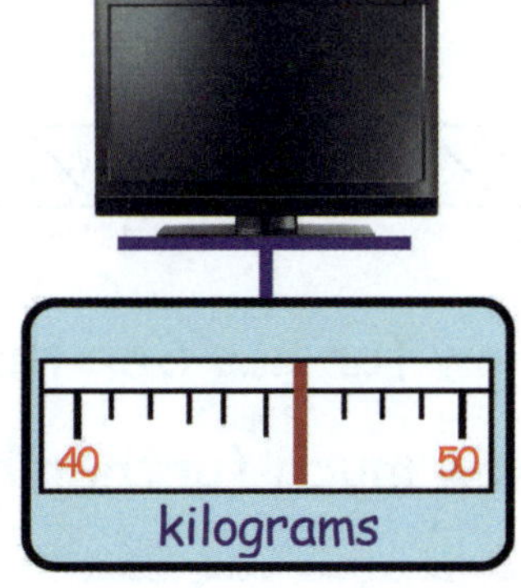

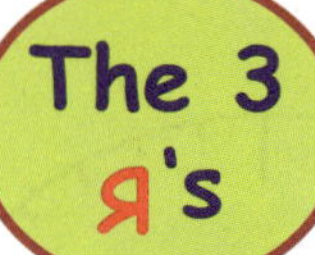

Revisit - Review - Revise

1. Write these numbers using **digits** :-

   a sixty three   b one hundred and sixty two.

2. Write these numbers **in words** :-

   a 78   b 409   c 753   d 999.

3. Write the number that comes :-

   a just **after** 149   b just **before** 800   c ten **after** 360.

4. Put these numbers in order, starting with the **smallest** :-

   229, 188, 282, 314, 179, 220.

5. What numbers do the arrows point to ?

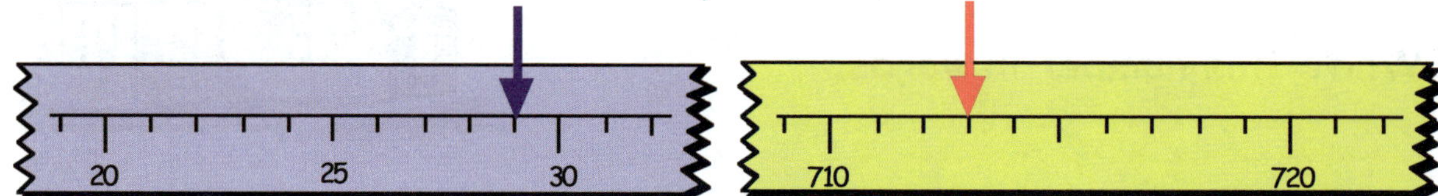

6. Bobby got 5 new £10 bank notes, **all in order** starting at NUMBER ***000 711***.

   a What was the **highest number** on his notes ?

   Bobby's sister, Fran, got **two** new £10 notes **just before** Bobby.

   b What was the **lower number** on her notes ?

7. Jay, Ian and Ger were in a Javelin throwing competition.

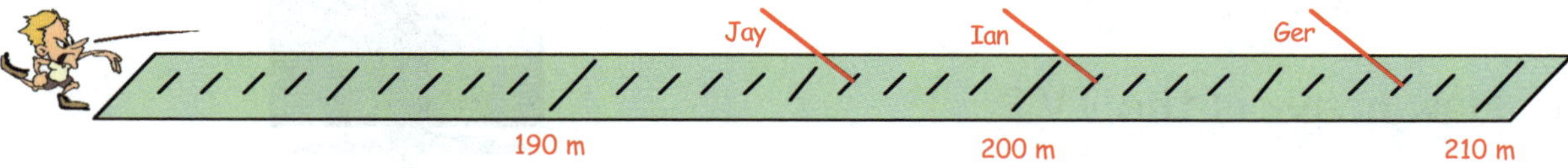

   a How far has Ger thrown ?   b How far has Jay thrown ?

   How much further has Ian thrown than Jay ?

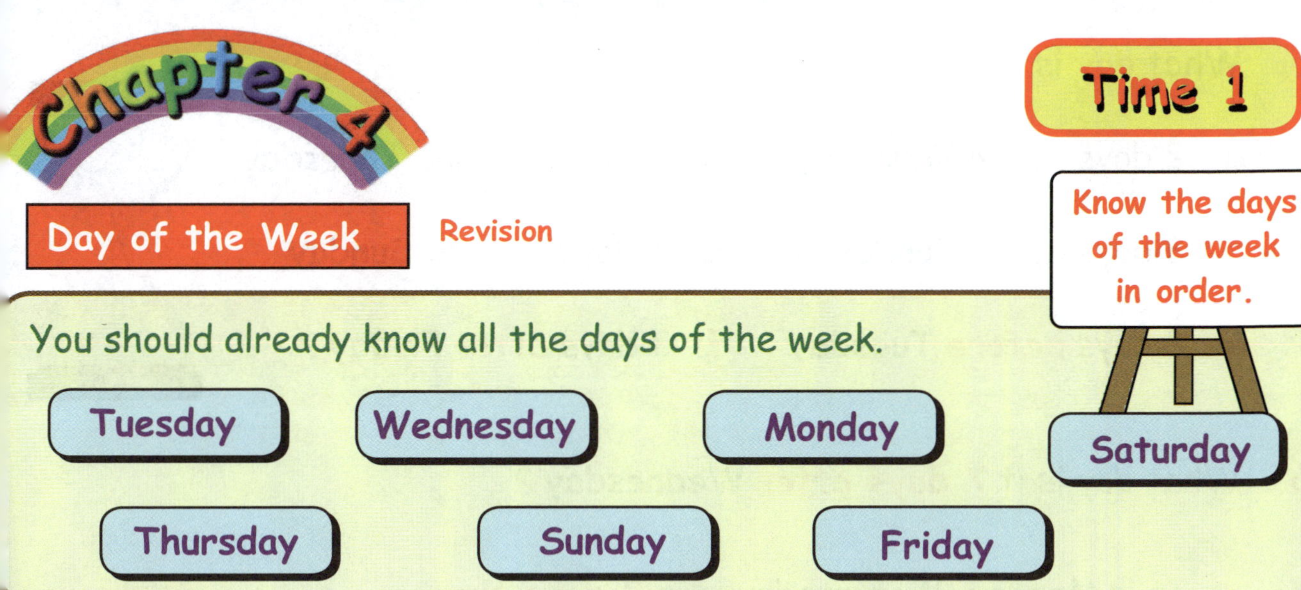

Chapter 4
Time 1
Day of the Week
Revision
Know the days of the week in order.
You should already know all the days of the week.
Tuesday
Wednesday
Monday
Saturday
Thursday
Sunday
Friday

Exercise 1

1. **Write** the days of the week in the **correct** order. Start with Monday.

2. a Write down the days of the week you go to school.

   b Which days do you **NOT** go to school ?

3. Write down the missing days :-

   a Monday, ... , Wednesday, Thursday, ... , Saturday, Sunday

   b .... , Wednesday, Thursday, ... , ... , ... , Monday.

4. a What is the day just **after Thursday ?**

   b What is the day just **before Saturday** ?

   c What is the day just **after Wednesday** ?

   d What is the day just **after Monday** ?

   e What is the day just **before Sunday** ?

5. What day is it :-

a 2 days after Thursday

b 2 days before Thursday

c 3 days after Sunday

d 3 days before Sunday

e 2 days before Tuesday

f 3 days after Friday ?

6. What day is it 7 days after Wednesday ?

7. a It is Monday. My birthday is in 2 days time.
On what day is my birthday ?

b Today is Thursday. My sister's birthday was yesterday.
On what day was her birthday ?

c Today is Friday. I am going to the pantomime tomorrow.
On what day am I going to the pantomime ?

d My party is today, Sunday. My birthday was 1 week ago.
On what day was my birthday ?

e Today is Sunday. Christmas Day is in 3 days time.
On what day is Christmas ?

f

Today is Monday. I am going skating the day after tomorrow.
On which day am I going skating ?

y is Tuesday. I go on holiday in 6 days time.
at day do I leave for my holiday ?

Months of the Year

Know the months of the year in order.

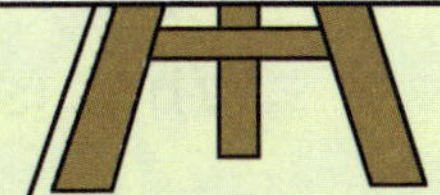

You will also need to know **all** the months of the year.

Exercise 2

1. **Copy** out the months of the year in the correct order.

2. Write down the **missing months** :-

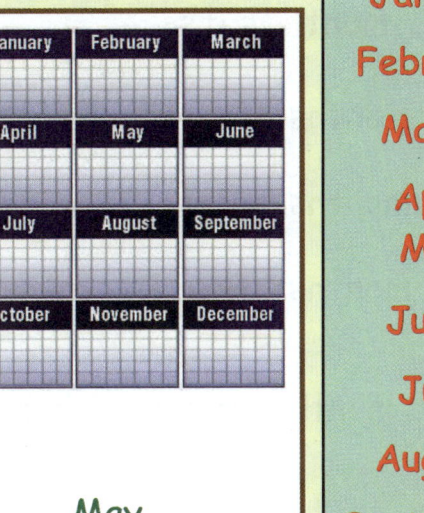

   a January, February, March, ... , May

   b June, July, ... , September, October

   c November, ... , January, ... , March

   d April, ... , June, ... , ... , September

   e December, ... , February, ... , April

   f .... , October, ... , ... , ... , February.

3. a What is the month just **after March** ?

   b What is the month just **before July** ?

   c What is the month just **after September** ?

   d What is the month just **before December** ?

3. e What is the month just **after April** ?

f What is the month just **before November** ?

g What is the month just **after February** ?

h What is the month just **before January** ?

4. What **month** is it :-

a 2 months **after** June

b 2 months **after** September

c 2 months **before** July

d 2 months **before** March

e 3 months **after** December

f 2 months **before** February ?

5. What month is it **12 months after** May ?

6. a What is the **3rd** month of the year ?

b What is the **6th** month of the year ?

c What is the **last** month of the year ?

d What is the **2nd last** month of the year ?

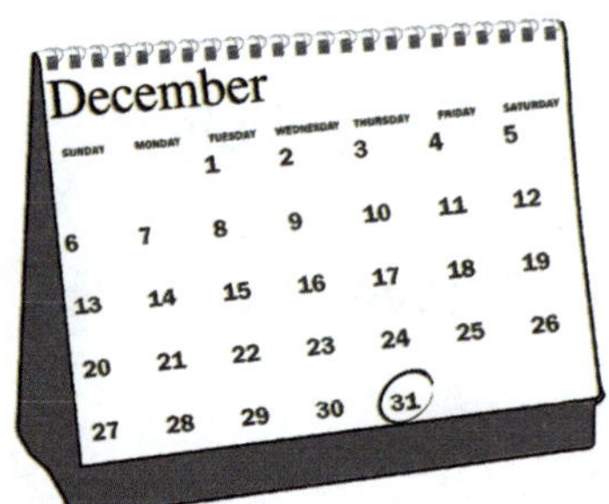

7. a Use a calendar to find how many days there are in each month.

For example, **December** has 31 days and **June** has 30 days.

b Here is a small rhyme that tells you how many days there are in each month.

Check that the rhyme works ...ach month of the year.

... learn the rhyme.

30 days has September,
April, June and November.
All the rest have 31, except February,
which has 28 days clear, and 29 days
each leap year.

Telling the Time on the Hour

Be able to tell the time - o'clock only.

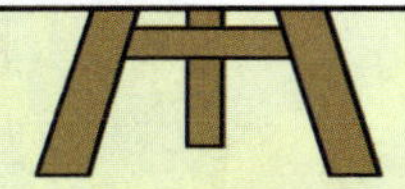

When the **BIG** hand is pointing to 12, the small hand tells you what the hour (**o'clock**) is.

This clock reads **4 o'clock**.

4 o'clock

Exercise 3

1. Write the time shown on each clock :-

a 

.... o'clock

b 

.... o'clock

c 

d 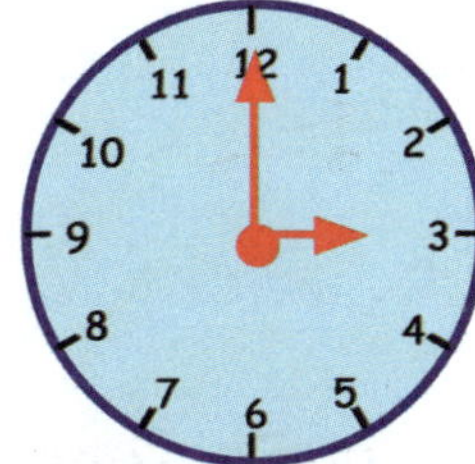

e 

f 

g 

h 

i 

j 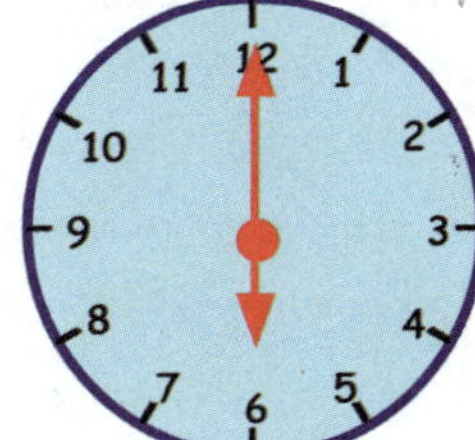

k 

l 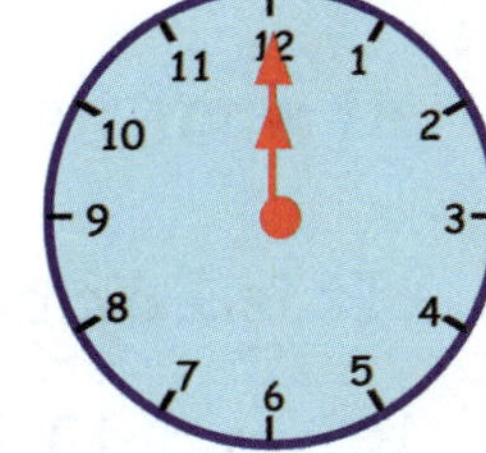

2. Write the time on each of these clocks :-

Worksheet 4·1

a

b

c

d

e

f

3. Draw a clock face. Put hands on it to show **8 o'clock**.

4. Draw a clock face. Put hands on it to show **3 o'clock**.

5. a It is 10 o'clock. What time will it be in **1 hour** ?

   b It is 7 o'clock. I arrived home **1 hour ago**.

   At what time did I arrive home ?

   c It is 6 o'clock. My favourite programme is on in **1 hour's time**.

   At what time will my programme start ?

   d My plane left at 4 o'clock. The flight takes **3 hours**.

   At what time will my plane land ?

6. a It is 11 o'clock in the morning. I leave for work in **3 hours**.

   At what time must I leave for work ?

   b It is 1 o'clock in the afternoon. I drank tea **2 hours ago**.

   When did I have my cup of tea ?

Telling the Time

Be able to tell the time using half past and quarter to/past.

When the **BIG** hand moves **half-way** round the clock, it is at the **6**.

The time reads as **half past** the hour.

This clock reads **half past 2**.

Exercise 4

1. Write the time shown on each clock :-

a 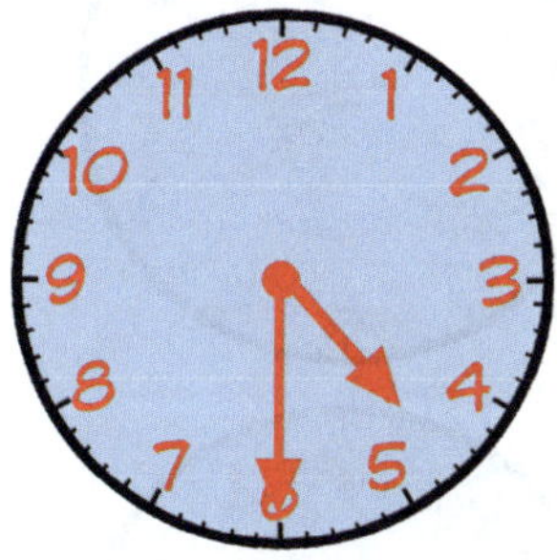

b 

c 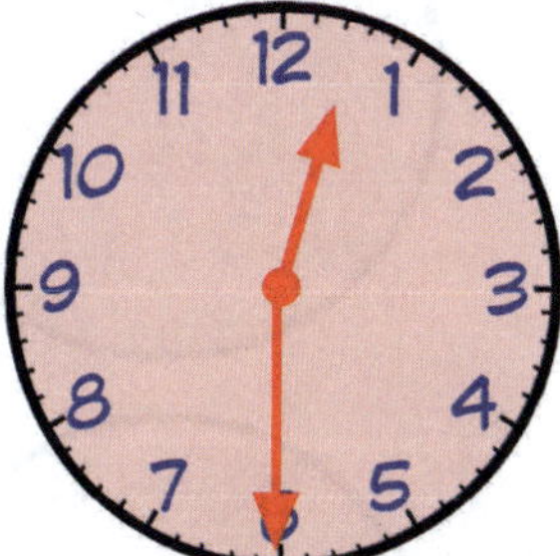

d 

e 

f 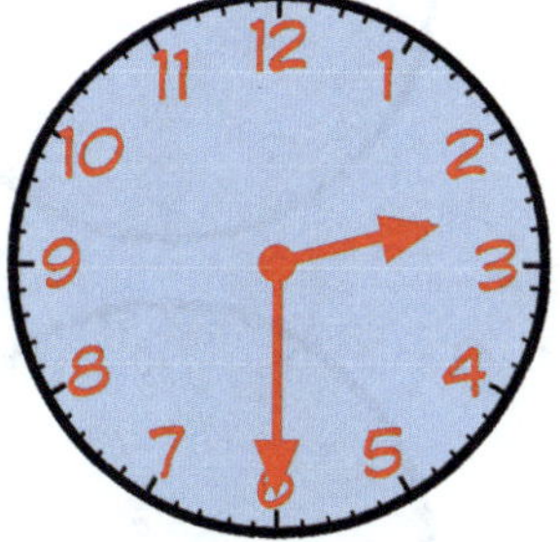

g 

h 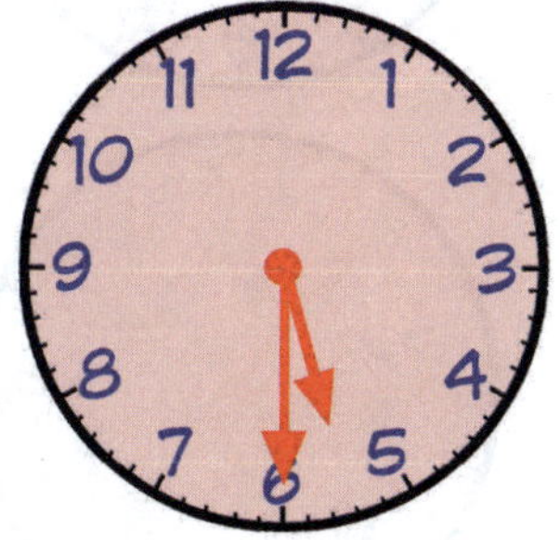

i 

Worksheet 4·2

When the **BIG** hand is at the **3** the time reads as **quarter past** the hour.

When the **BIG** hand is at the **9** the time reads as **quarter to** the hour.

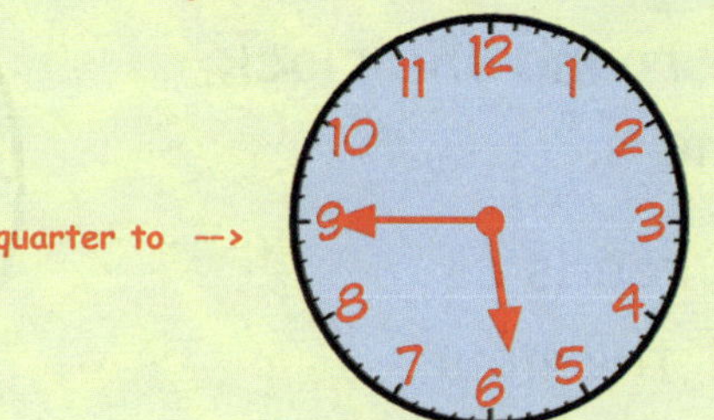

<-- quarter past

quarter to -->

This clock reads **quarter past 8**.

This clock reads **quarter to 6**.

2. Write the time shown on each clock :-

a

b

c

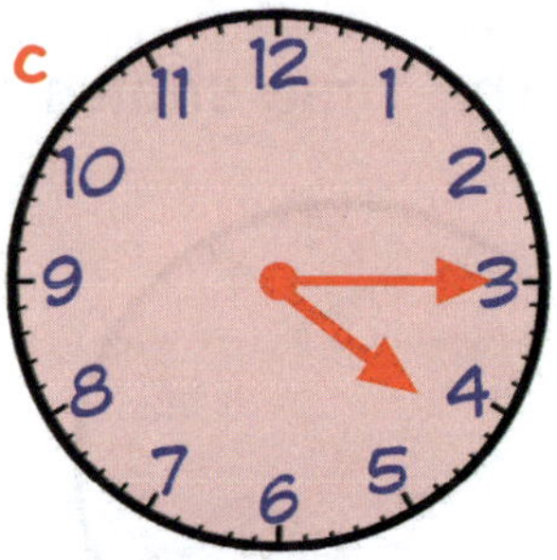

d

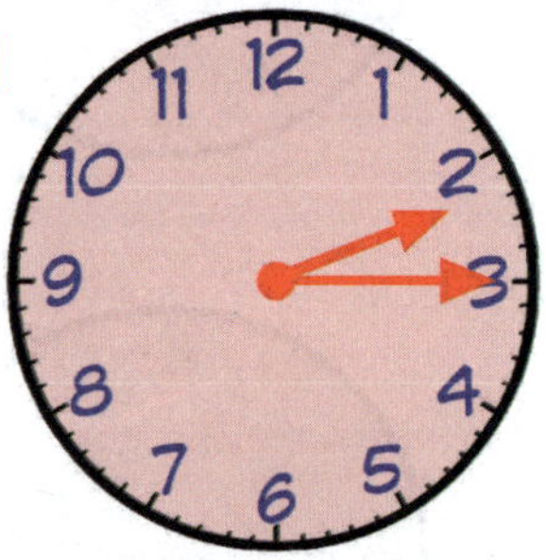

e

f

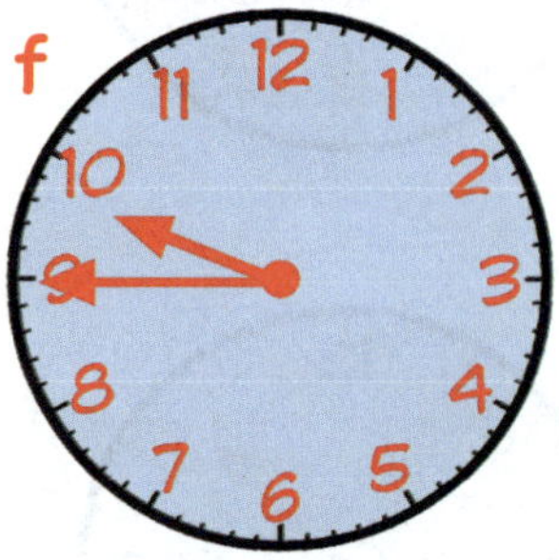

g

h

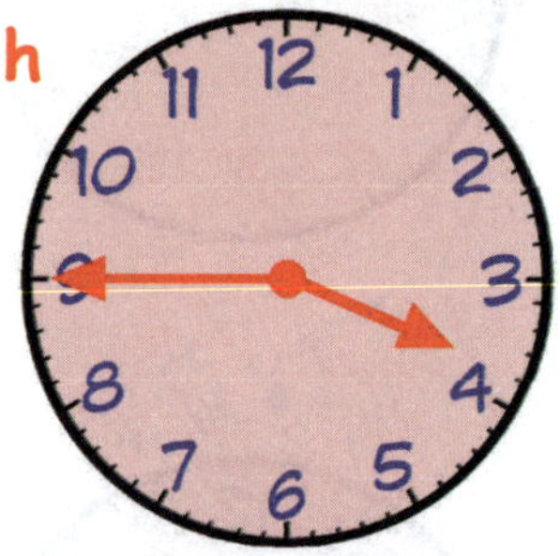

i

j

k

l

Worksheet 4·3

3. A mixture. Write the time shown on each clock :-

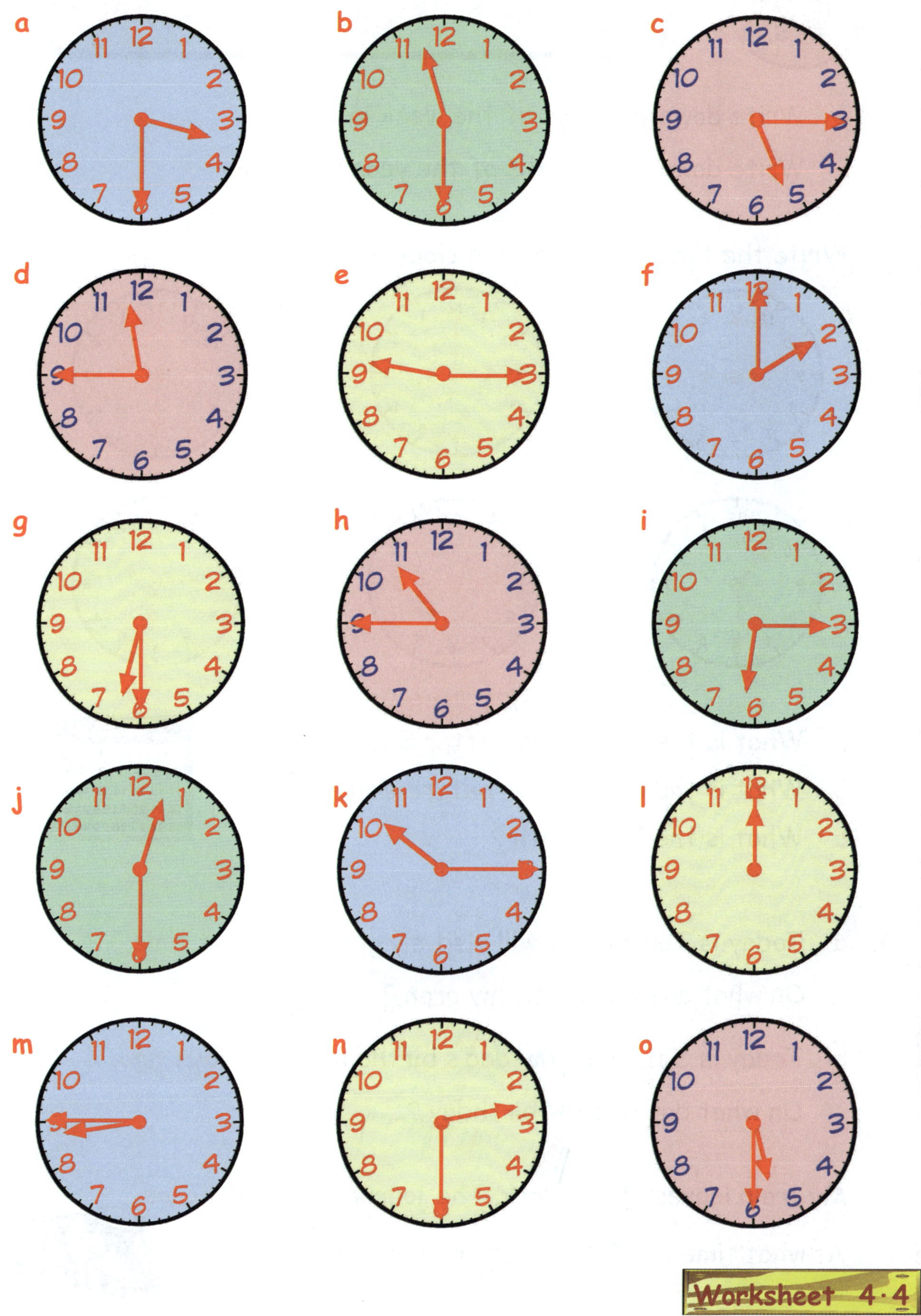

Worksheet 4·4

The 3 R's

Revisit - Review - Revise

1. a Write down the days of the week **in order**.

   b Write down the months of the year **in order**.

2. Write the time shown on each clock :-

   a

   b

   c

   d

   e 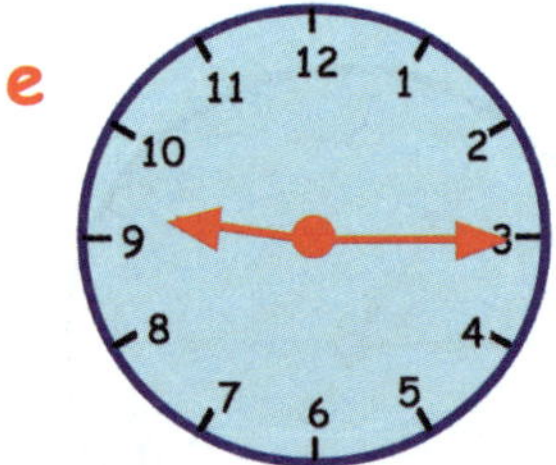

   f 

3. a What is the month just **after** September ?

   b What is the month just **before** January ?

   c What is the **7th** month ?

4. a Today is Tuesday. I will visit my gran in **3 days** time.

   On what day will I visit my gran ?

   b Today is Saturday. My dad's birthday was **2 days ago**.

   On what day was his birthday ?

5. My train leaves at 9 o'clock. The journey takes **4 hours**.

   At what time will I arrive at my destination ?

Chapter 5

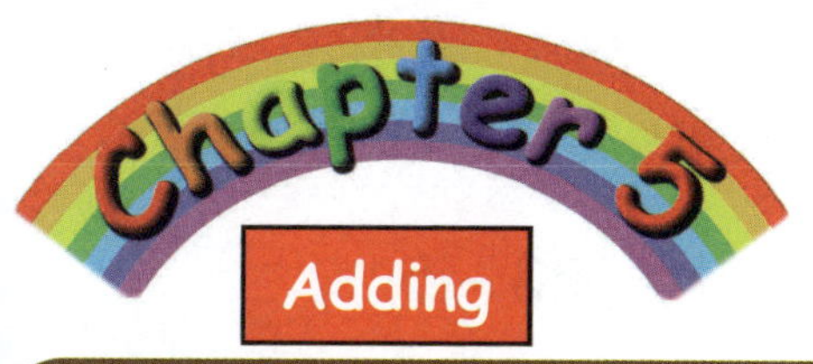

Adding

Adding whole numbers up to 2 digits with no "carrying".

You can use coins or counters to help you add.

Example Add :- 14 + 3.

14 + 3

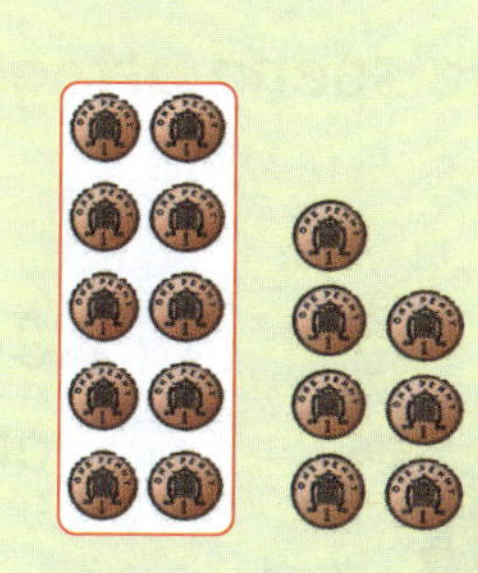

14 + 3 = 17

This can be written as

T	U
1	4
+	3
1	7 ✓

When **adding**, the numbers must be **in line**.

Example Add :- 32 + 7.

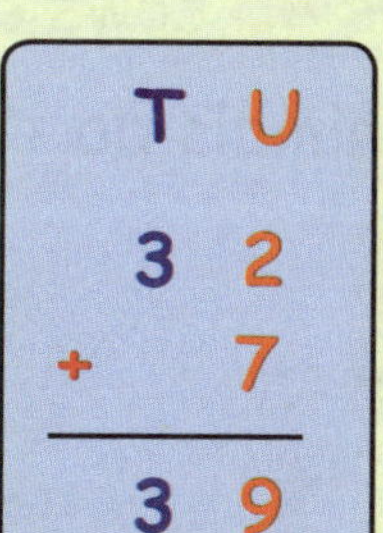

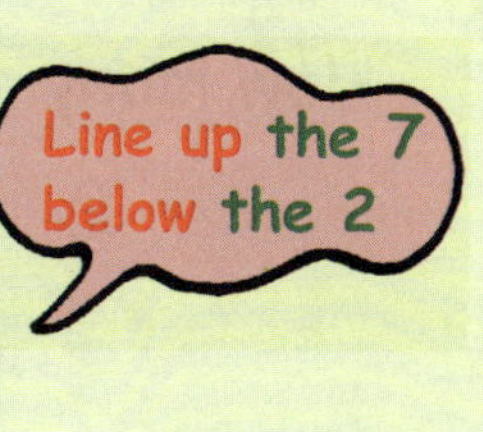

	T	U
	3	2
+		7
	3	9

Line up the 7 below the 2

Exercise 1

Worksheet 5·1

1. **Copy** and **complete** these additions :- (You may use counters to help you)

a $14 + 5$

b $23 + 2$

c $67 + 1$

d $51 + 8$

e $84 + 4$

f $91 + 3$

g $30 + 6$

h $42 + 7$

i $63 + 4$

j $5 + 22$

k $6 + 53$

l $1 + 77$

2. Set down the sums like Question 1 and work out :-

a 36 + 2 b 8 + 20 c 15 + 1 d 83 + 5

e 42 + 7 f 30 + 4 g 6 + 22 h 9 + 70.

3. Katia bought a sugar mouse and a chocolate bar.

How much did she spend **altogether** ?

6p

32p

4. 

James spent **61p** on a doughnut and **8p** on an apple.

How much did he spend **altogether** ?

5. A farmer has **45** cows and **4** sheep.

How many animals do they have ?

6. 

There are **62** ducks and **3** swans in a pond.

How many birds is that **altogether** ?

7. Helen sent out invitation cards to her birthday party.

12 were sent to school friends and **5** were sent to friends from her street. How many children were asked to the party ?

8. 

Eric has **21** chips and a piece of fish on his plate.

His mum brings him **6** more chips from the oven and his wee sister gives him **2** of hers.

How many chips does Eric have now ?

Adding with Tens

Example What's the answer to :- 32 + 21 ?

This can be written as

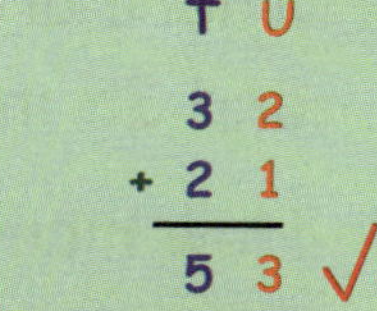

32 + 21 = + =

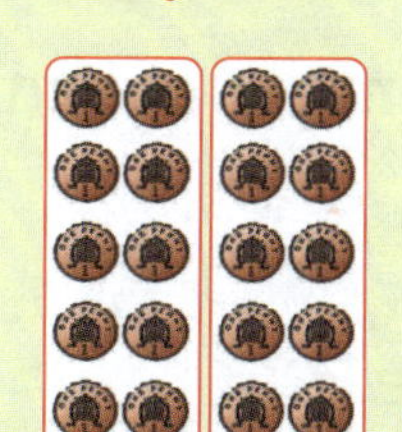

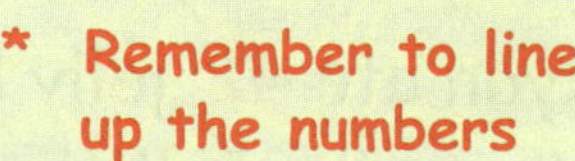

* Remember to line up the numbers

32 + 21 = 53

Exercise 2

Worksheet 5·2

1. **Copy** and **complete** :-

a 16 + 12	b 23 + 15	c 17 + 11	d 26 + 33
e 51 + 25	f 77 + 11	g 47 + 32	h 43 + 35
i 59 + 40	j 35 + 24	k 13 + 56	l 24 + 71

2. **Line up** these sums, then work them out :-

a 19 + 10	b 36 + 11	c 45 + 13	d 57 + 22
e 62 + 33	f 78 + 20	g 61 + 18	h 47 + 31
i 55 + 44	j 44 + 11	k 41 + 14 + 33	l 41 + 25 + 13.

3. There are 23 scarecrows in one field and 35 in another.

How many are there **in total** ?

4. 

At present, there are 52 dogs in the Cat & Dog Home.

There are 26 cats there too.

How many animals **altogether** ?

5. Ryan ate 42 jelly beans. Nan ate 33.
How many jelly beans did they eat **in total** ?

6. 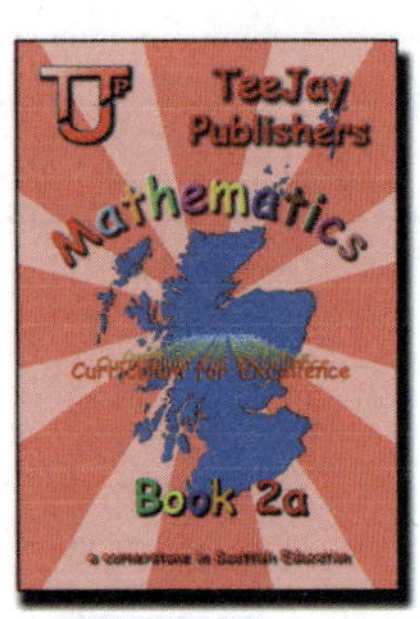

One classroom has 26 maths books in it.

The classroom next door has 63.

How many maths books **altogether** ?

7. Mrs Amos planted 21 marigolds in the garden.

Her daughter Jenny planted 37 dahlias.

What's the **total** number of plants in the garden ?

8. Goudies Garage has 55 cars on sale.

Paton's have only 14 ready for sale.

How many cars **altogether** are for sale ?

9. KareFit Tyre Company have 55 new tyres in stock.

They also have 34 part worn tyres for sale.

How many tyres do they have **altogether** ?

Adding in Hundreds

Adding whole numbers up to 3 digits with no "carrying".

Example Do this sum :- 216 + 473

Set down as shown.

* Remember to line up the numbers

216 + 473 = 689

6 + 3 = 9

1 + 7 = 8

2 + 4 = 6

Exercise 3

1. Copy and complete :-

a 104 + 123	b 429 + 260	c 315 + 134	d 426 + 172
e 506 + 391	f 572 + 225	g 609 + 140	h 681 + 217
i 801 + 177	j 856 + 123	k 900 + 87	l 637 + 52

2. Line up each addition sum, then work out the answers :-

a 215 + 372	b 148 + 531	c 396 + 102	d 424 + 265
e 300 + 200	f 356 + 423	g 482 + 311	h 501 + 198
i 572 + 116	j 677 + 210	k 603 + 345	l 714 + 273
m 814 + 72	n 888 + 110	o 900 + 3	p 946 + 12.

3. A laptop is on sale for **£380**.

The printer costs **£105**.

What is the **total** price ?

4.

216 people work in the Glynhall Hotel.

The Firs Hotel has **172** workers.

How many hotel workers **altogether** ?

5. There are **243** pages in a maths book and **621** pages in a store catalogue.

How many pages **in total** are there ?

6.

508 seagulls are nesting on a cliff.

There are **191** puffins there too.

How many birds are on the cliff ?

7. Jack has **£2·35** and Jill has **£4·42**.

They both change their money into **1p** pieces.

a How many pennies does Jack have ?

b How many pennies does Jill have ?

c How many pennies do they have **altogether** ?

8.

The teacher of Primary 3 has **415** coloured pencils to give out.

The Primary 4 teacher has **354**.

How many coloured pencils do they have in total ?

Addition with Carrying

Again, you can use counters to help you add.

Example Add :- 15 + 9.

15 + 9

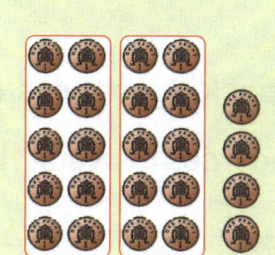

+

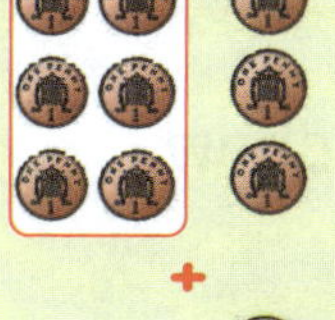

=

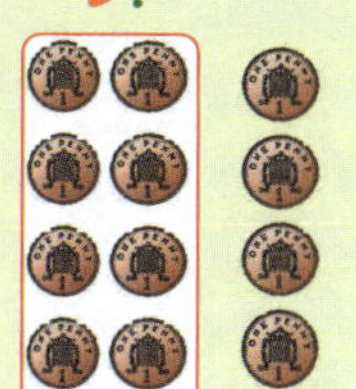

+

=

This can be written as

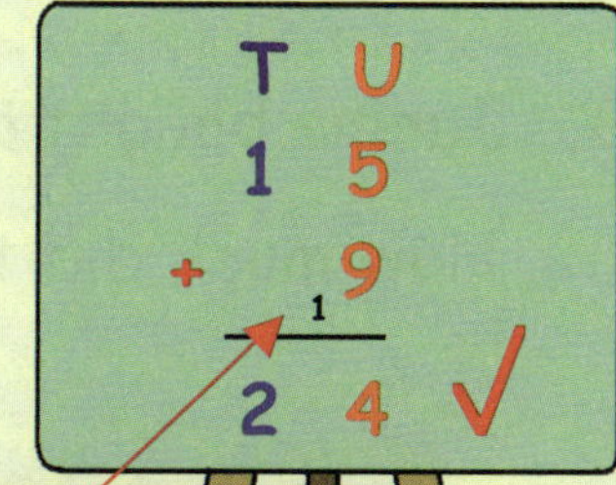

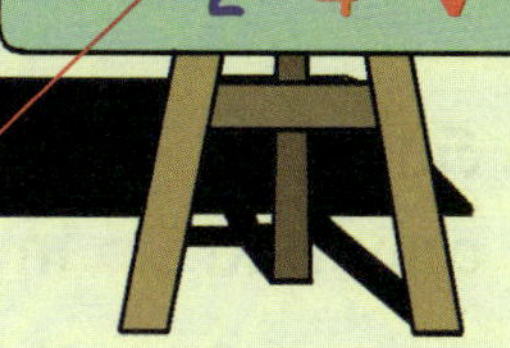

9 + 5 = 14
= 4 units
carry 1 (ten)

15 + 9 = 24

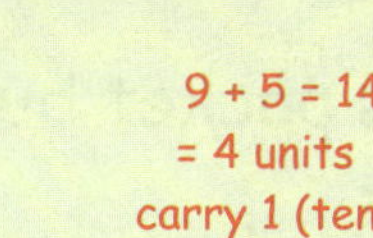

Remember, the numbers must be **in line**.

Example Add :- 58 + 7.

T	U
5	8
+	$_1$7
6	5

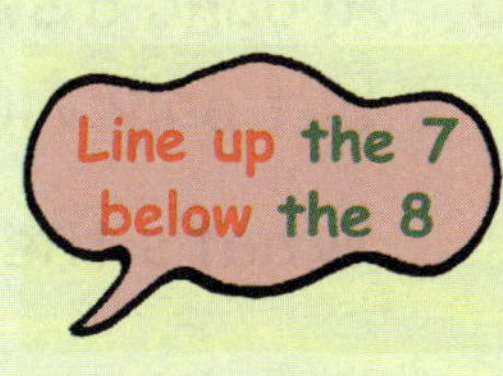

Don't forget to add the number you have carried !

Exercise 4

Worksheet 5·4

1. **Copy** and **complete** these additions :- (You may use counters to help you)

a) 49 + 5 = ____
b) 27 + 4 = ____
c) 58 + 2 = ____
d) 68 + 6 = ____

e) 77 + 7 = ____
f) 86 + 8 = ____
g) 31 + 9 = ____
h) 49 + 4 = ____

i) 89 + 2 = ____
j) 8 + 37 = ____
k) 9 + 89 = ____
l) 1 + 29 = ____

2. Set down the sums like Question 1 and work out :-

a 38 + 8 b 9 + 22 c 79 + 1 d 87 + 5

e 88 + 7 f 31 + 9 g 6 + 59 h 9 + 77.

3. Janine bought a packet of gums and a chew.

How much did they cost **altogether** ?

4. Sam had **46p** in his pocket but Alice only had **9p** in hers.

How much did they have **altogether** ?

5. Around a swimming pool there are **25** sunbeds, but only **7** umbrellas.

What's the **total** number of sunbeds and umbrellas ?

6.  

A cafe sold **67** glasses of cola and only **4** glasses of cherryade.

How many glasses is that **altogether** ?

7. In a zoo, there are **39** lions and **2** tigers.

How many lions and tigers **altogether** ?

8. 

A bus holds **59** people, compared to a taxi which can only take **5** people.

How many **in total** can one of each hold ?

Addition in Tens (with carrying)

Example Add :- 38 + 54.

This can be written as

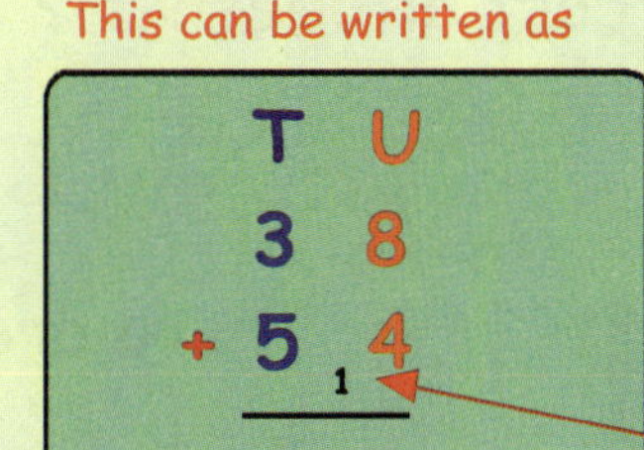

Set down like this :-

8 + 4 = 12
= 2 units
carry 1 (ten)

38 + 54 = 92

* Remember to line up the numbers

* Remember to add the numbers you have carried

Exercise 5

1. Copy and complete :-

a 58 + 23	b 47 + 16	c 45 + 38	d 29 + 47
e 25 + 59	f 61 + 19	g 79 + 19	h 58 + 24
i 31 + 29	j 65 + 48	k 68 + 56	l 33 + 67

2. Line up these sums, then work them out :-

a 39 + 44	b 67 + 27	c 55 + 25	d 19 + 78
e 37 + 25	f 23 + 59	g 46 + 19	h 66 + 24
i 78 + 15	j 12 + 29	k 17 + 77	l 99 + 3.

3. Tony bought a burger for **55p** and a drink for **37p**.

How much did it cost **altogether** ?

4. 

There are **48** cars in a car/bus park.

There are **18** buses there too.

How many **altogether** ?

5. Davie went away in May for **27** days and for **16** days in September.

How many days **in total** was he away for ?

6. Mr Taylor is **65** years old.

His wife is **59**.

What is their **total** age ?

7. In her garden, Maisie planted **75** pansies and **27** roses.

What's the **total** number of flowers in her garden ?

8. 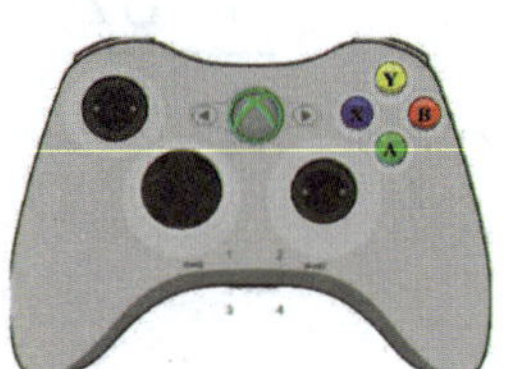

Pauline bought two computer games.

One cost **£39**, the other cost **£28**.

How much **altogether** for the games ?

9. Freddie bought a newspaper for **35p** and rolls for **37p**.

   a How much did that cost ?

   b He went back into the shop and bought an apple for **19p**.
   What was the **total** cost of the three items ?

Addition in Hundreds (with carrying)

Adding whole numbers up to 3 digits with "carrying".

Example Add :- 328 + 297.

Set down like this :-

328 + 297 = 625

This can be written as

7 + 8 = 15
= 5 units
carry 1 (ten)

1 + 9 + 2 = 12
= 2 tens
carry 1 (hundred)

* Remember to line up the numbers

* Remember to add the numbers you have carried

Exercise 6

Worksheet 5·6

1. Copy and complete :-

a 108 + 135	b 437 + 129	c 348 + 442	d 666 + 219
e 545 + 376	f 397 + 218	g 419 + 492	h 688 + 188
i 801 + 109	j 444 + 366	k 887 + 99	l 999 + 1

2. Line up each addition sum, then work out the answers :-

a 234 + 346	b 456 + 108	c 567 + 228	d 119 + 449
e 450 + 150	f 255 + 555	g 487 + 178	h 169 + 376
i 897 + 79	j 88 + 189	k 903 + 27	l 899 + 12.

3. Kenny earns **£385** per week.

Kerry gets **£565** per week.

What is their **total** wage ?

4. 

216 people are swimming at Greenock Baths.

194 are at Renfrew Baths.

How many people swimming **altogether** ?

5. Last year, John paid **£567** for a holiday to Paris.

He later spent **£377** going to London.

How much **in total** did he spend ?

6. In an orchard, there are **666** apple trees
and **285** pear trees.

How many fruit trees ?

7. Rena bought a table for **£259** and two chairs for **£258**.

a Which was cheaper - the table or the chairs ?

b What was the **total** cost ?

c She also bought a rug for **£99**.

How much did Rena spend **altogether** ?

8. Three children play a game.

Yasmin scores **258** and **103**.
Trevor scores **177** and **192**.
Micky scores **304** and **179**.

The winner has the highest **total** score.

Who was that ?

Addition - A Mixture

Adding any numbers up to 3 digits - a mixture

Exercise 7

1. Copy and complete :-

a   24 + 5

b   8 + 37

c   41 + 56

d   54 + 76

e   209 + 18

f   48 + 723

g   114 + 368

h   559 + 286

2. Find the answers to these sums after lining them up :-

a   47 + 99   b   106 + 392   c   11 + 899   d   995 + 100.

3. Arith scores 239 runs at cricket.

Erin scores 77.

What is their total number of runs ?

4.  

In a shop window there are 35 gold bracelets and 84 gold necklaces.

How many bits of gold altogether ?

5. Chef has 7 starters, 15 main courses and 6 puddings on his menu.

Line up the numbers and add to find the total number of choices.

6. The top three goalscorers in Division 1 last season were :-

Dargo 32   Johnston 28   Thomson 25

How many goals did they score altogether ?

Adding with a Calculator

Adding whole numbers up to 3 digits using a calculator.

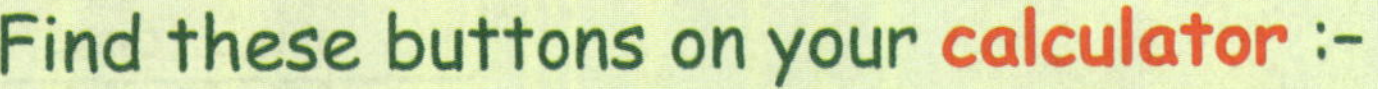

Find these buttons on your **calculator** :-

[+] means **add**

[=] means **equals**

Examples

Press [4][6] [+] [2][9] [=] → The answer is **75.**

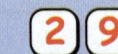

[1][4][8] [+] [7][2][6] [=] → The answer is **874.**

Exercise 8

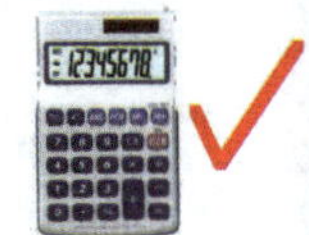

1. a Press [5][8] [+] [3][4] [=]. Write down your answer.

   b Press [2][7][9] [+] [3][6][8] [=]. Write down your answer.

2. **Find** :-

a 39 + 17	b 37 + 69	c 12 + 177	d 86 + 752
e 234 + 176	f 507 + 203	g 888 + 75	h 536 + 286
i 44 + 956	j 800 + 400	k 750 + 550	l 888 + 222.

3. Donna scores **142** points, **76** points and **102** points on her dartboard.

   What is her **total** score ?

4.   

   One bee hive has **38** bees.
   Another has **99** bees.
   A third bee hive has **167** bees.

   How many bees **altogether** ?

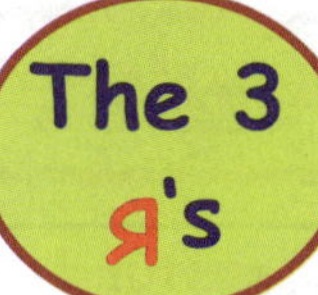

Revisit - Review - Revise

1. **Copy** and **work out** :-

a	b	c	d
$\begin{array}{r} 18 \\ +\ 7 \\ \hline \end{array}$	$\begin{array}{r} 9 \\ +\ 64 \\ \hline \end{array}$	$\begin{array}{r} 62 \\ +\ 29 \\ \hline \end{array}$	$\begin{array}{r} 74 \\ +\ 96 \\ \hline \end{array}$

e	f	g	h
$\begin{array}{r} 375 \\ +\ 485 \\ \hline \end{array}$	$\begin{array}{r} 57 \\ +\ 846 \\ \hline \end{array}$	$\begin{array}{r} 183 \\ +\ 599 \\ \hline \end{array}$	$\begin{array}{r} 784 \\ +\ 216 \\ \hline \end{array}$

2. **Line them up** and **add** :-

   a 39 + 79 b 207 + 481 c 22 + 388 d 899 + 201.

3. I gave my postie **£18** at Christmas and the bin collectors got **£15** from me.

   What did it cost me ?

4. 

   Ryanjet has a fleet of **106** planes.

   Flyby has **95** planes.

   How many planes **altogether** ?

5. I travelled **147** miles from Glasgow to Stanley, then moved on **204** miles to Brixmouth.

   How far had I travelled **in total** ?

6.  

   Mr Moore needed **785** bricks to build a porch and **105** to build a barbecue.

   How many bricks had he to buy ?

An Angle

Understand that when two lines meet angles are formed.

When two straight lines meet at a point, an **angle** is formed.

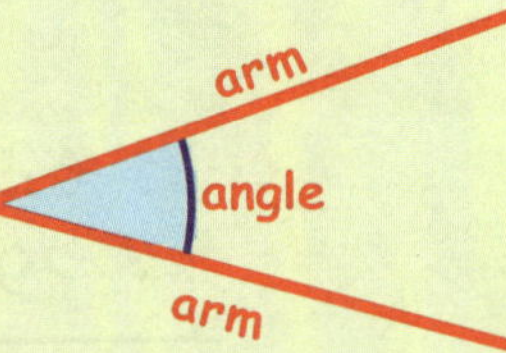

The two lines are called the **arms** of the angle.

Sometimes, more than one angle is formed.

Exercise 1

1. **Trace** these angles (or copy them).

   Mark in any angle you see with and colour each one.

   a like this

   b

   c

   d

   e

   f

   g

Worksheet 6·1

2. How many angles can you see in each picture ?

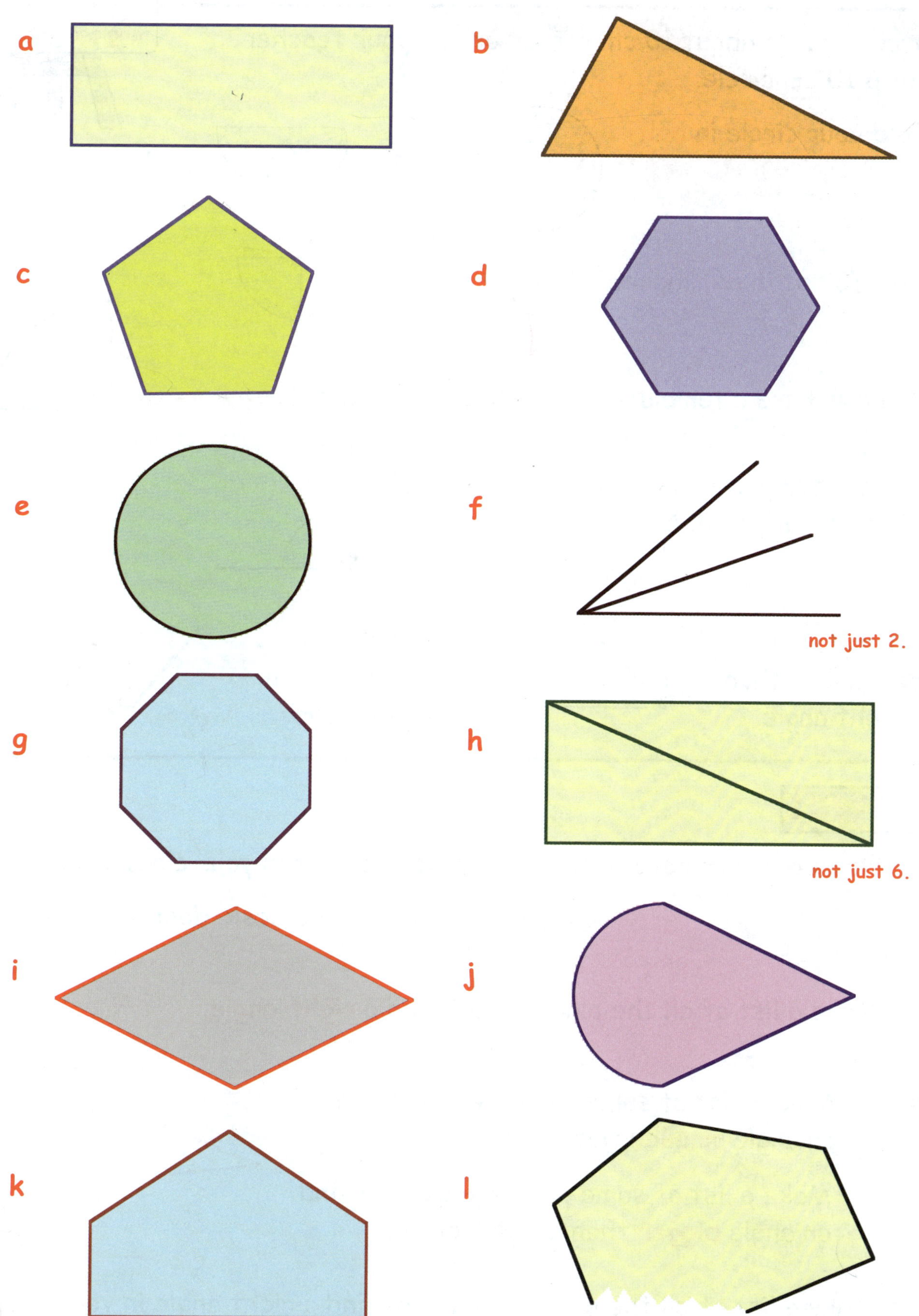

A special angle - A Right Angle

Be able to identify a right angle from any angle or shape.

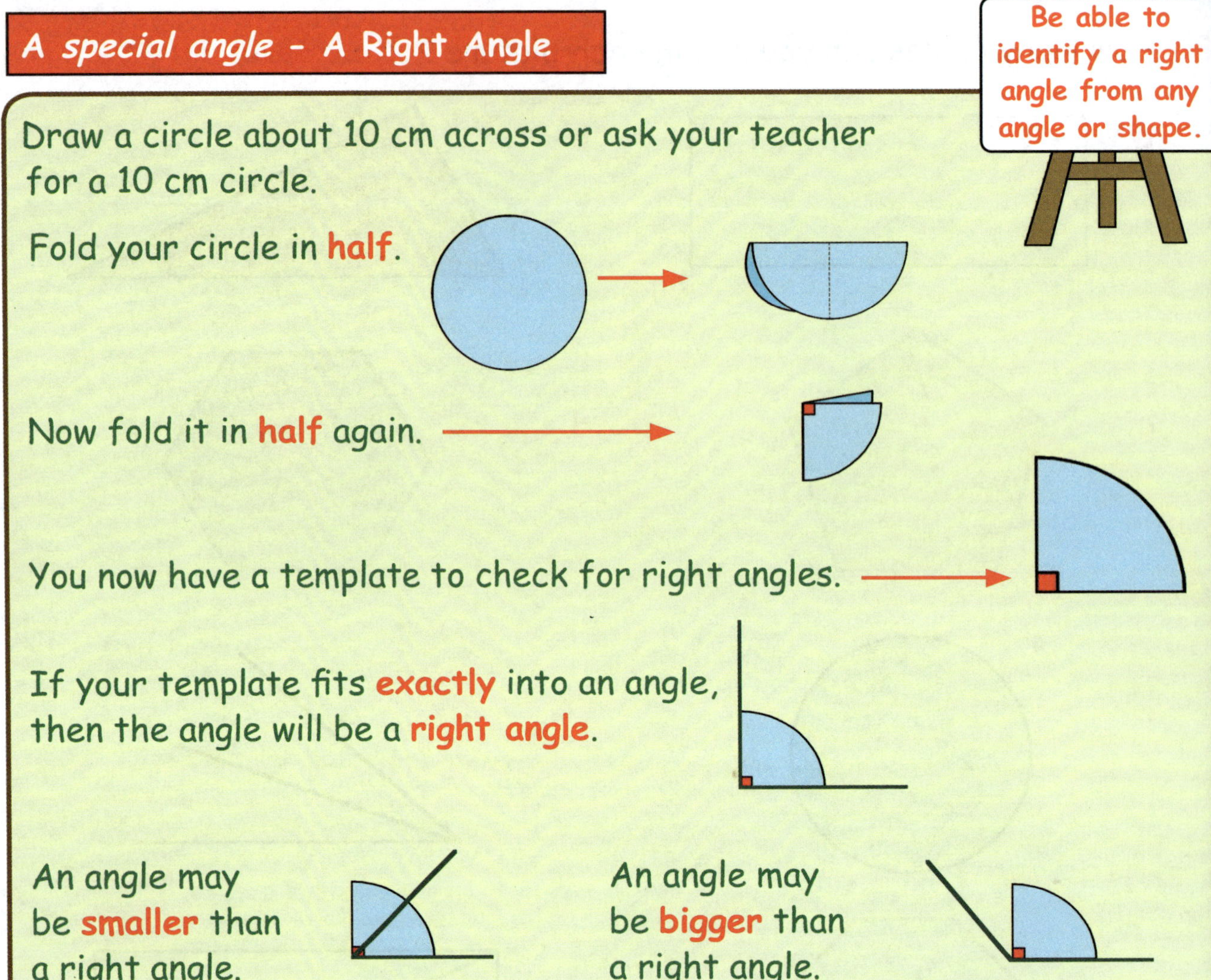

Draw a circle about 10 cm across or ask your teacher for a 10 cm circle.

Fold your circle in **half**.

Now fold it in **half** again.

You now have a template to check for right angles.

If your template fits **exactly** into an angle, then the angle will be a **right angle**.

An angle may be **smaller** than a right angle.

An angle may be **bigger** than a right angle.

Exercise 2

1. **Use your template -** try to find right angles in your classroom.

   (Try your jotter, book, desk, door.........).

2. Make a list of all the places you found a **right angle**.

3. a Make a list of some places you might find an angle **smaller** than a **right angle**.

   b Make a list of some places you might find an angle **bigger** than a **right angle**.

4. Make a list of all the places you might find a right angle in your house.

5. Use your template to decide which of these are right angles.

Answer **YES** or **NO**.

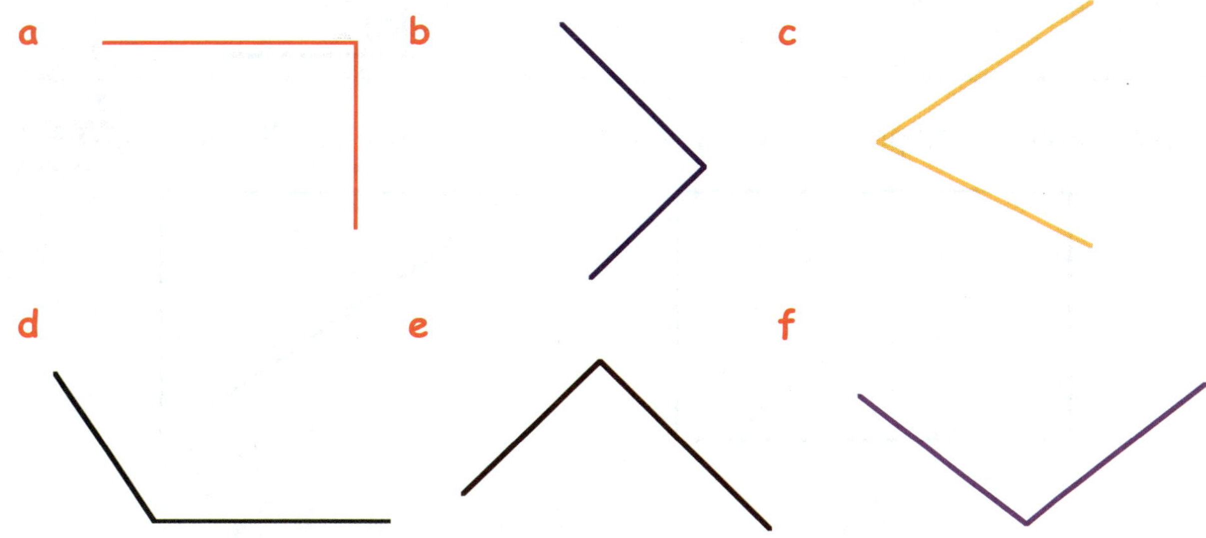

6. Use your template to find out how many **right angles** there are in the 3 figures shown here :-

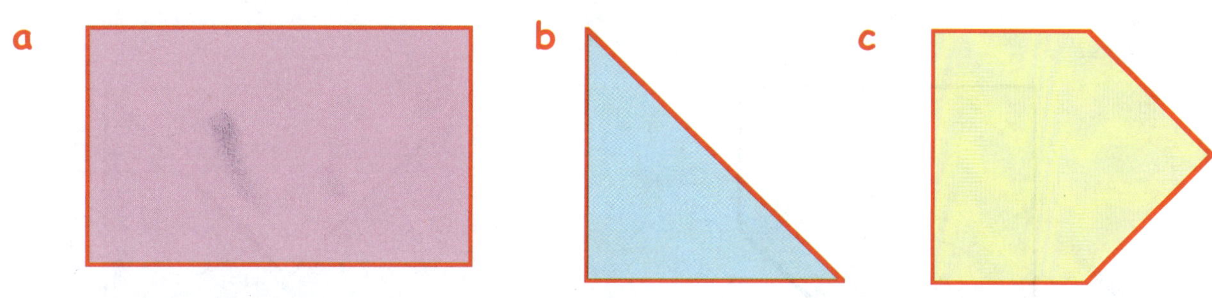

7. How many **right angles** can you see in this picture of a house ?

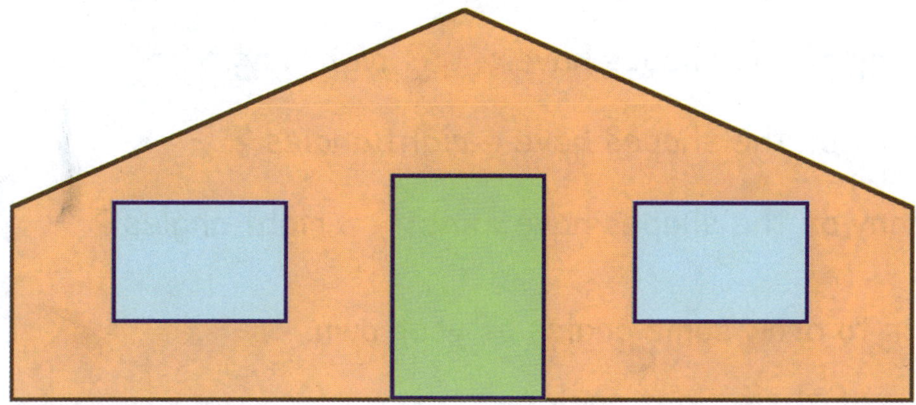

When we draw a right angle, we mark its corner with a **small box**.

8. **Trace** each shape. Mark any right angles with a small box :- **Worksheet 6·2**

a

b

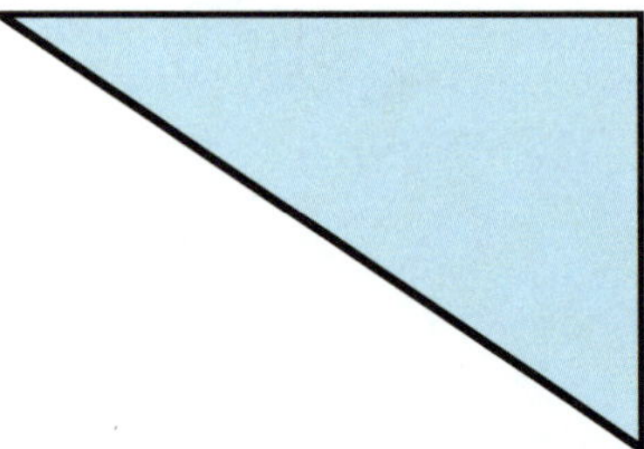

c

d

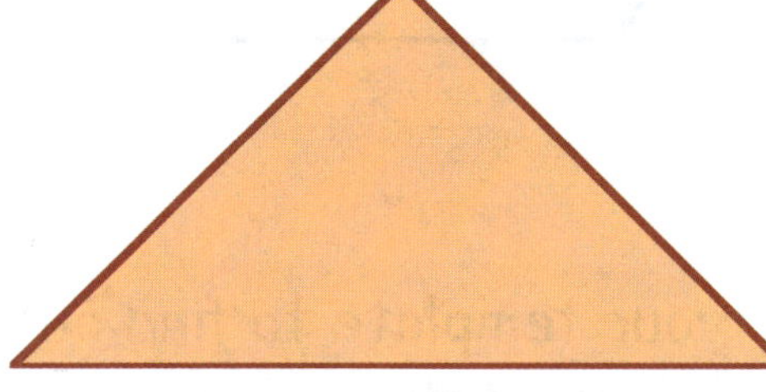

e

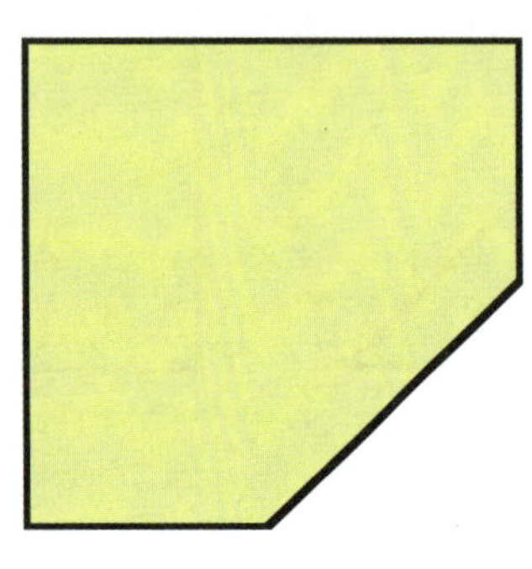

f

9. Look at the 6 shapes in question **8**.

a How many of the shapes have **only 1** right angle ?

b How many of the shapes have **4** right angles ?

c How many of the shapes have **exactly 3** right angles ?

10. Use a ruler to draw some angles of your own.

Make **some** of them right angles.

The 3 ЯʼS

Revisit - Review - Revise

1. How many **angles** can you see in each picture ?

a

b

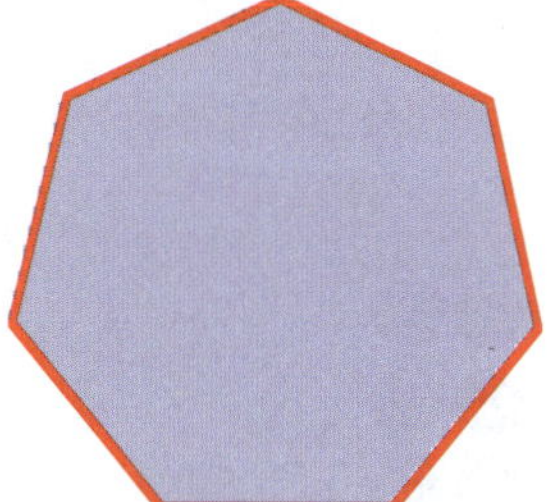

c

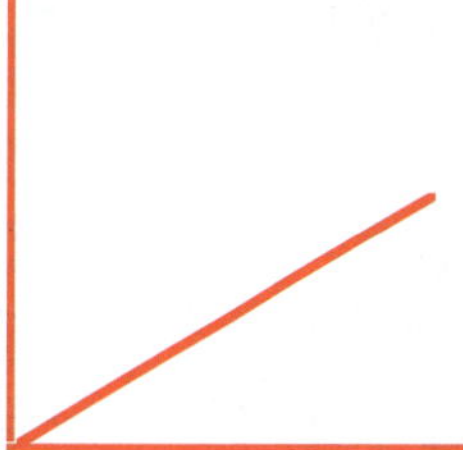

2. Which of these angles are **right angles** ?

a

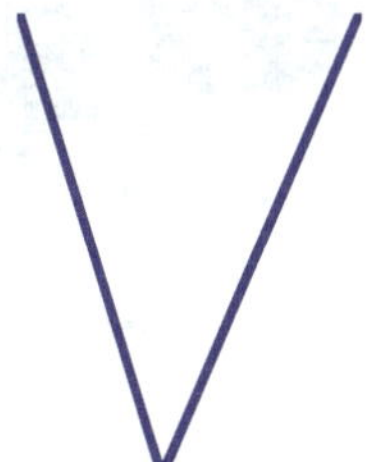

b

c

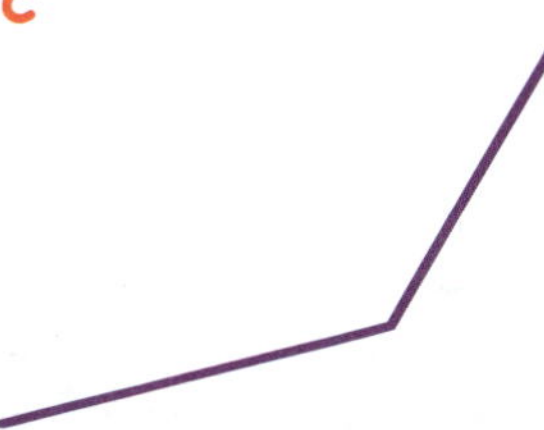

3. How many **right angles** can you see here ?

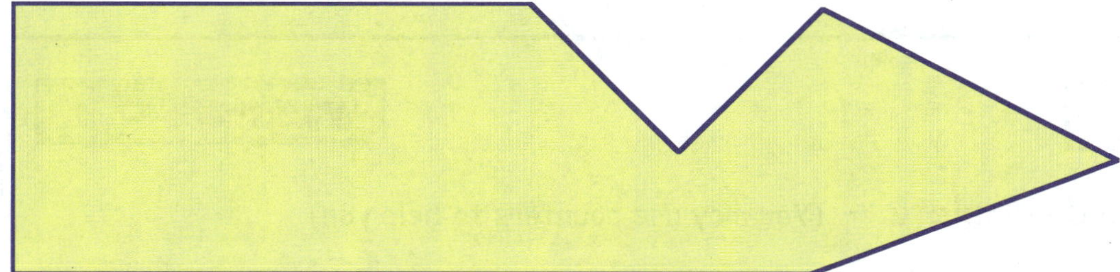

4. a **Trace** the shape above.

   b Mark all the **right angles** you can see.

Subtracting

Whole Numbers 4

Subtracting whole numbers up to 3 digits with no "carrying".

You can use coins to help you subtract (take away).

Example What is 17 - 4 ?

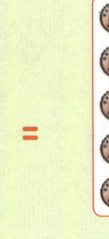

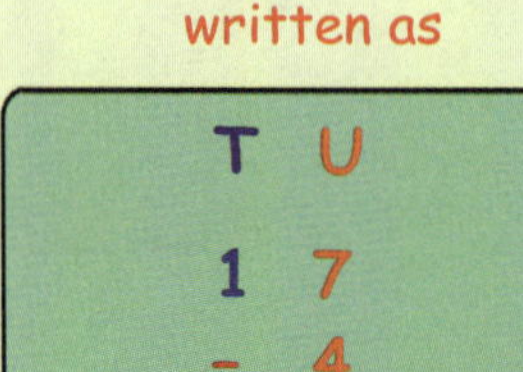

17 - 4 = 17 - 4 = 13

17 - 4 = 13

This can be written as

When subtracting, the numbers must be in line.

Example Subtract :- 48 - 3.

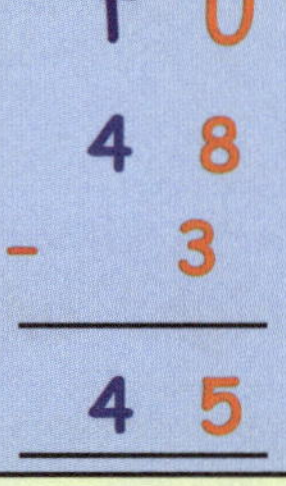

Line up the 8 below the 3

Exercise 1

Worksheet 7·1

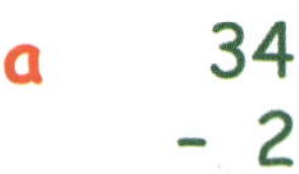

1. **Copy** and **complete** :- (You may use counters to help you)

a 34 - 2

b 27 - 4

c 76 - 1

d 59 - 3

e 89 - 5

f 48 - 8

g 38 - 7

h 49 - 9

2. Set down the subtractions like Question 1 and work out :-

a 22 - 1	b 38 - 2	c 47 - 3	d 58 - 4
e 69 - 5	f 78 - 6	g 87 - 7	h 99 - 8
i 18 - 7	j 49 - 6	k 55 - 5	l 76 - 4.

3. Dana asked **26** friends to her Halloween party.

4 of them could not come.

How many **turned up** ?

4. 

A cook was carrying **37** eggs.

6 dropped and they broke.

How many whole eggs **were left** ?

5. Newspapers usually **48p** are priced at **5p** less.

What do they cost **now** ?

5p OFF !

6. Oscar had **59** blocks of chocolate.

He ate a piece with **9** blocks.

How many blocks were **left** ?

7. A shopkeeper bought in **77** bags of potatoes and sold **5** of them right away.

How many were **left** ?

8. 

London Zoo had **68** snakes in the reptile house.

3 were moved to Chester Zoo and **4** to Edinburgh Zoo.

How many did that leave in London Zoo ?

Subtraction in Tens

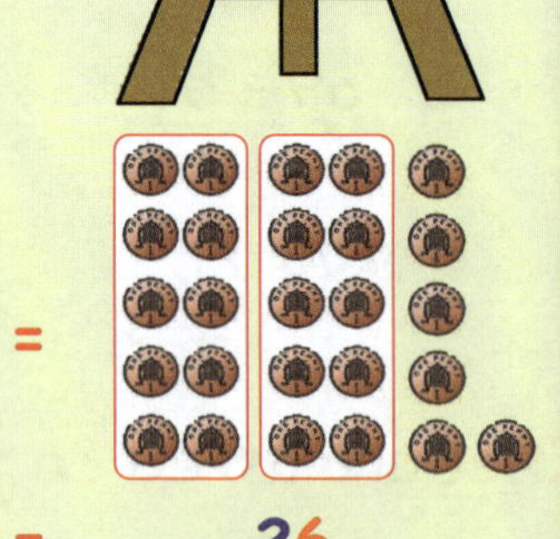

Example Work out :- 38 – 12.

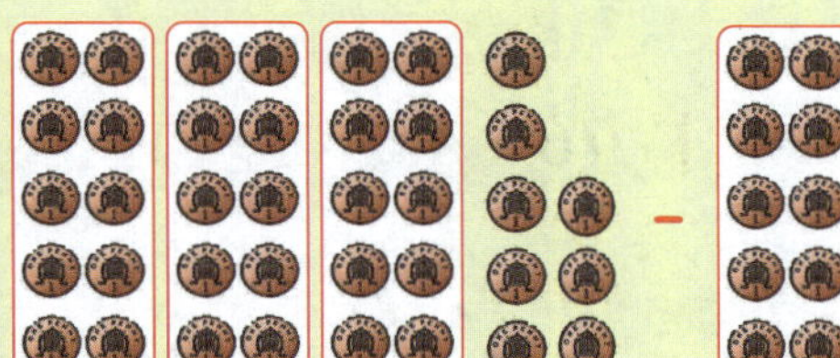

38 – 12 = 38 – 12 = 26

38 – 12 = 26

This can be written as

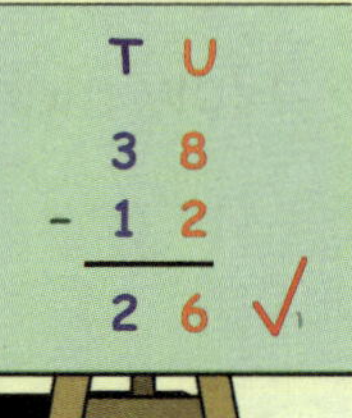

* Remember to line up the numbers

Exercise 2

Worksheet 7·2

1. **Copy and complete** :-

a	42 - 11	b	59 - 15	c	74 - 13	d	83 - 51
e	47 - 23	f	75 - 13	g	98 - 74	h	89 - 63
i	84 - 71	j	87 - 35	k	58 - 20	l	99 - 29

2. **Line up** the subtractions, then work them out :-

a	17 - 10	b	56 - 11	c	35 - 13	d	67 - 22
e	74 - 33	f	88 - 20	g	79 - 18	h	37 - 31
i	66 - 44	j	77 - 11	k	99 - 17	l	64 - 64.

3. There were **49** apples in a barrel.

23 of them went bad.

How many were still **good** ?

4. 

Jorge prints off **57** pages.

32 are in colour.

How many in **black and white** ?

5. **88** buses are parked outside a football stadium.

44 are green the rest are yellow.

How many are **yellow** ?

6. 

The monkeys in a zoo ate **92** bananas on Saturday, but on Sunday ate **21** fewer.

How many did they eat on Sunday ?

7. The school library gave **75** books to Primary 3 and **30** books **less** to Primary 2.

How many books did Primary 2 get ?

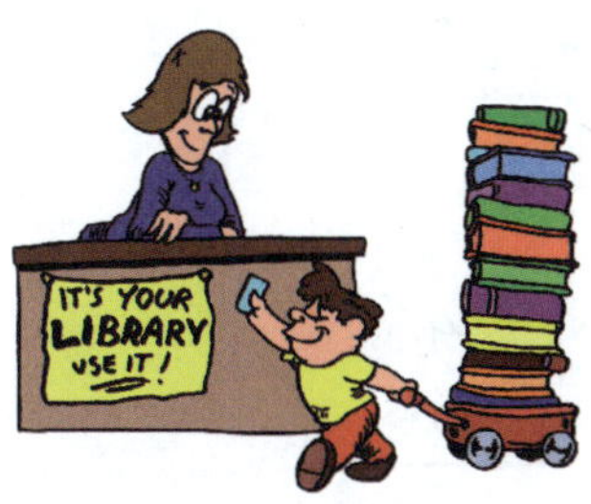

8. 

J P Sports had **46** football tops for sale.

They now have **11** left.

How many tops were sold ?

9. There are **59** coloured pencils in a box.

4 are red, **25** are yellow and the rest are blue.

How many blue coloured pencils are in the box ?

Subtraction in Hundreds

Subtracting 3 digits from 3 digits with no "carrying".

Example Try this :- 497 - 173

Set down as shown.

* Remember to line up the numbers

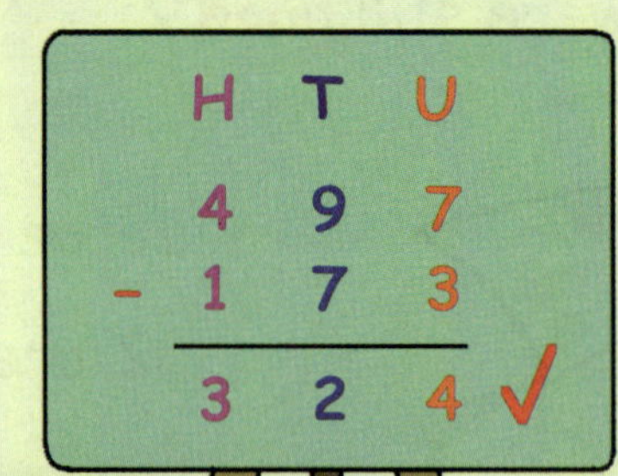

H	T	U
4	9	7
- 1	7	3
3	2	4 ✓

7 - 3 = 4
9 - 7 = 2
4 - 1 = 3

497 - 173 = 324

Exercise 3

Worksheet 7·3

1. **Copy** and **complete** :-

a 253 - 132	b 369 - 127	c 481 - 301	d 436 - 233
e 507 - 205	f 572 - 421	g 689 - 314	h 697 - 523
i 746 - 214	j 879 - 532	k 950 - 450	l 999 - 923

2. **Line up** each subtraction **before** working out the answers :-

a 193 - 82	b 768 - 17	c 254 - 253	d 375 - 212
e 398 - 194	f 406 - 102	g 499 - 357	h 501 - 301
i 575 - 263	j 622 - 601	k 695 - 344	l 728 - 413
m 797 - 525	n 888 - 274	o 900 - 700	p 999 - 666.

3. There are **382** tadpoles in a pond.

211 have turned into frogs.

How many tadpoles have still to change ?

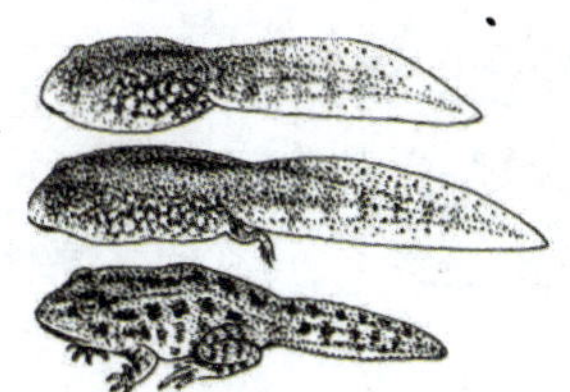

4. 

Out of **350** people asked, **40** said they did not like chicken curry.

How many did like the curry ?

5. Mr Greig gets paid **£885** per week.

Mr Peters gets paid **£112** less.

How much does Mr Peters get ?

6. 

I drove **279** miles from home to Edinburgh.

Later, I drove **118** miles back up the road.

How far had I still to go ?

7. Howard paid for **221** units of electricity in March.

In January, he had paid for **578** units.

How many units **less** did he pay for in March ?

8. 

£ ???

£999 - £720

Ed Baines paid **£999** for an HD television.

His fridge cost **£720 less** than that.

The vacuum cleaner he bought cost **£175 less** than the fridge.

What was the price of the vacuum cleaner ?

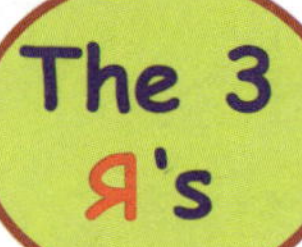

Revisit - Review - Revise

1. Work out :-

a $\begin{array}{r} 48 \\ -\ 7 \\ \hline \end{array}$ b $\begin{array}{r} 236 \\ -\ 24 \\ \hline \end{array}$ c $\begin{array}{r} 457 \\ -\ 136 \\ \hline \end{array}$ d $\begin{array}{r} 809 \\ -\ 203 \\ \hline \end{array}$

2. Find :-

a 68 - 5 b 484 - 63 c 769 - 368 d 957 - 205.

3. Tina texted her mum **368** times last month.
Una texted her mum **122** times fewer.
How many times did Una text her mum ?

4. 

A baker has a tray of **237** steak pies.
He puts **25** into the oven to heat.
How many have still to be heated ?

5. VMH Stores had **396** copies of the PC game "Green Ghost" in stock.
They sold **273** on the first day they were on sale.
How many did they have left ?

6. 

Mr Marsh ordered **589** bedding plants from Gardening Mail ..... **223** Pansies, **130** Marigolds, the rest were Asters.

a How many Asters ?

b How many **more** Asters than Marigolds ?

Using Coins

Money 1

Be able to work with money up to £1.

Here are some coins you might use every day.

1p piece

2p piece

5p piece

10p piece

20p piece

50p piece

Example 1  is the same as 

Example 2  is the same as    

Example 3  is the same as 

Exercise 1

1. a How many  are in  ?

   b How many  are in  ?

   c How many 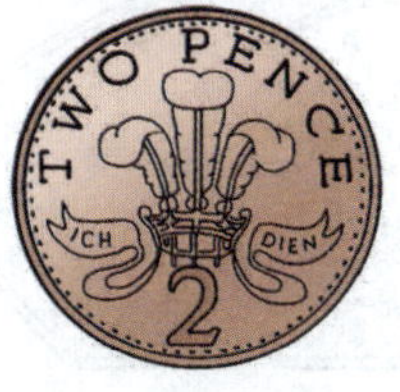 are in  ?

1. d How many 

are in 

?

e How many 

are in 

?

f How many 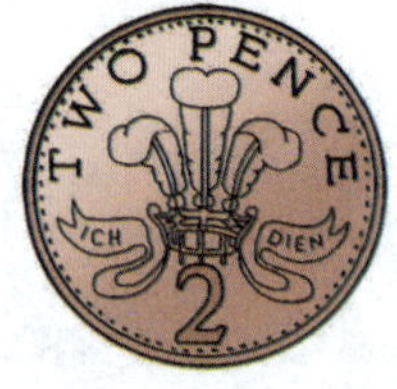

are in 

?

2. How many **1p** coins can I get for :-

a 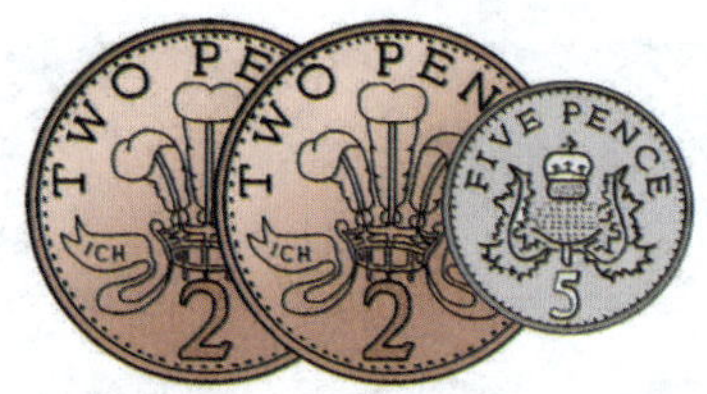

b 

3. How many **2p** coins can I get for :-

a 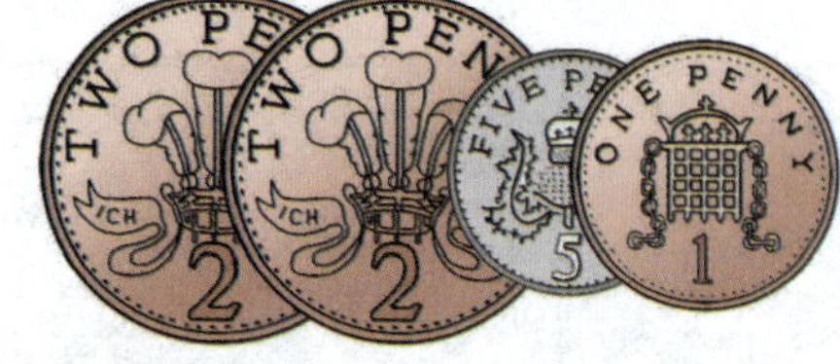

b 

4. How many **5p** coins can I get for :-

a 

b 

5. How many **10p** coins can I get for :-

a 

b 

Here is another coin you might use every day.

£1 coin

There are 100 pence in £1.

6. How many  pieces are in  ?

7. a How many 20p pieces can I get for £1 ?

b How many 10p pieces can I get for £1 ?

c How many 5p pieces can I get for £1 ?

d How many 2p pieces can I get for £1 ?

8. List the coins you might use to pay for each item exactly :-

a 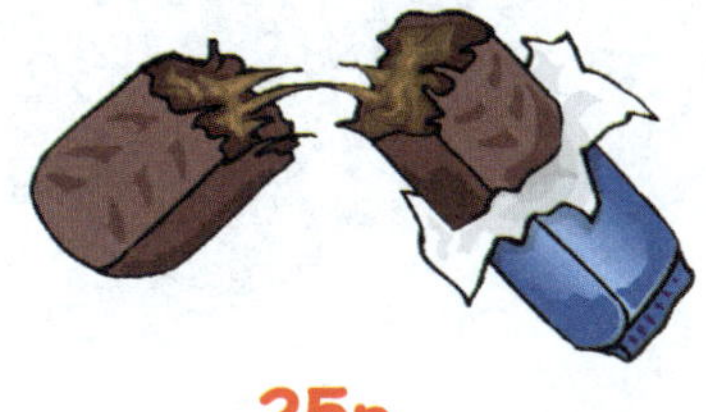
25p

b 
80p

c  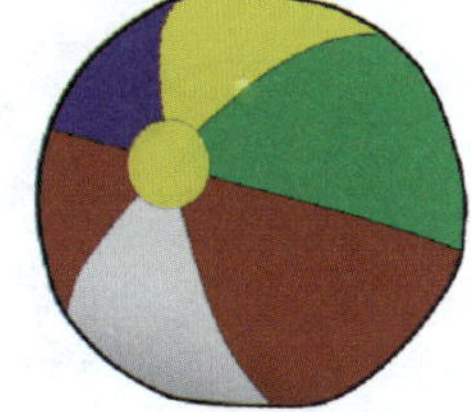
57p

d 

76p

e 
48p

f  
99p

9. Make up some questions of your own, similar to question 8.

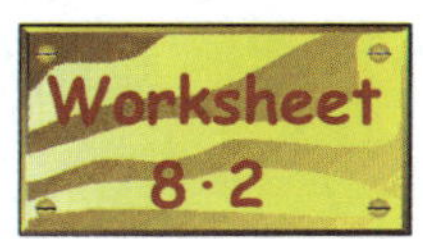

Adding and Subtracting Money up to £1

Be able to add or subtract money up to £1.

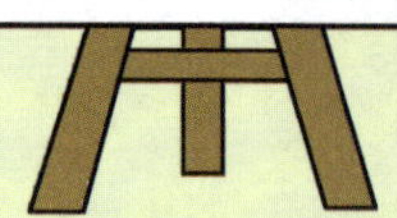

Jamie has 

Amy has 

Altogether they have **89p**.

$$\begin{array}{rl} & 35 \text{ Jamie} \\ + & 54 \text{ Amy} \\ \hline & 89 \end{array}$$

Exercise 2

1. How much does each pair of children have altogether ?

 a Lee 

 Olive 

 b Penny 

 Kia 

2. Sara has 

 Kevin has 

 a How much do 3a and Kevin have **altogether** ?

 b How much **more** does Sara have than Kevin ?
 (hint - subtract).

3. Jack has  Gary has 

Maisie has  Annie has 

a How much do the boys have **altogether** ?

b How much do the girls have **altogether** ?

c How much **more** do the boys have than the girls ?

4. Ian has  Harry **too** has some money.

Altogether they have 76p. How much does Harry have ?

5. Yari has  Bud has 

They put their money together.

Do they have enough money to buy a Whizz magazine costing 95p ?

6. Frank has a one pound coin.

He buys a drink costing 67p.

a How much change will he get ?

b List the coins he could get in his change ?

The 3 Я's

Revisit - Review - Revise

1. a How many  are in  ?

   b How many  are in  ?

   c How many  are in  ?

2. List the coins you might use to pay for each item **exactly** :-

   a 

   75p

   b 

   49p

   c 

   66p

3. Brad has  Bart has 

   a How much does each boy have ?

   b How much do they have **altogether** ?

   c How much **more** does Brad have than Bart ?

Chapter 9

Whole Numbers 5

Subtraction with Carrying (or Borrowing)

Subtracting 1 digit number from 2 digit number with "carrying".

Example Subtract :- 24 − 8.

24 − 8 = 10 + 14 − 8 = 10 + 6 = 16

This can be written as

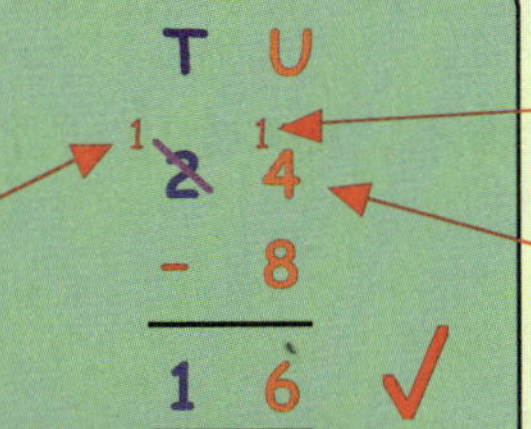

*We **cannot** take 8 away from 4.*

*We need to **borrow** (or **carry**) 1 ten and **change** this to 10 units.*

This means the 4 becomes 14.

Then the 2 tens become 1 ten.

Now we can do the subtraction.

24 − 8 = 16

Exercise 1

Worksheet 9·1

1. **Copy and complete** :- (You can use counters to help you)

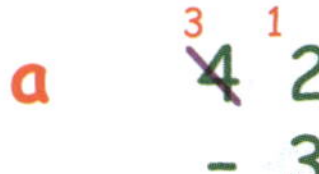

a	42 − 3	b	31 − 8	c	66 − 7	d	45 − 8
e	23 − 4	f	74 − 5	g	92 − 9	h	50 − 1
i	41 − 2	j	83 − 7	k	57 − 8	l	90 − 9

2. Set down these like Question 1 and find :-

a 44 - 5 b 80 - 2 c 62 - 4 d 35 - 7

e 71 - 3 f 53 - 9 g 76 - 8 h 91 - 6.

3. Len has a pack of playing cards with **52** cards in it.

He lays **6** cards down on the table.

How many cards are left in the pack ?

4. 

An ice cream van sold **74** cones.

7 of them had a flake.

How many didn't have a flake ?

5. Of the **60** people at the station
9 were waiting for the Ayr train.

How many were **not** waiting for the train ?

6. A waiter was carrying **25** plates.

They dropped and broke **8** of them.

How many were left unbroken ?

7. Irene has only sold **5** raffle tickets from a book of **93** tickets.

How many has she still to sell ?

8. 

There are **82** library books on a trolley.

9 of them are old and have to be thrown out.

How many are being kept ?

Subtraction in Tens (with carrying) (or Borrowing)

Subtracting 2 digit number from 2 digit number with "carrying".

Subtract :- 45 - 18.

This can be written as

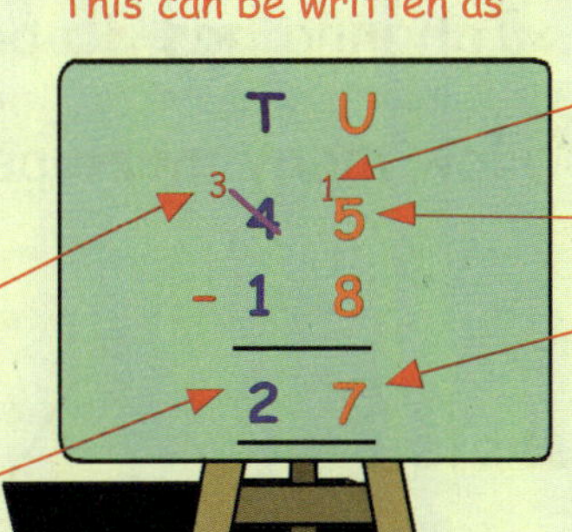

We cannot take 8 away from 5.

We need to borrow (or carry) 1 ten and change this to 10 units.

So the 5 becomes 10 + 5 = 15.

8 away from 15 is 7.

Then the 4 tens become 3 tens.

Now we can do the subtraction.

1 ten away from 3 tens is 2 tens.

45 - 18 = 27

Exercise 2

1. **Copy** and **complete** :-

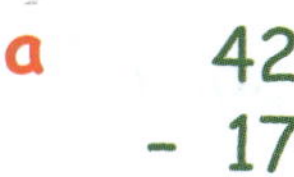

a 42 - 17	b 51 - 28	c 74 - 35	d 63 - 46
e 95 - 57	f 80 - 61	g 91 - 67	h 92 - 73
i 95 - 16	j 84 - 38	k 94 - 29	l 90 - 49

2. Set down these subtractions like Question 1, then try them :-

a 62 - 14	b 55 - 19	c 43 - 27	d 67 - 49
e 70 - 11	f 60 - 28	g 93 - 45	h 104 - 95.

3. Mrs Hendrie is **56**.

Mr Hendrie is **48**.

How much **younger** is Mr Hendrie ?

4. 

Johanna has **35** pencils and **19** pens.

How many **more** pencils than pens ?

5. Barry's golf score was **93** shots.

He played Val, who scored **69**.

a Who won ?

b By how many shots **less** ?

6. 

Mansell had to give up after **27** laps.

Moss lasted **61** laps before stopping.

How many **more** laps did Moss finish than Mansell ?

7. There are **85** sweets in a large tin.

Lenny eats **38** of them.

How many sweets are left ?

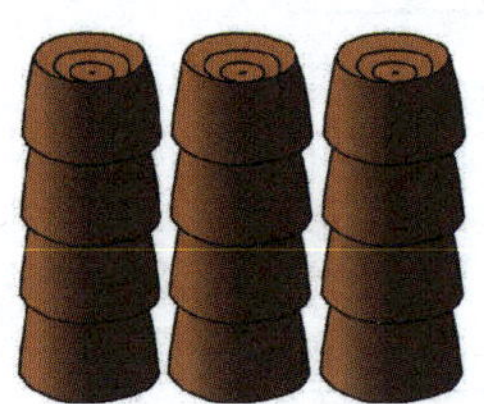

8. Sandie has **£70** in her bank account.

She takes out **£15** to buy new earphones.

How much has she left ?

Subtraction in Hundreds (with carrying)

Example Look at :- 7 4 6 - 1 5 9.

Your teacher will explain this.

This can be written as

	H	T	U
	6 ~~7~~	13 ~~4~~	16
-	1	5	9
	5	8	7

We cannot take 9 away from 6.

We need to borrow (or carry) 1 ten and change this to 10 units.

=> the 6 becomes 10 + 6 = 16.

9 away from 16 is 7.

Then the 4 tens become 3 tens.

Now we can try to do the subtraction.

But we cannot take 5 away from 3.

We need to borrow (or carry) 1 hundred and change this to 10 tens.

=> the 3 becomes 10 + 3 = 13.

5 tens away from 13 tens is 8 tens.

Then the 7 hundreds become 6 hundreds.

Now we can do the subtraction.

1 hundred away from 6 hundreds is 5 hundreds

746 - 159 = 587

Exercise 3

1. **Copy** and **complete** :-

a	b	c	d
303 − 124	431 − 158	622 − 187	710 − 246
e 763 − 294	**f** 397 − 318	**g** 419 − 275	**h** 725 − 389
i 801 − 488	**j** 804 − 507	**k** 887 − 89	**l** 912 − 178

2. **Line up** each subtraction, then work out the answers :-

a 834 - 547	**b** 856 - 592	**c** 961 - 635	**d** 802 - 687
e 903 - 705	**f** 830 - 764	**g** 900 - 816	**h** 926 - 878
i 807 - 371	**j** 800 - 408	**k** 903 - 59	**l** 1000 - 234.

3. Mrs Allan's new laptop cost her **£312**.

   Her new phone cost **£124**.

   How much **dearer** was the laptop ?

4. 

   A holiday to Australia costs **£805**.

   A holiday to France costs **£349**.

   What's the **difference** in price ?

5. A large bottle of syrup holds **500 ml**.

   The smaller bottle holds **185 ml**.

   How many **more ml** is in the large bottle ?

6. The chemist has a jar full of **510** flu tablets.

   Abbie buys **28** tablets from the chemist.

   How many are left ?

7. A secretary has **1000** envelopes.

   He has put stamps on **555** but has still to do the rest.

   How many has he still to do ?

8. 

   A farmer has **823** haystacks to move over the weekend.

   On Saturday, they move **595** of them and leave the rest for Sunday - but they only manage to move **200**.

   How many are left to be moved the next day ?

Subtraction - A Mixture

Exercise 4

Subtracting up to 3 digits - a mixture

1. Copy and complete :-

a	b	c	d
83 - 6	125 - 9	74 - 28	703 - 91

e	f	g	h
81 - 36	800 - 235	724 - 368	1010 - 525

2. Line these up and try them :-

a 75 - 28   b 109 - 63   c 411 - 136   d 852 - 275.

3. Jordan has lived on a farm for **24** years.

Maureen has lived there for **7** years **less**.

How long has Maureen lived on the farm ?

4. 

45 ordinary dustbins are ready for collection.

There are **73** recycling bins there too.

How many **more** recycling bins ?

5. Mr Samson's gas bill came to **£212**.

Next door, Mr Watt's bill was **£94**.

What's the **difference** in price ?

6. 

Last year I paid **£345** to get my car serviced !

This year it cost me **£189**.

How much cheaper was that ?

Subtracting with a Calculator

Subtracting whole numbers up to 3 digits using a calculator.

Find these buttons on your **calculator** :-

[−] means **subtract**

[=] means **equals**

Examples

Press [5][6] [−] [2][9] [=] → The answer is **27**.

[8][4][1] [−] [4][5][6] [=] → The answer is **385**.

Exercise 5

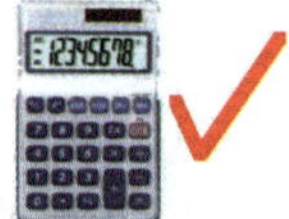

1. a Press [7][3] [−] [2][9] [=]. Write down your answer.

   b Press [8][0][1] [−] [2][7][6] [=]. Write down your answer.

2. **Find** :-

a 38 - 29	**b** 66 - 48	**c** 53 - 47	**d** 71 - 15
e 172 - 88	**f** 148 - 99	**g** 576 - 218	**h** 892 - 876
i 665 - 167	**j** 500 - 222	**k** 630 - 480	**l** 1000 - 775.

3. Amy Baker scored **61** goals last year.

   This year she has scored **25** goals **less**.

   How many goals has she scored ?

4. 

   A tree had **450** oranges on it, but a high wind blew off **264** of them.

   How many oranges are still on the tree ?

Revisit - Review - Revise

1. **Work out** :-

a $62 - 8$

b $415 - 57$

c $647 - 369$

d $701 - 409$

2. **Find** :-

a 74 - 6 b 603 - 72 c 317 - 148 d 626 - 479.

3. There were **341** fashion shops in the area.

Sadly **95** of them closed down last year.

How many are left open ?

4.  

There are two sizes of hose available in a garden centre - **35** metres and **16** metres.

How much **longer** is one than the other ?

5. Sally sold **£578** worth of books last weekend, compared to Hazel who sold **£917** worth.

How much less were Sally's sales ?

6. 

534 people were asked about their favourite pet.

257 said dogs and **169** said cats.
The rest chose something else.

a How many people chose something else ?

b How many **more** people chose dogs than chose cats ?

Chapter 10

Money 2

Be able to handle and use decimal money up to £1.

Money and Decimals

£1 can be written as £1·00.

93p can be written as £0·93.

52p can be written as £0·52.

30p can be written as £0·30.

This is called a **decimal point**.

Always have **two** numbers to the right of the decimal point when working with **money**.

Exercise 1

Worksheet 10·1

1. Write these amounts using a **decimal point** :- (37p = £0·37).

   a 95p b 36p c 20p d 13p

   e 99p f 10p g 80p h 100p.

2. Write each of these as pence without a **decimal point** :-

   a £0·45 b £0·72 c £0·80 d £0·21

   e £0·50 f £0·75 g £1·00 h £0·04.

Ninety four pence can be written as **94p** or **£0·94**

3. Write each amount in **two ways** (as above) :-

   a seventy one pence b twenty two pence

   c sixty pence d thirty pence.

Adding and Subtracting Money with Decimals

When you add or subtract money, you **MUST** line up the **decimal points**.

Examples

Addition

43p + 14p
= 57p
or £0·57

Subtraction

78p − 13p
= 65p
or £0·65

Exercise 2

Worksheet 10·2

1. **Copy** and **complete** these **additions** :-

a £0·34 + £0·15

b £0·47 + £0·31

c £0·44 + £0·34

d £0·55 + £0·16

e £0·54 + £0·38

f £0·66 + £0·26

g £0·30 + £0·50

h £0·25 + £0·55

i £0·40 + £0·60

j £0·57 + £0·29

k £0·86 + £0·14

l £0·29 + £0·69

m £0·53 + £0·26

n £0·26 + £0·58

o £0·22 + 49p

p £0·76 + £0·23

q £0·54 + 56p

r £0·61 + 59p.

2. Copy and complete these subtractions :-

a
$$\begin{array}{r} £0{\cdot}34 \\ -\ £0{\cdot}12 \\ \hline \end{array}$$

b
$$\begin{array}{r} £0{\cdot}56 \\ -\ £0{\cdot}41 \\ \hline \end{array}$$

c
$$\begin{array}{r} £0{\cdot}65 \\ -\ £0{\cdot}35 \\ \hline \end{array}$$

d
$$\begin{array}{r} £0{\cdot}47 \\ -\ £0{\cdot}25 \\ \hline \end{array}$$

e
$$\begin{array}{r} £0{\cdot}87 \\ -\ £0{\cdot}75 \\ \hline \end{array}$$

f
$$\begin{array}{r} £0{\cdot}76 \\ -\ £0{\cdot}66 \\ \hline \end{array}$$

g
$$\begin{array}{r} £0{\cdot}80 \\ -\ £0{\cdot}50 \\ \hline \end{array}$$

h
$$\begin{array}{r} £0{\cdot}72 \\ -\ £0{\cdot}57 \\ \hline \end{array}$$

i
$$\begin{array}{r} £0{\cdot}45 \\ -\ £0{\cdot}28 \\ \hline \end{array}$$

j
$$\begin{array}{r} £0{\cdot}67 \\ -\ £0{\cdot}49 \\ \hline \end{array}$$

k
$$\begin{array}{r} £0{\cdot}86 \\ -\ £0{\cdot}68 \\ \hline \end{array}$$

l
$$\begin{array}{r} £0{\cdot}98 \\ -\ £0{\cdot}89 \\ \hline \end{array}$$

m £0·76 - £0·24

n £0·45 - £0·18

o £0·62 - 38p.

3. a Frank has **£0·74**. His dad gives him **£0·25**.

How much does Frank have now ?

b Jo spent **£0·26** in a chemist and **£0·65** in a newspaper shop.

How much did Jo spend in **total** ?

c Li bought a sweet for **£0·16** and a lolly for **£0·36**.

How much did Li spend **altogether** ?

d Lewis had **£0·47**. He found **£0·25** in coins lying on the street.

How much did Lewis then have **in total** ?

4. **Alan** has **£0·70**. **Amy** has **£0·47**. **Jack** has **£1**.

They visit a shop and look at these items :-

Comic £0·45

£0·36

£0·14

Pizza £0·68

Show all your working for each of these questions :-

a How much money would **Amy** have left if she bought a **comic** ?

b How much money would **Alan** have left if he bought a **comic** ?

c How much money would **Alan** have left if he bought **nuts** ?

d How much money would **Amy** have left if she bought **2 pencils** ?

e How much money would **Jack** have left if he bought a **pizza** ?

f How much money would **Jack** have left if he bought a **pencil** ?

g Does **Alan** have enough to buy a **comic and** a **pencil** ?

h Does **Alan** have enough to buy **nuts and 2 pencils** ?

i **Amy** buys **3 pencils**. How much does she have left ?

j **Jack** buys a **comic and nuts**. How much does he have left ?

k How many **pencils** can **Jack** buy **altogether** ?

l How much money do the **3 children** have **altogether** ?

Money and Decimals up to £5

Be able to use and handle all money up to £5.

Another coin you will use is a £2 coin.

Shown below is £3·88.

Exercise 3

1. How much does each person have ?

a Katie

b Keith

c Neil

d Abraham

e Krish

f Heather

2. **Copy** and **complete** these calculations :-

a
  £2·34
+ £1·12

b
  £1·56
+ £1·41

c
  £3·65
+ £1·35

d
  £3·47
- £1·25

e
  £2·87
- £1·75

f
  £4·76
- £4·67

g
  £1·80
+ £1·50

h
  £5·72
- £3·57

i
  £3·45
+ £1·28

j
  £4·67
- £4·49

k
  £3·86
+ £1·68

l
  £5·98
- £1·89

m £4·76 - £1·24

n £2·45 + 218p

o £3·62 - 138p.

3. a Sarah has **£2·76**. Her gran gives her **£1·75**.

How much does Sarah have now ?

b Zak spent **£2·45** in a sweet shop and **£1·85** in a newspaper shop.

How much did Zak spend in **total** ?

c Sally spent **£4·28** of her pocket money.
Stefan spent **£3·36** of his pocket money.

How much **more** did Sally spend than Stefan ?

Exercise 4 **Money up to £10**

1. How much does each person have ?

a Caitlin

b Bob

2. Calculate :-

a £3·34 + £2·12

b £6·53 + £2·45

c £5·65 + £4·35

d £7·47 - £4·25

e £9·87 - £6·75

f £8·76 - £6·21

g £7·80 + £1·53

h £8·72 - £6·57

i £4·45 + £3·78

j £9·67 - £7·59

k £5·86 + £3·68

l £9·18 - £8·89

m £7·82 - £5·78

n £4·72 + 167p

o £9·07 - 493p.

3. Gary has £7·28. He buys a sandwich costing £3·66 and a juice at £1·48.

Does he have enough money left to buy a cake which costs £2·20 ?

The 3 Я's

Revisit - Review - Revise

1. Write these amounts using a **decimal point** :- (54p = £0·54).

   a 62p b 9p c 257p

   d fifty one pence e ninety pence f six pounds and 1p.

2. **Copy** and **complete** these :-

   a £0·43 + £0·17

   b £0·75 - £0·46

   c £1·55 + £1·27

   d £4·47 - £2·25

   e £4·17 - £3·75

   f £5·76 + £2·67

   g £4·06 - £1·42 h £3·33 + £4·83 i £8·67 - 55p.

3. How much does each person have ?

   a Bob b Carol  c Jai 

4. a Jack has £3·24. Charlie has £4·78.

   How much do they have altogether ?

   b 

   Sharon has £3·35. Gary has some money.
   Altogether they have £8·99.

   How much money does Gary have ?

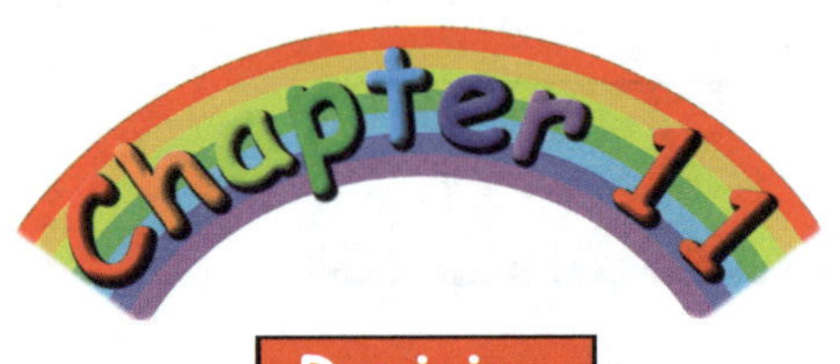

Revision

Time 2

Revise Time from Chapter 4 and know the four Seasons

In Chapter 4 we learned :-

Days of the Week	Months of the Year	"*Some*" clock times
Monday,	January, February,	This clock reads half past 4.
Tuesday,	March, April,	
Wednesday,	May, June,	
Thursday,	July, August,	
Friday,	September, October,	
Saturday,	November,	
Sunday.	December.	This clock reads quarter to 7.

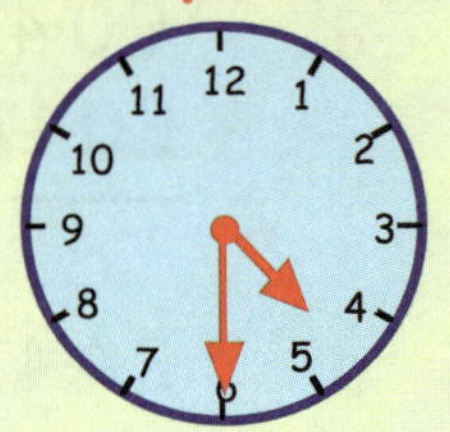

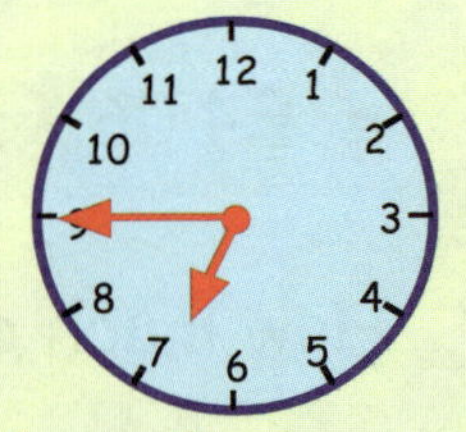

Seasons of the Year

Know the seasons of the year in order.

You also need to know about the seasons of the year.

Spring | Summer | Autumn | Winter

Discuss what kind of things happens during each of the 4 seasons.

Worksheet 11·1

Exercise 1

Worksheet 11·2

1. a Write the **days** of the week in the correct order.

   b Write the **months** of the year in the correct order.

   c Write the **seasons** of the year in the correct order.

2. Write down the missing words :-

   a Monday, ... , ..., Thursday, ..., Saturday, ...

   b April, ... , ... , July, ... , ..., October

   c Spring, ... , ... , Winter, ... , ... , Autumn, ...

3. a What is the day just **after Thursday** ?

   b What is the month just **before June** ?

   c What season follows **after Spring** ?

4. Write the time shown on each clock :-

a 

b 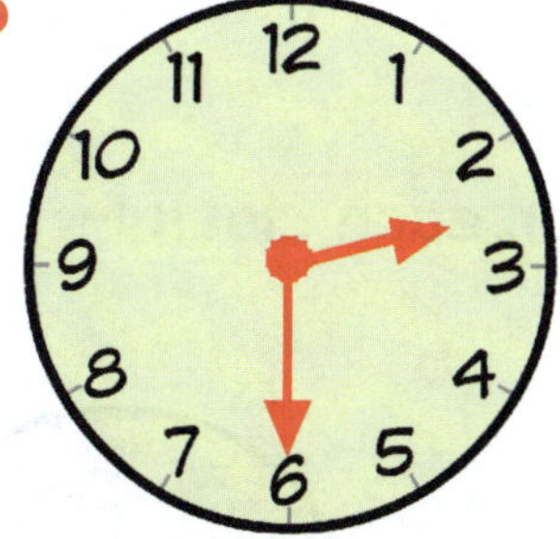

c 

5. a Today is Thursday. I am going to the cinema in **3 days time**.

   On what day am I going to the cinema ?

   b It is September. I went on holiday **last month**.

   What month did I go on holiday ?

Telling the Time

Be able to tell the time from an analogue clock.

Remember :- There are 60 minutes in an hour.

When the big hand is between the 6 and the 12 we say it is **to** the *(next)* hour.

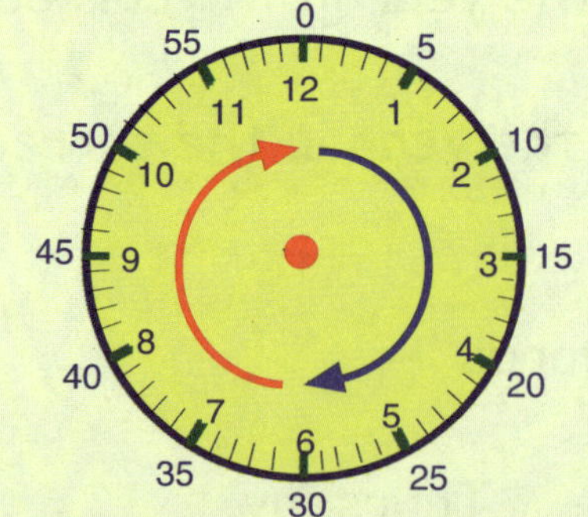

When the big hand is between the 12 and the 6 we say it is **past** the *(last)* hour.

This clocks says
10 minutes past 7

This clocks says
5 minutes to 2

This clocks says
20 minutes past 6

Exercise 2

1. Write down the time on each clock :-

a

b

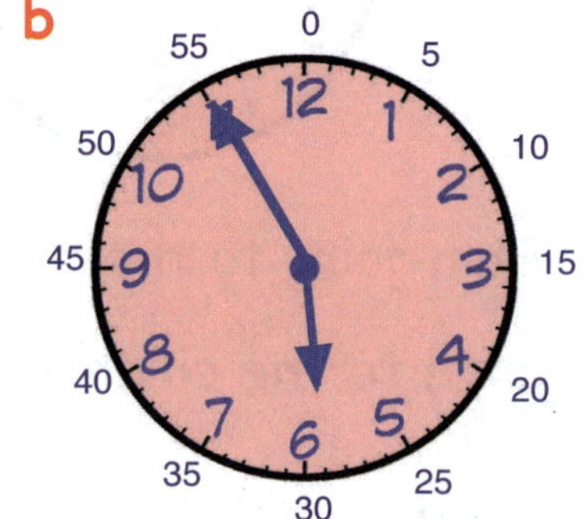

c

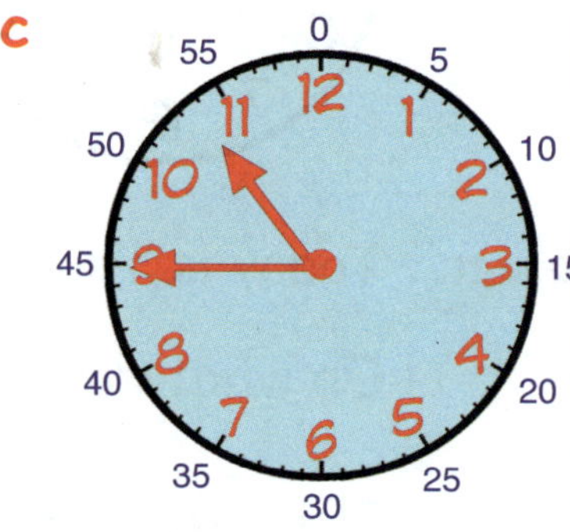

1. d

e

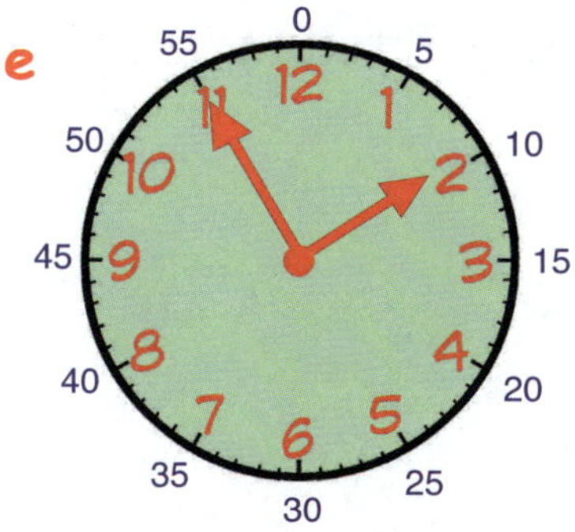

f

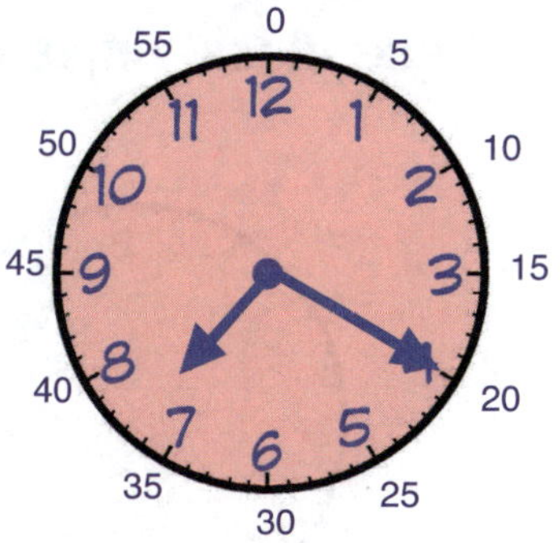

g

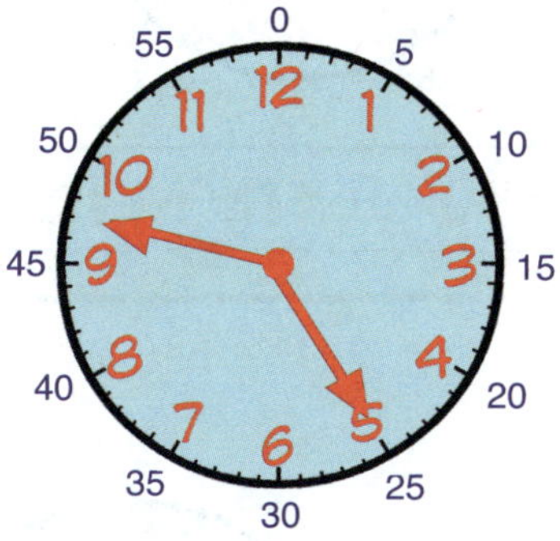

h

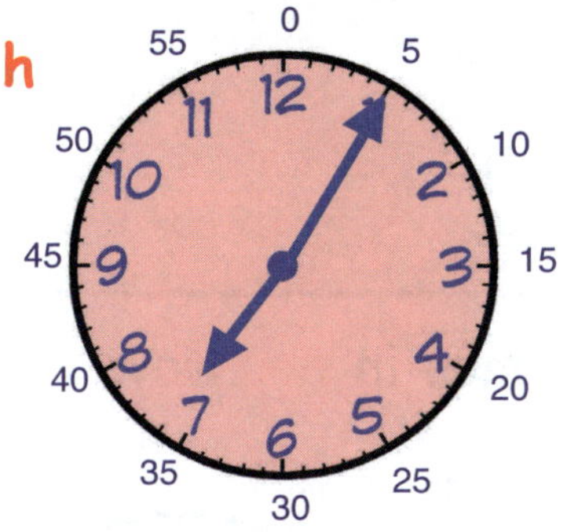

i

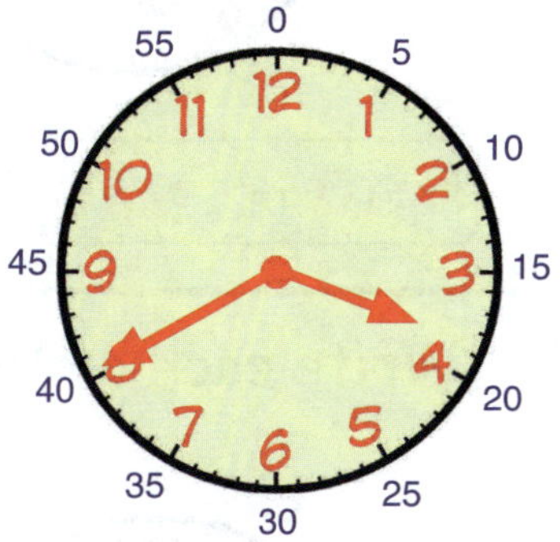

j

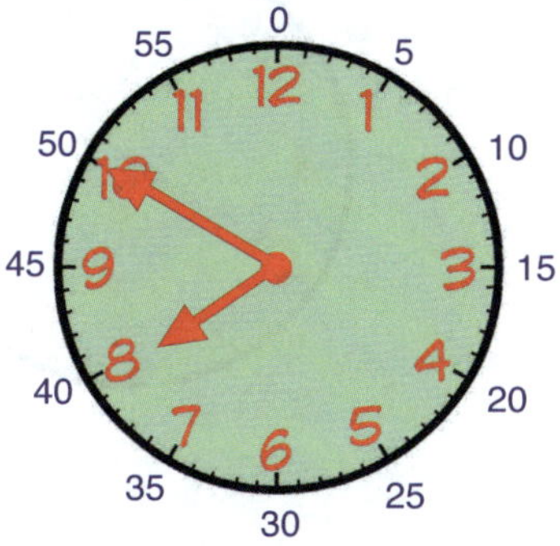

k

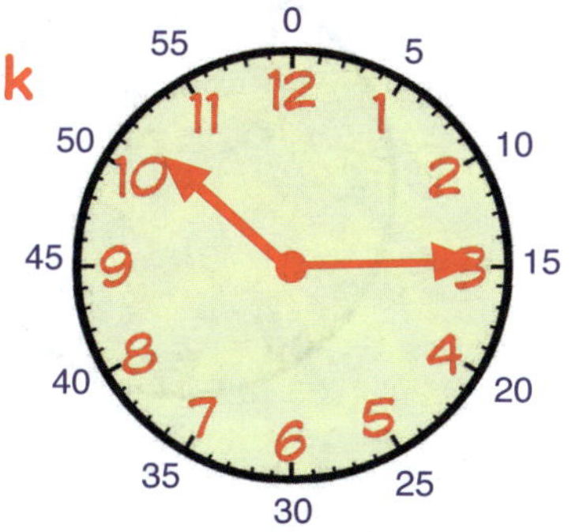

l

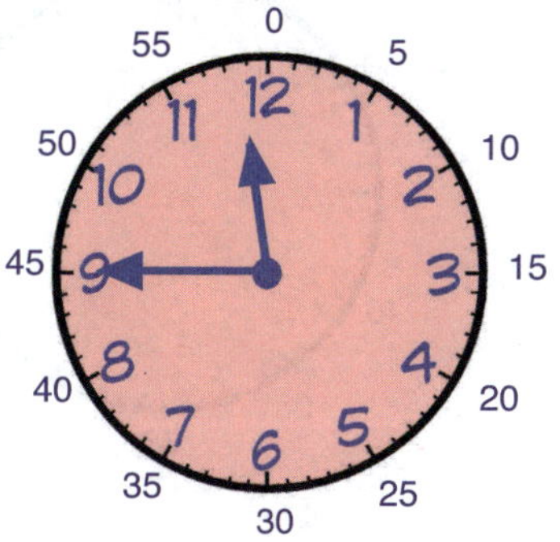

m

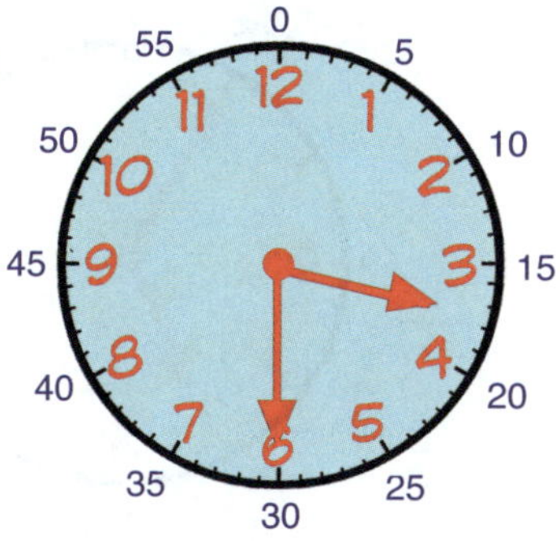

n

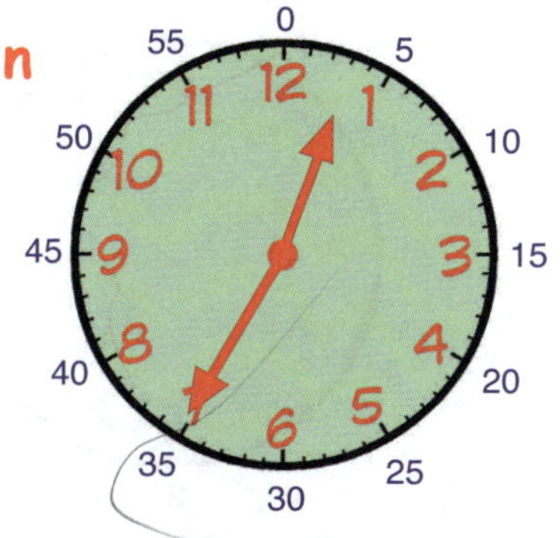

o

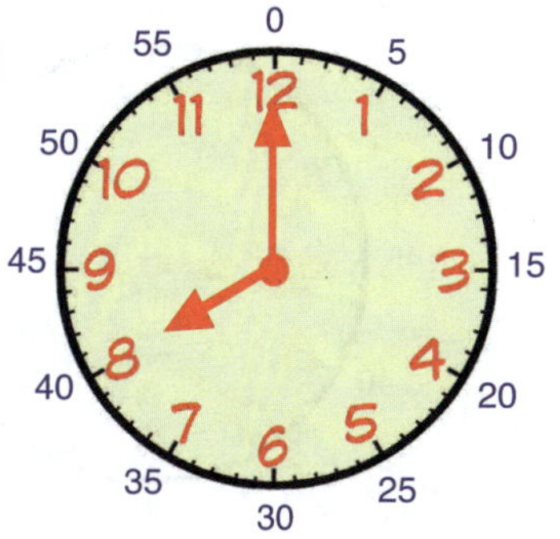

p

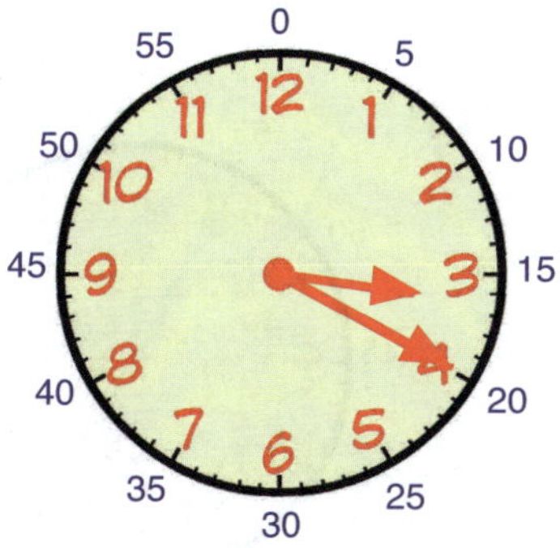

q

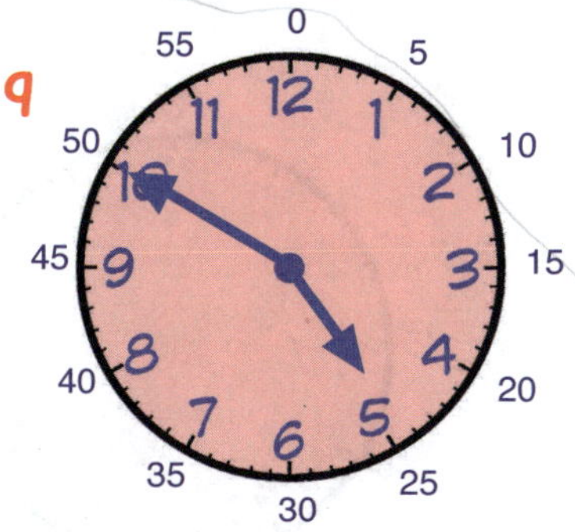

r

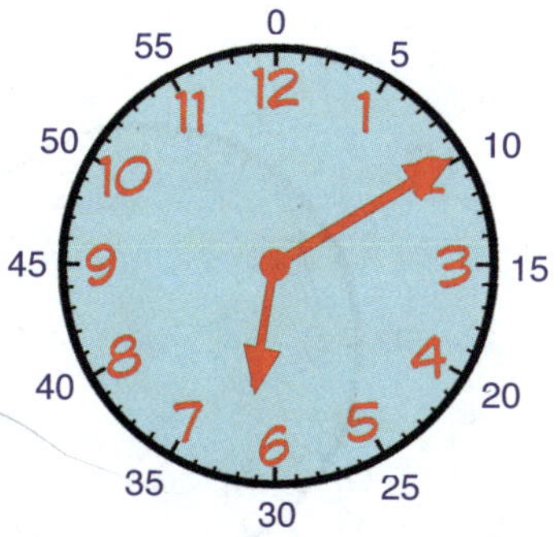

2. Draw some clock faces of your own .

Show the different times of the day when you do things.

These clock times can be written in two ways.
9:10 or ten past nine
1:50 or ten to two

3. Write each of these times in **two** ways :-

a

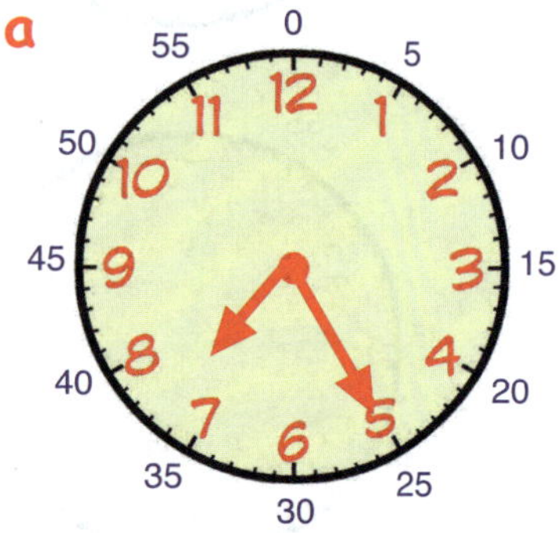

b

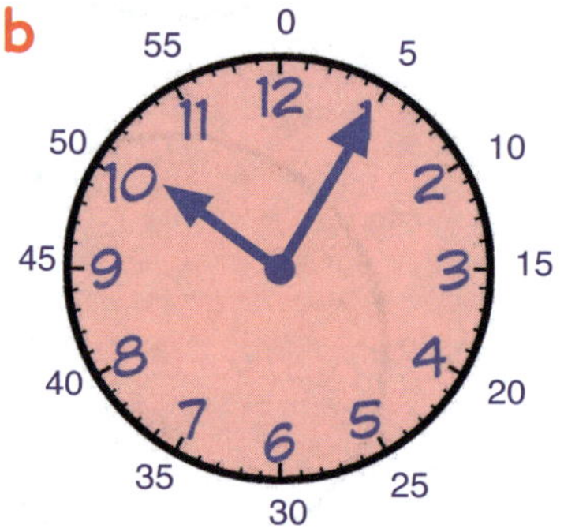

c

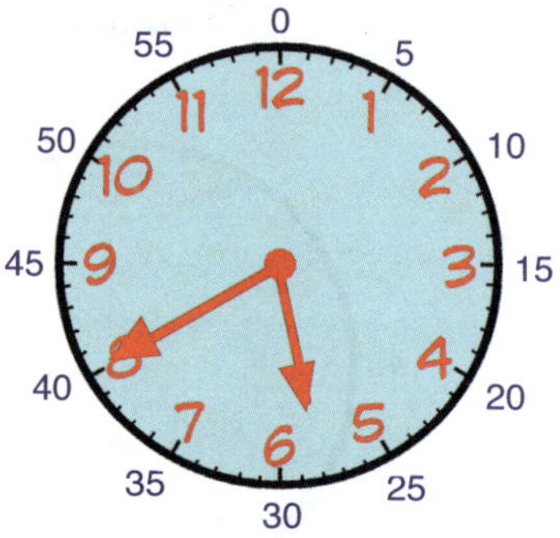

d

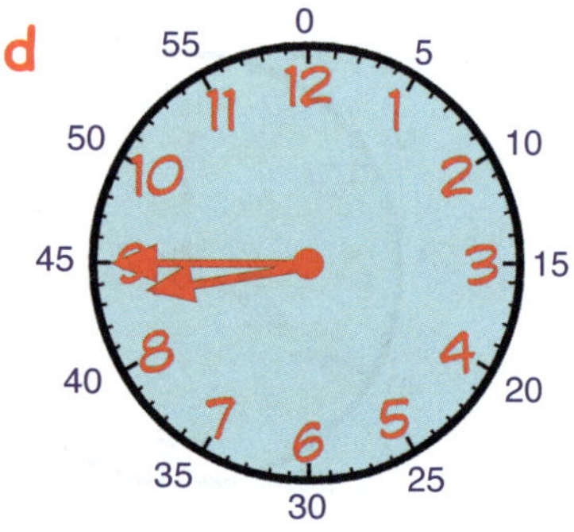

e

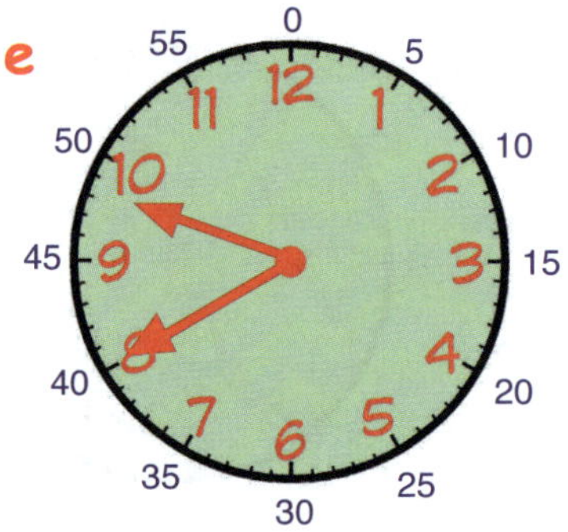

f

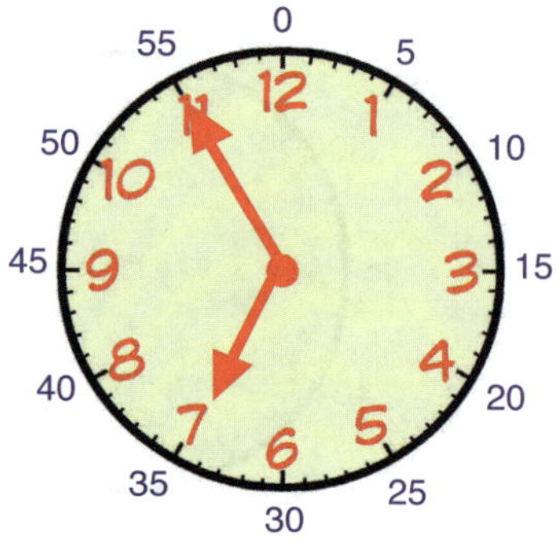

g

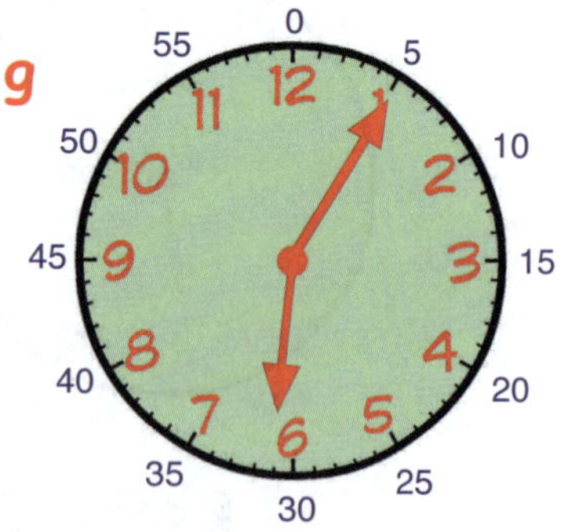

h

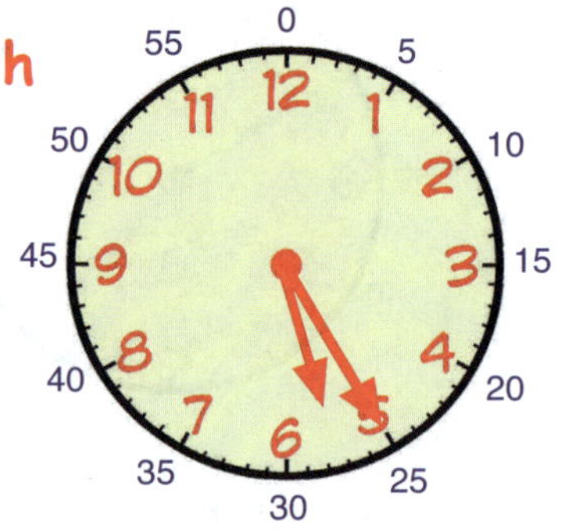

i

Revisit - Review - Revise

1. a Write the **days of the week** in order starting on Monday ....

   b Write the **months of the year** in order.

2. Write the time shown on each clock :-

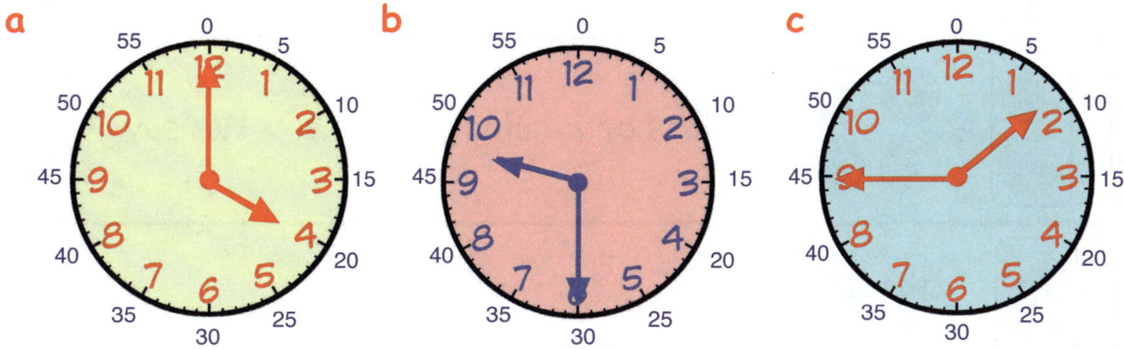

3. Write down the time on each clock **in 2 ways** :-
   (***Example*** - *quarter past 8* or *8·15 pm*)

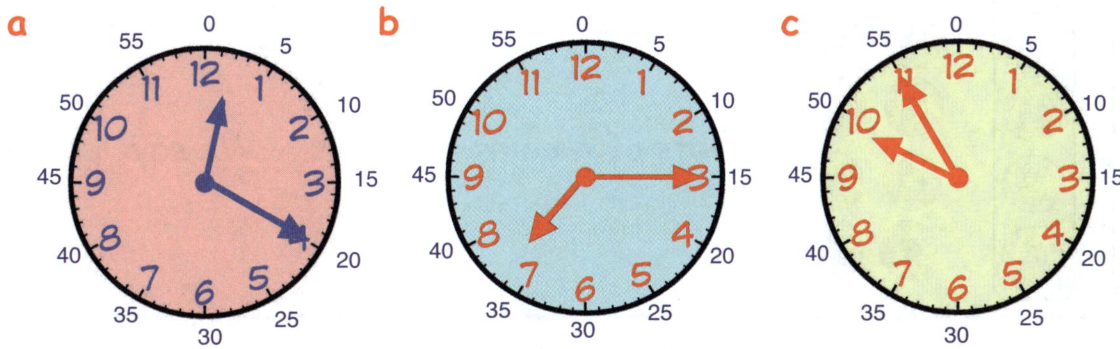

4. a What is the **5th** month of the year ?

   b Today is Tuesday. What day was it **3 days ago** ?

   c Today is Sunday. My birthday is in **6 days time**.
   When is my birthday ?

   d It is 1 o'clock in the afternoon. I arrived home **3 hours ago**.
   At what time did I arrive home ?

2 Times Table

Whole Numbers 6

Multiplying by 2

The 2 times table.

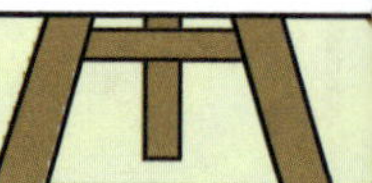

Look at what happens when you have **pairs** of sets of coins :-

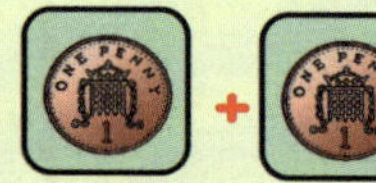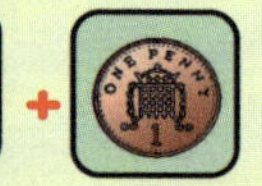

2 lots of 1 coin = 2 coins. We say $2 \times 1 = 2$

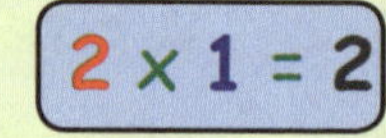
2 times 1 is 2

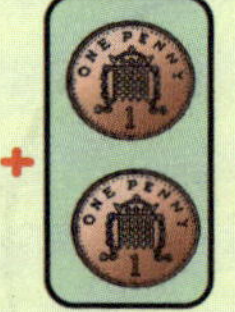

2 lots of 2 coins = 4 coins. We say $2 \times 2 = 4$

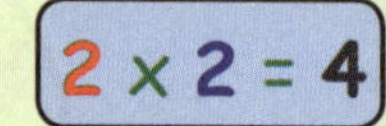
2 times 2 is 4

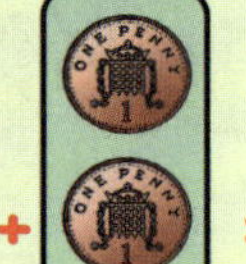

2 lots of 3 coins = 6 coins. We say $2 \times 3 = 6$

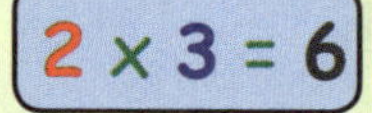
2 times 3 is 6

2 lots of 4 coins = 8 coins. We say $2 \times 4 = 8$

2 times 4 is 8

The sign $\times$ is called the **multiply** or **times** sign.

When we write :- 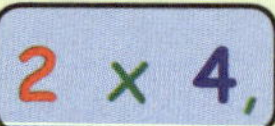 2×4, we mean 2 lots of 4 which gives us 8.

We read this as **2 times 4 equals 8.**

Use **coins** or **counters** to find out the following :-

- 2 lots of 5 coins, ($2 \times 5 = ?$)
- 2 lots of 6 coins, ($2 \times 6 = ?$)
- 2 lots of 7 coins, ($2 \times 7 = ?$)
- 2 lots of 8 coins, ($2 \times 8 = ?$)
- 2 lots of 9 coins, ($2 \times 9 = ?$)
- 2 lots of 10 coins, ($2 \times 10 = ?$)

Exercise 1

1. Copy and complete :- (For example, $2 \times 1 = 2$).

   a $2 \times 2 =$ ..... b $2 \times 3 =$ ..... c $2 \times 4 =$ .....

   d $2 \times 5 =$ ..... e $2 \times 6 =$ ..... f $2 \times 7 =$ .....

   g $2 \times 8 =$ ..... h $2 \times 9 =$ ..... i $2 \times 10 =$ .....

2. Write out and learn the "two times table" by heart.

   Say to yourself, $2 \times 1 = 2$, $2 \times 2 = 4$, $2 \times 3 = 6$, $2 \times 4 = 8$, ...

   Practise it with someone at home.

3. What numbers are missing ?

   a $2 \times$ .... $= 4$ b $2 \times$ .... $= 8$ c $2 \times$ .... $= 12$

   d $2 \times$ .... $= 18$ e $2 \times$ .... $= 0$ f $2 \times$ .... $= 14$

   g $2 \times$ .... $= 16$ h $2 \times$ .... $= 10$ i $2 \times$ .... $= 20$.

4. a There are 2 nests in a barn.

   Each nest has 4 chicks.

   How many chicks are there altogether ?

   b Every room in my house has 2 electric sockets.

   My house has 7 rooms.

   How many sockets in total ?

   c 

   Beryl and Meryl both have 8 plums each.

   What's their total number of plums ?

Multiplying Two Digit Numbers by 2

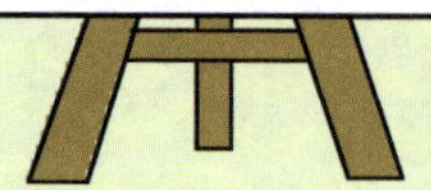

Be able to multiply a 2 digit number by 2.

We can **multiply** a 2 digit number, (or **times it**) by 2.

Example 1 What is 73 x 2?

Example 2 Find 69 x 2.

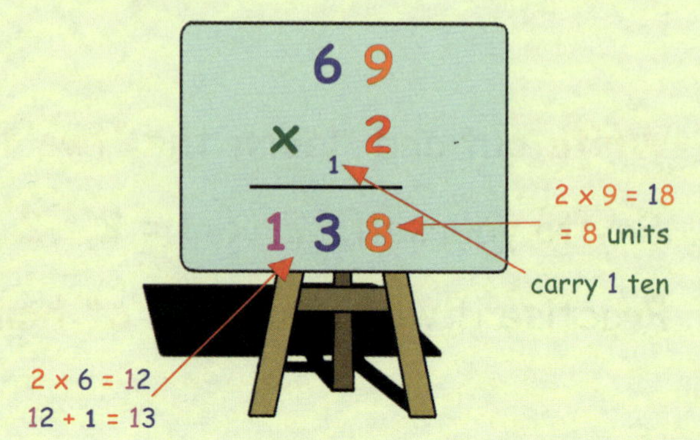

Exercise 2

Worksheet 12·1

1. **Copy** and **complete** :-

a	12 x 2	b	26 x 2	c	34 x 2
d	56 x 2	e	75 x 2	f	87 x 2
g	49 x 2	h	53 x 2	i	28 x 2

2. Find :-

a	14 x 2	b	45 x 2	c	36 x 2
d	54 x 2	e	80 x 2	f	67 x 2
g	79 x 2	h	83 x 2	i	98 x 2.

3. There are **43** builders working on blocks of flats.

Each of them has brought **2** sandwiches for lunch.

How many sandwiches **in total** ?

43
x 2

4. Sadie and her sister both weigh **58** kg.

What's their **total** weight ?

5. A hot dog costs **75p**.

Bernie bought **2** of them.

How much did he pay ?

6. 

The monkeys in a zoo are fed **2** times a day.

As well as bananas, each monkey gets **36** nuts.

How many nuts do they get each day ?

7. John took in **2** Munchies for everyone in his class.

There are **26** children **and** John in the class.

How many Munchies did he take in ?

Doubling a number is the same as **x by 2**.

8. **Find** :-

a double 18	**b** double 33	**c** double 46
d double 65	**e** double 78	**f** double 97.

Be able to muliply by 3. The 3 times table.

This time, we have 3 sets of coins :-

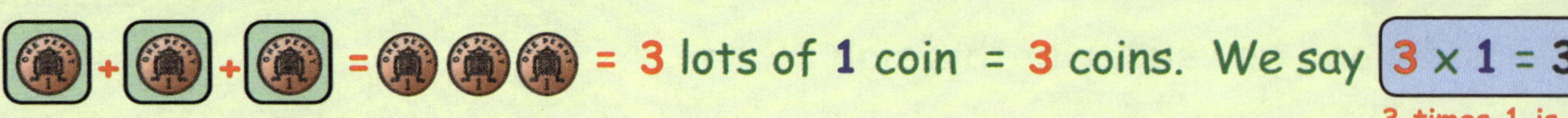

= 3 lots of 1 coin = 3 coins. We say 3 x 1 = 3
3 times 1 is 3

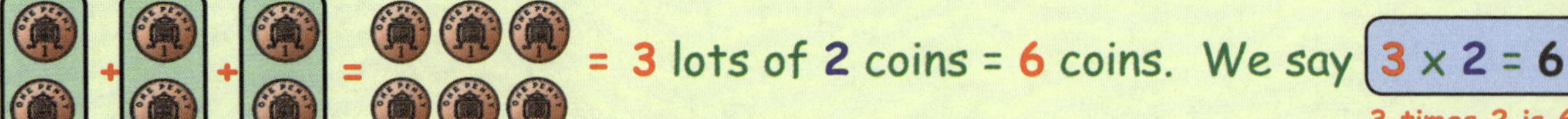

= 3 lots of 2 coins = 6 coins. We say 3 x 2 = 6
3 times 2 is 6

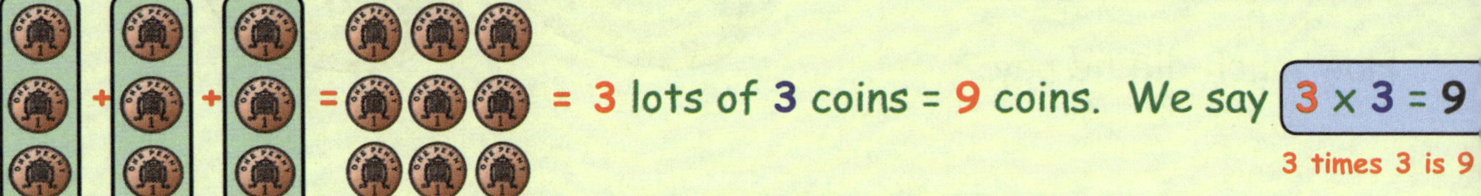

= 3 lots of 3 coins = 9 coins. We say 3 x 3 = 9
3 times 3 is 9

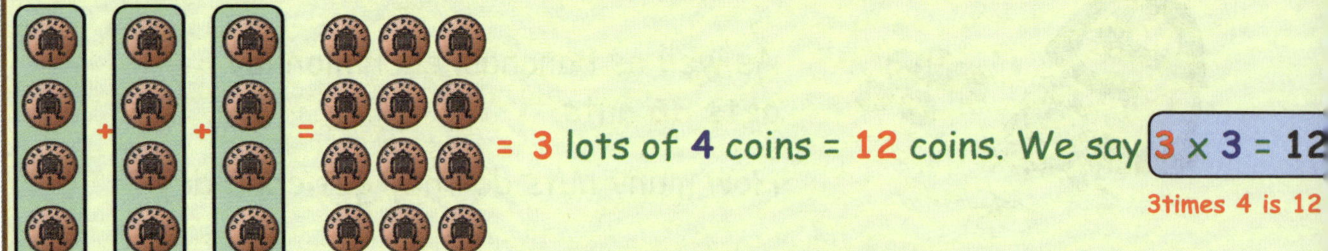

= 3 lots of 4 coins = 12 coins. We say 3 x 3 = 12
3times 4 is 12

Again, the sign **x** is called the **multiply** or **times** sign.

When we write :- 3 x 4 we mean 3 lots of 4 which gives us 12.

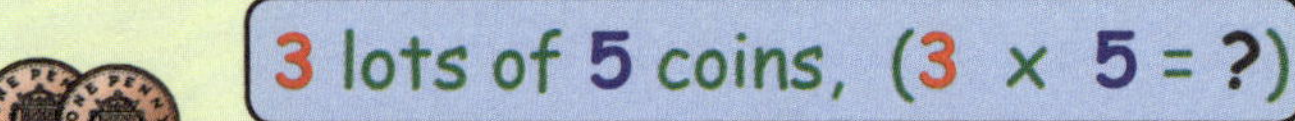

We read this as 3 times 4 equals 12.

Use **coins** or **counters** to find out the following :-

3 lots of 5 coins, (3 x 5 = ?)	3 lots of 6 coins, (3 x 6 = ?)
3 lots of 7 coins, (3 x 7 = ?)	3 lots of 8 coins, (3 x 8 = ?)
3 lots of 9 coins, (3 x 9 = ?)	3 lots of 10 coins, (3 x 10 = ?)

Exercise 3

1. Copy and complete :- (For example, 3 x 1 = 3).

a 3 x 2 = ...   b 3 x 3 = ...   c 3 x 4 = ...

d 3 x 5 = ...   e 3 x 6 = ...   f 3 x 7 = ...

g 3 x 8 = ...   h 3 x 9 = ...   i 3 x 10 = ...

2. Write out and learn the "three times table" by heart.

Say to yourself, 3 x 1 = 3, 3 x 2 = 6, 3 x 3 = 9, 3 x 4 = 12, ...

Practise it with someone at home.

(Remember to keep practising your "2 times table" as well).

3. What numbers are missing ?

a 3 x .... = 9   b 3 x .... = 18   c 3 x .... = 21

d 3 x .... = 15   e 3 x .... = 24   f 3 x .... = 30

g 3 x .... = 27   h 3 x .... = 12   i 3 x .... = 0.

4. a At tea time each of the Reid family get 3 potatoes.

If there are 5 people in the family,
how many potatoes are used ?

b In a sponsored cycle event 3 participants each travel 9 miles. What is the total number of miles ?

c

7 songs are downloaded by 3 friends.

How many songs do they have altogether ?

Multiplying Two Digit Numbers by 3

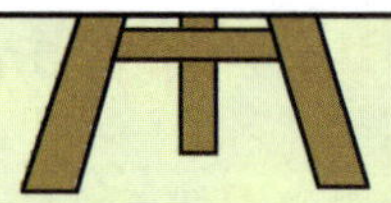
Be able to
multiply a 2 digit
number by 3.

We can **multiply** a 2 digit number (or **times it**) by 3.

Example 1 What is 8 2 x 3 ?

8 2
× 3
2 4 6
3 x 2 = 6
3 x 8 = 24

Example 2 Find 9 8 x 3.

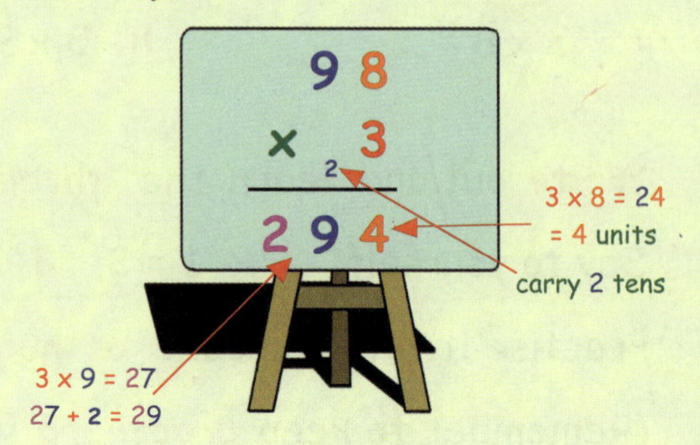
9 8
× 3
2
2 9 4
3 x 8 = 24
= 4 units
carry 2 tens
3 x 9 = 27
27 + 2 = 29

Exercise 4

Worksheet 12·2

1. **Copy** and **complete** :-

a	14 x 3	b	25 x 3	c	31 x 3
d	92 x 3	e	73 x 3	f	46 x 3
g	57 x 3	h	89 x 3	i	49 x 3

2. Find :-

a	17 x 3	b	13 x 3	c	25 x 3
d	39 x 3	e	58 x 3	f	67 x 3
g	44 x 3	h	80 x 3	i	96 x 3.

3. a A football team can have **25** players in their squad.

How many players are there in **3** squads ?

b A pack of balloons costs **70p**.

How much would **3** packs cost ?

c This bus holds **47** people.

How many people would **3** buses hold ?

4. **A mixture** Find :-

a	13×2	b	23×3	c	41×2
d	42×3	e	86×2	f	45×3
g	58×2	h	97×3	i	69×2

5. **69** telephone poles have to be repaired.

If it takes **2** hours to repair each one,
how long will the whole job take ?

6. 

3 people are playing darts and each score **87**.

What is their total score ?

7. This jacket costs **£78**.

If Ami is to buy one for herself **and** her two sisters,
how much will it cost her ?

£78

The 3 Я's

Revisit - Review - Revise

1. **Work out** :-

a	b	c	d
63	82	59	75
x 2	x 3	x 2	x 3

2. **Find** :-

a 2 x 44	b 3 x 62	c 2 x 38	d 3 x 69
e 85 x 2	f 71 x 3	g 94 x 2	h 87 x 3.

3. Donnie's car service costs him **£76** every year.

   What has he paid out over the past **2** years ?

4. 

   A motorcycle goes **68** km each hour.

   How far will it go in **2** hours ?

5. An adult flight to London with Ryanjet costs **£85**.

   A child's flight costs **£69**.

   a What's the cost for **3** adults ?

   b What's the cost for **2** children ?

   c What's the **total** cost for **3** adults and **2** children?

6. 

   Anna buys **3** pears at **65p** each.

   Jill buys **2** melons at **94p** each.

   a How much did Anna pay ?

   b How much did Jill pay ?

   c How much **more** did Anna pay than Jill ?

Chapter 13

2 Dimensions

Naming 2D Shapes

Be able to recognise and name some 2 Dimensional Shapes.

You should already know these **2 dimensional** shapes : -

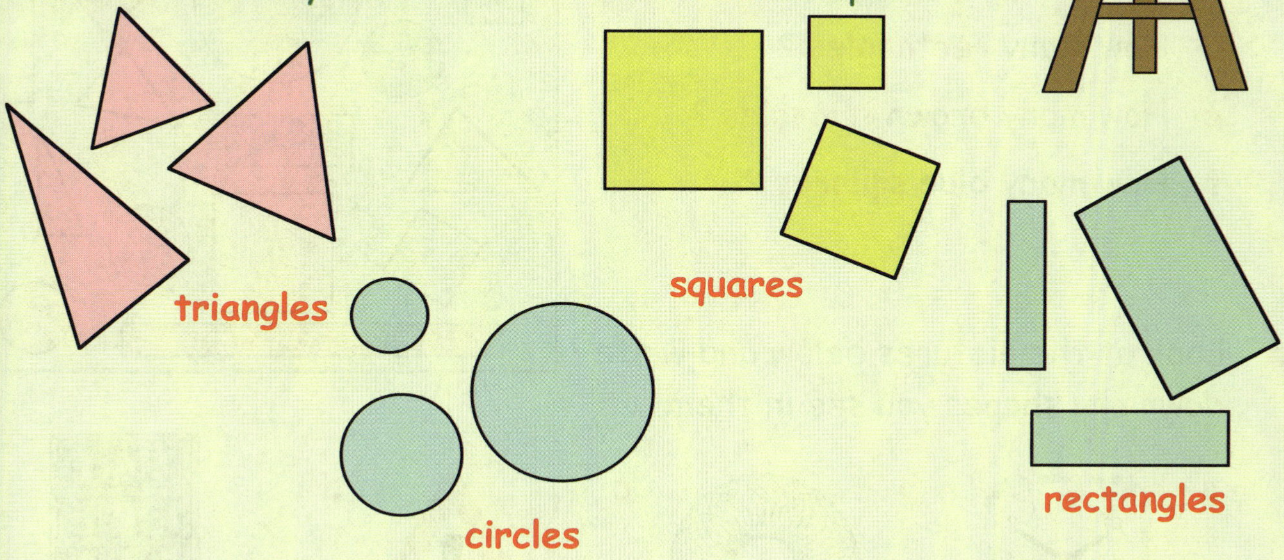

triangles

squares

circles

rectangles

Exercise 1

1. What do you call this shape ?

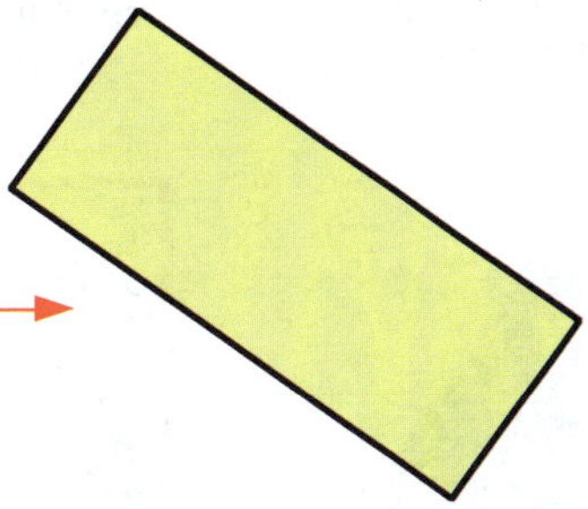

2. What is this shape called ?

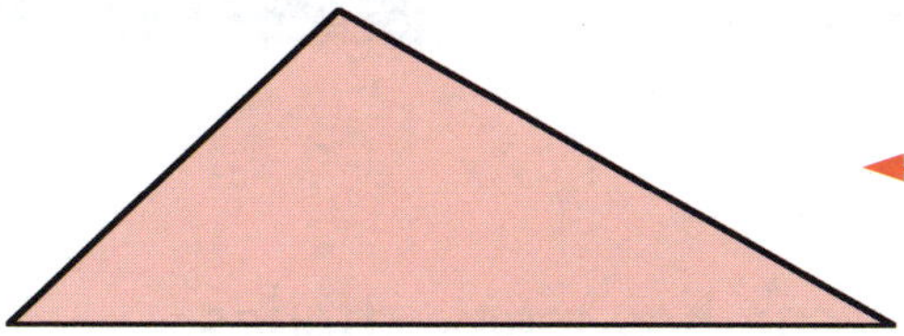

3. What is this shape known as ?

4. What's the name of this shape ?

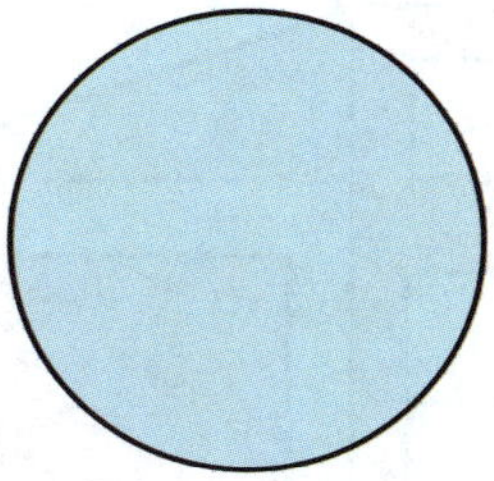

5. Look at the group of shapes.

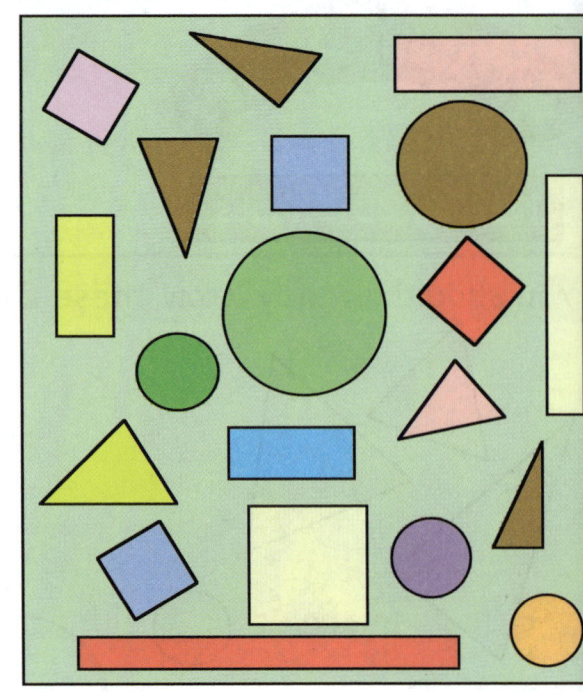

a How many **triangles** are there ?

b How many **circles** ?

c How many **squares** ?

d How many **rectangles** ?

e How many **brown triangles** ?

f How many **blue squares** ?

6. Look at the pictures below and write down any shapes you see in them.

a 

b 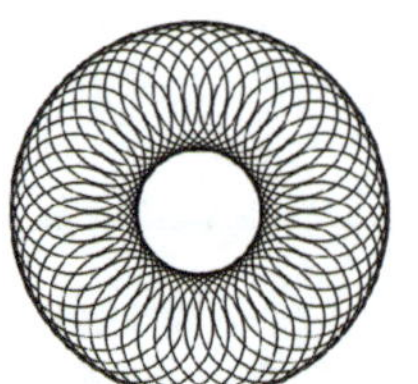

c 

d 

e 

f 

g 

h 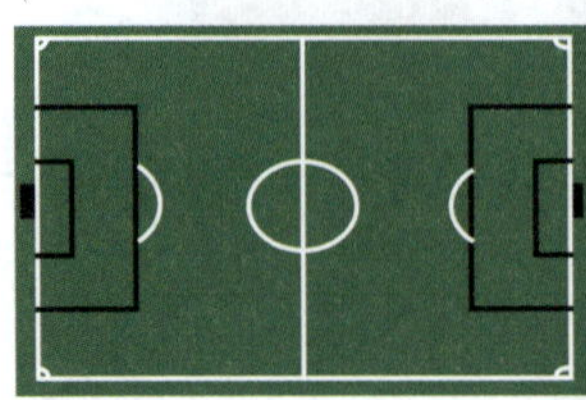

7. This picture of a house and garage in the sun has many shapes.

How many :-

a squares

b triangles

c rectangles

d circles

e **red** rectangles ?

Number of Sides, Corners and Angles

Know how many sides, corners and angles 2D shapes have.

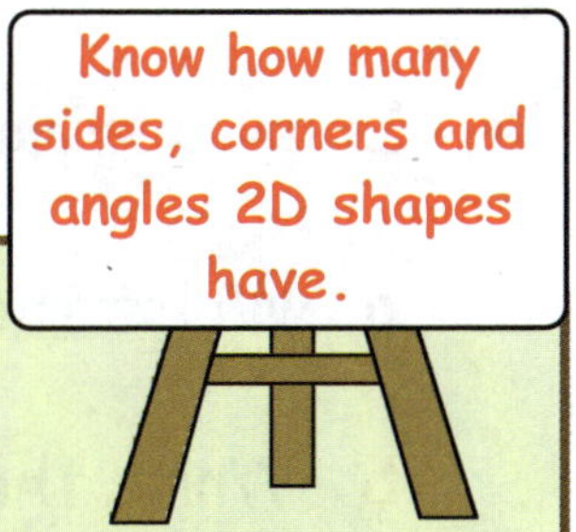

Look at the square.

It has :-

- 4 corners
- 4 sides
- 4 angles

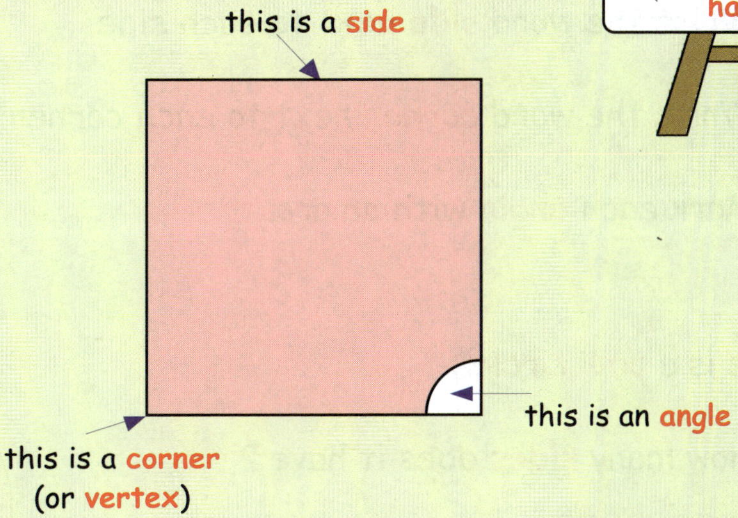

this is a side

this is an angle

this is a corner (or vertex)

Exercise 2

Ruler and Coloured Pencils needed !

Worksheet 13·1

1. Draw a rectangle like this and colour it blue.

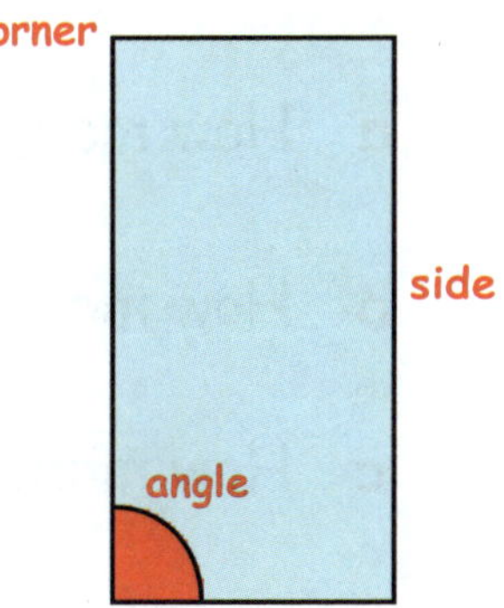

   a Write the word side next to each side.

   b Write the word corner next to each corner.

   c Mark each angle with an arc like this :- 

2. Draw a square like this and colour it green.

   a Write the word side next to each side.

   b Write the word corner next to each corner.

   c Mark each angle like this :- 

3. Write down one thing which makes a square different from a rectangle.

4. **Draw** a **triangle** like this and colour it **purple**.

   a Write the word **side** next to each side.

   b Write the word **corner** next to each corner.

   c Mark each **angle** with an arc.

5. Here is a **pink circle** :-

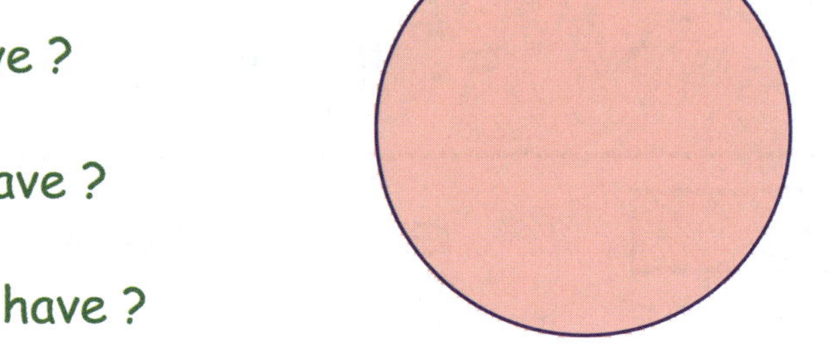

   a How many **sides** does it have ?

   b How many **angles** does it have ?

   c How many **corners** does it have ?

6. a How many **corners** does a **rectangle** have ?

   b How many **sides** does it have ?

   c How many **angles** does it have ?

7. a How many **angles** does a **square** have ?

   b How many **corners** does it have ?

   c How many **sides** does it have ?

8. a How many **sides** does a **triangle** have ?

   b How many **angles** does it have ?

   c How many **corners** does it have ?

9. **Copy** or **trace** this shape and colour it in.

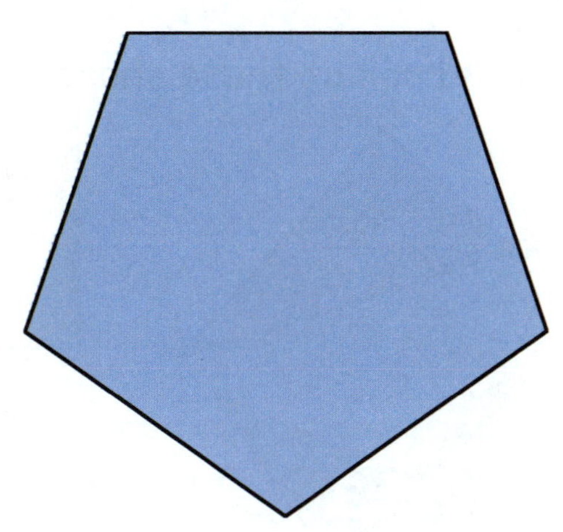

a How many **sides** does this shape have ?

b How many **corners** does it have ?

c How many **angles** does it have ?

d Find out what this shape is called.

10. **Copy** or **trace** this shape and colour it in.

a How many **sides** does this shape have ?

b How many corners does it have ?

c How many **angles** does it have ?

d Find out what this shape is called.

11. a How many **sides** does this shape have ?

b How many **angles** does it have ?

c How many **corners** does it have ?

12.

a How many **sides** does this shape have ?

b How many **corners** does it have ?

c How many **angles** does it have ?

13. Look at these shapes :-

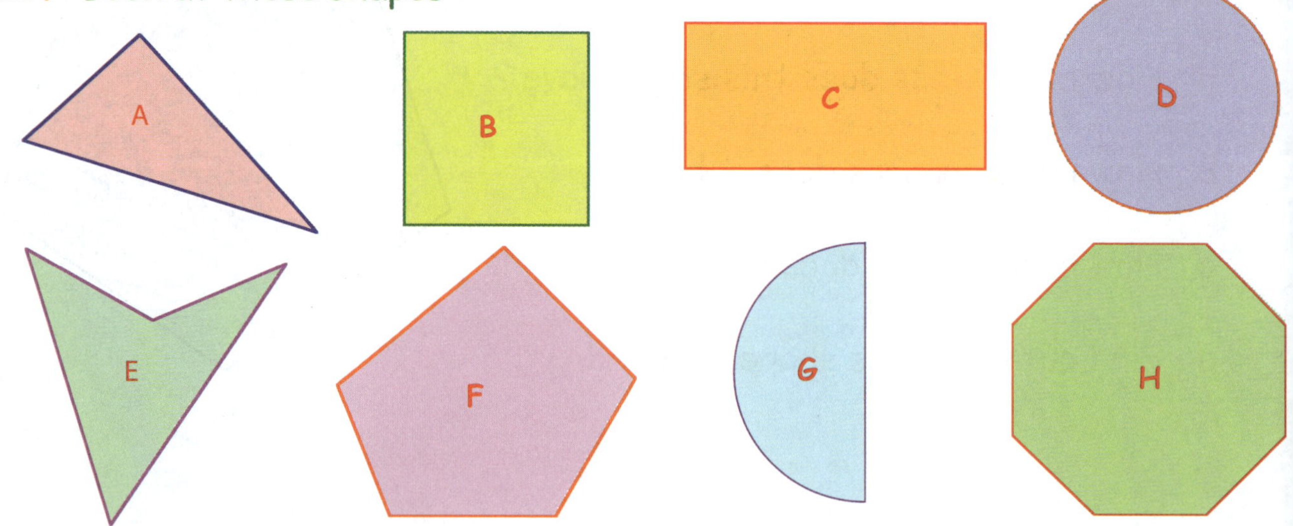

a Which shapes have 4 sides ?

b Which shape has 3 angles ?

c Which shape has 5 corners ?

d Which shape has 8 sides ?

e Which shape has 1 curved side only ?

f Which shape has 1 curved and 1 straight side ?

Give this shape a name !

14. Use a ruler, when needed, to draw these shapes :- (Colour them.)

a A shape with 3 angles.

b A shape with 4 sides.

c A shape with 5 sides.

d A shape with 6 corners.

e A shape with 4 angles.

f A shape with 7 sides.

g A shape with 1 curved side.

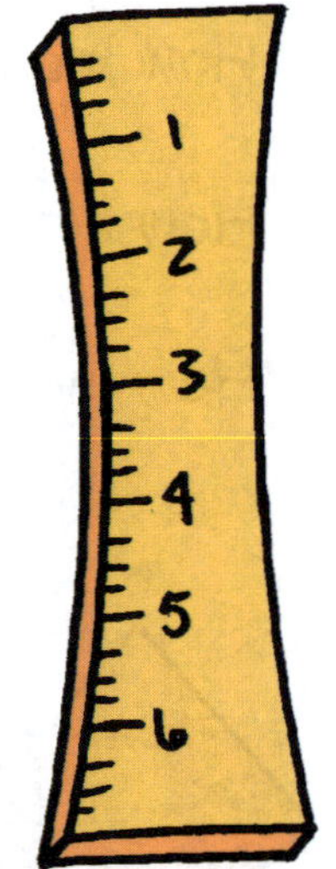

15. Use an encyclopaedia or the internet to name a shape with :-

a 8 sides b 9 sides c 10 sides d 12 sides.

The 3 Я's

Revisit - Review - Revise

1. What are the **names** given to these 2 dimensional shapes ?

a 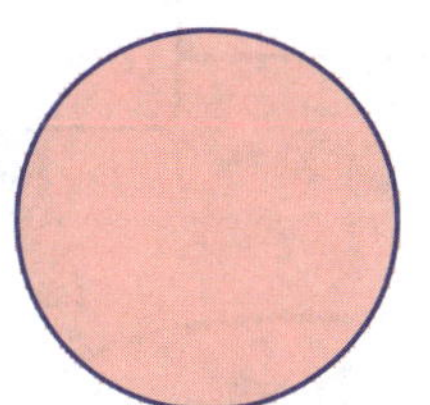

b 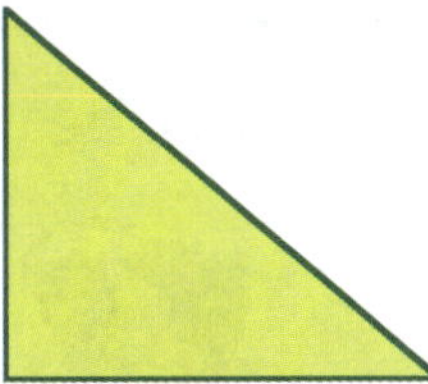

c 

d 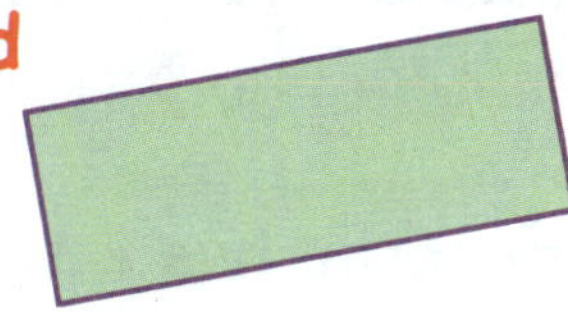

2. List what shapes are in the picture and **how many** of each there are.

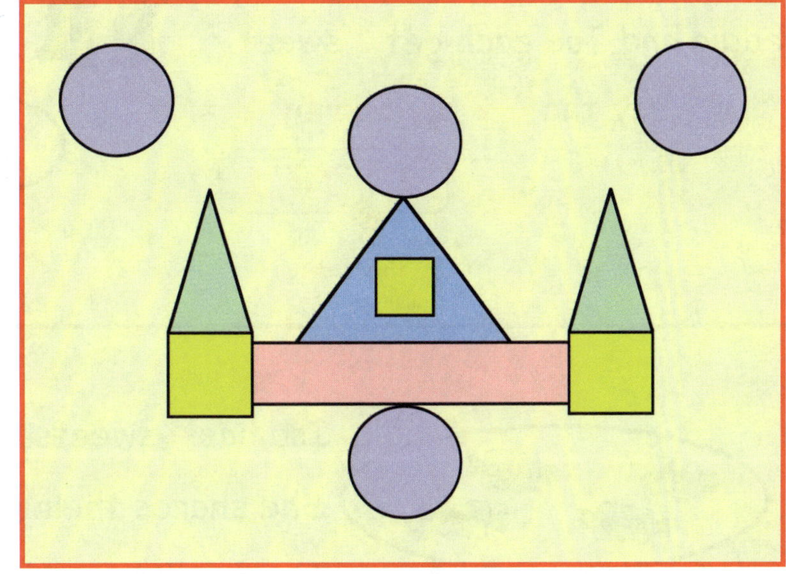

3. How many :-

a corners are in a square

b sides are in a rectangle

c angles are in a triangle

d sides are in a circle

e corners are in a rectangle

f angles are in a square

g sides are in a square

h corners are in a circle

i angles are in a rectangle

j sides are in a triangle

k angles are in a circle

l corners are in a triangle ?

4. Find **one difference** between :-

a a square and a rectangle

b a rectangle and a triangle.

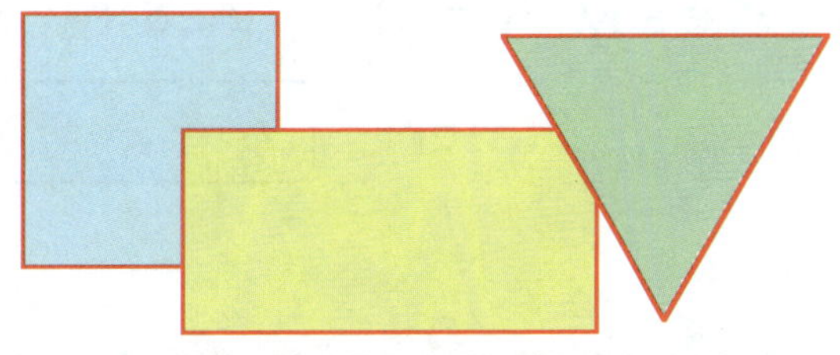

Dividing by 2

Be able to divide a quantity by 2.

Dividing by **2** is the same as **sharing** equally between **two**.

Freddie has **2** sweets.

He shares them with Joe.

Freddie and Joe each get **1** sweet.

÷ 2

We say that **2 divided by 2 = 1**.

or 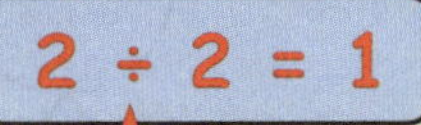

this is the dividing sign

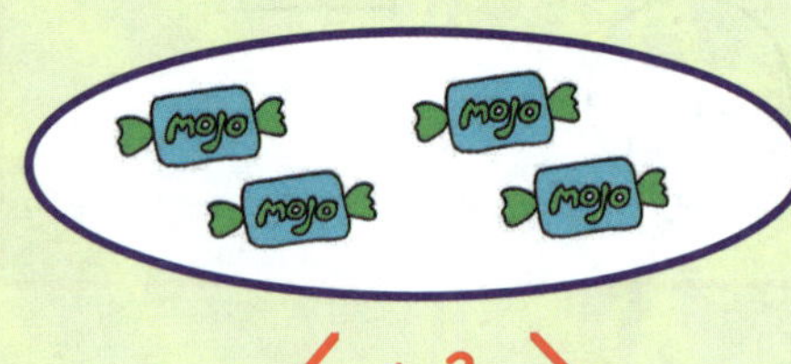

÷ 2

Isa has **4** sweets.

She shares them with Kylie.

Isa and Kylie each get **2** sweets.

We say that **4 divided by 2 = 2**.

or 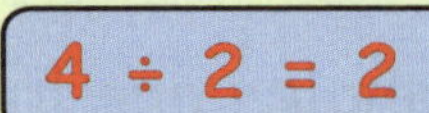

Tommy has **6** sweets.

He shares them equally with Jenny.

Tommy and Jenny each get **3** sweets.

We say that **6 divided by 2 = 3**.

or **6 ÷ 2 = 3**

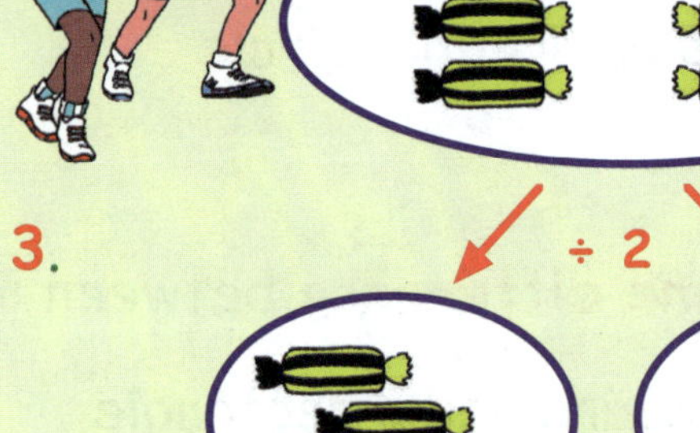

÷ 2

Exercise 1 You will need small cubes here, or sweets, coins or counters. Possibly work in pairs.

1. a Count out 8 small cubes, or coins, counters etc.

   b Share them equally between you and your friend.

   c How many did each of you get ?

   d Copy and complete :- 8 divided by 2 = ... => 8 ÷ 2 = ...

2. a This time count out 10 small cubes.

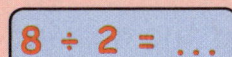

   b Share them equally between you and your friend.

   c How many did each of you get ?

   d Copy and complete :- 10 divided by 2 = ... => 10 ÷ 2 = ...

3. a This time count out 12 cubes.

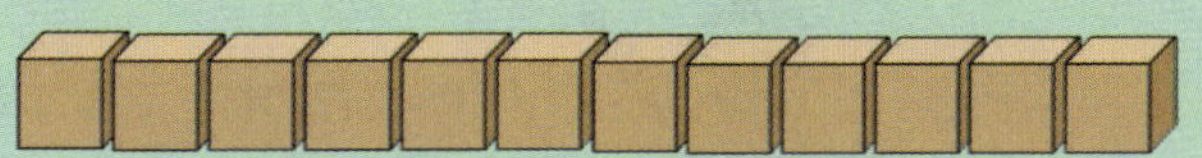

   b Share them equally again. How many did each of you get ?

   c Copy and complete :- 12 divided by 2 = ... => 12 ÷ 2 = ...

4. a Count out 14 small cubes and share them equally between you.

   b Copy and complete :- 14 divided by 2 = ... => 14 ÷ 2 = ...

5. a Share 16 cubes, then 18 cubes, then 20 cubes between you.

   b Find :- 16 ÷ 2 = ... 18 ÷ 2 = ... 20 ÷ 2 = ...

Exercise 2

1. Copy each of these and complete :-

a $4 \div 2 = ...$ b $8 \div 2 = ...$ c $6 \div 2 = ...$

d $12 \div 2 = ...$ e $10 \div 2 = ...$ f $14 \div 2 = ...$

g $18 \div 2 = ...$ h $16 \div 2 = ...$ i $20 \div 2 = ...$.

2. Find the missing numbers :-

a $\square \div 2 = 3$ b $\bigcirc \div 2 = 6$ c $\triangle \div 2 = 9$

d $\triangle \div 2 = 8$ e $\square \div 2 = 7$ f $\bigcirc \div 2 = 10$.

3. Do these questions mentally.

a 8 lollies are shared equally between 2 pupils.

How many lollies did each pupil get ?

b 

12 carrots are shared equally between 2 rabbits.

How many carrots did each rabbit get ?

c 14 strawberries are shared equally between 2 friends.

How many strawberries did each friend get ?

d 

6 muffins are shared between Terry and June.

How many muffins did each get ?

e 20 one pence coins are shared equally between 2 children.

How much money did each child get ?

Methods of Dividing

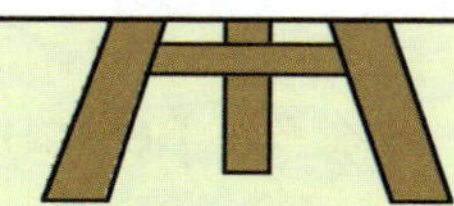

Be able to divide by 2 using a standard method.

Example 1

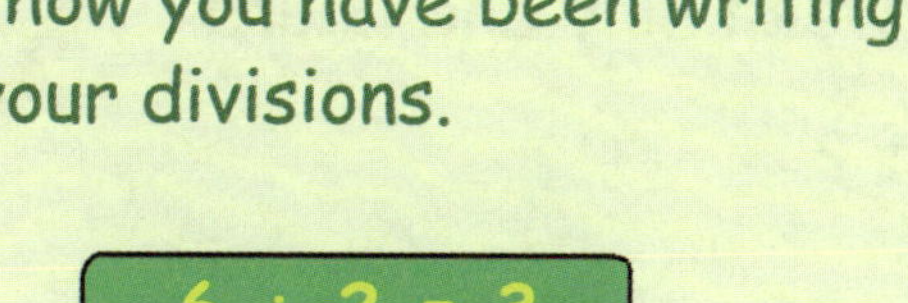

This is how you have been writing down your divisions.

6 ÷ 2 = 3
8 ÷ 2 = 4
4 ÷ 2 = 2

Here is another way of setting out your divisions.

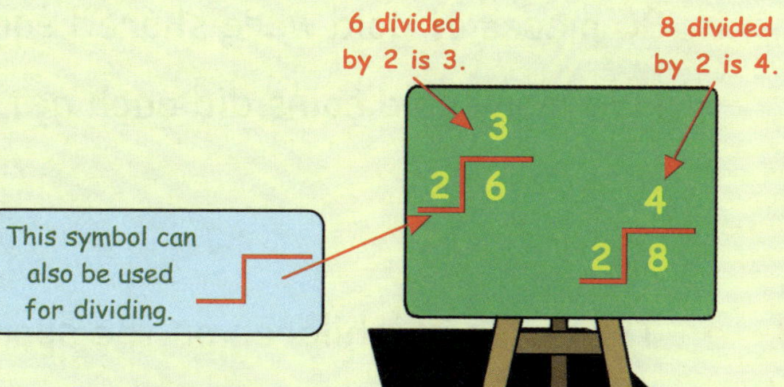

6 divided by 2 is 3.
8 divided by 2 is 4.
This symbol can also be used for dividing.
3
2 | 6
4
2 | 8

$6 \div 2 = 3$ can be read as :-

- 6 divided by 2 is 3.
- 2 into 6 goes 3 times.
- 6 shared equally by 2 is 3.

When **dividing** into **larger numbers** you have to do so in 2 steps.

Example 2 What is $86 \div 2$?

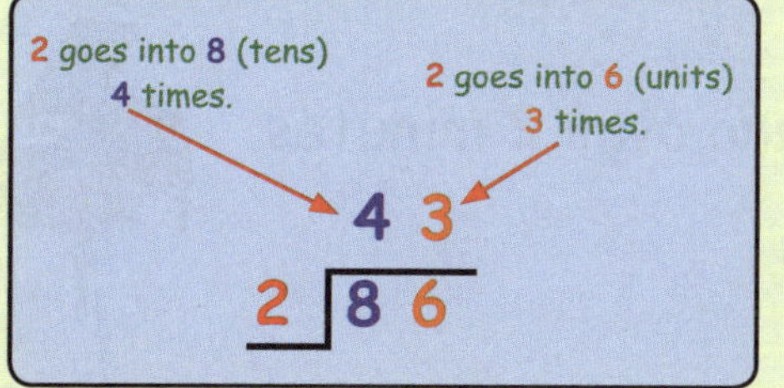

2 goes into 8 (tens) 4 times.
2 goes into 6 (units) 3 times.
4 3
2 | 8 6

$86 \div 2$
$= 43$

Example 3 What is $48 \div 2$?

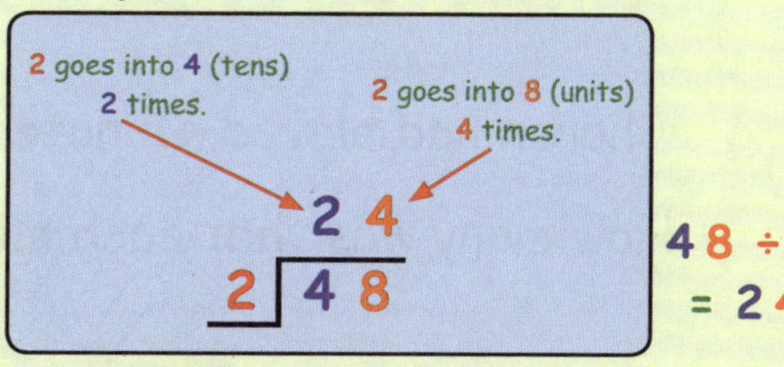

2 goes into 4 (tens) 2 times.
2 goes into 8 (units) 4 times.
2 4
2 | 4 8

$48 \div 2$
$= 24$

Exercise 3

Worksheet 14·1

1. **Copy** and **complete** :-

a 2⟌26 b 2⟌46 c 2⟌22 d 2⟌44

e 2⟌62 f 2⟌68 g 2⟌84 h 2⟌82

i 2⟌64 j 2⟌88 k 2⟌42 l 2⟌28.

Show how you do each of these. Use the ⟌ sign when dividing.

2. a **46** pencils were divided equally between Lilly and Laura.

   How many pencils did they each get ?

   b **80** pieces of gold were shared equally between **two** pirates.

   How many gold coins did each get ?

3. a There are **26** children on the sports field.

   Divide them into teams of **2**. How many teams ?

   b Mary had phoned her mum **28** times over Saturday and Sunday.

   She had phoned the same number of times each day.

   How many did she phone on Sunday ?

4. a Sharon had played **42** notes on the piano over **2** minutes.

   How many was that each minute ?

   b 

   George practised his three times table **64** times over **2** days.

   What does that work out at each day ?

5. a How many **two** pence coins can I get for **30p** ?

   b How many **two** pound coins make up **£40** ?

Be able to divide by 3 when there is no remainder.

Dividing by **3** is the same as **sharing** equally among **3**.

Flo has **3** apples.

She shares them with Jen and Anna.

Flo, Jen and Anna each get **1** apple.

We say that **3 divided by 3 = 1**.

or

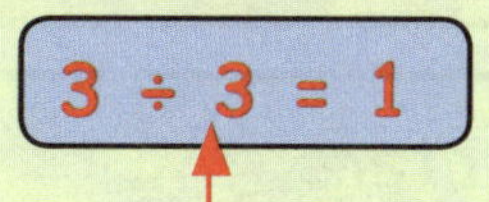

the dividing sign again.

Ben has **6** donuts.

He shares them with Tom and Paul.

Ben, Tom and Paul each get **2** donuts.

We say that **6 divided by 3 = 2**.

or **6 ÷ 3 = 2**

Tom has **9** biscuits.

He shares them equally with Dick and Harry.

Tom, Dick and Harry each get **3** biscuits.

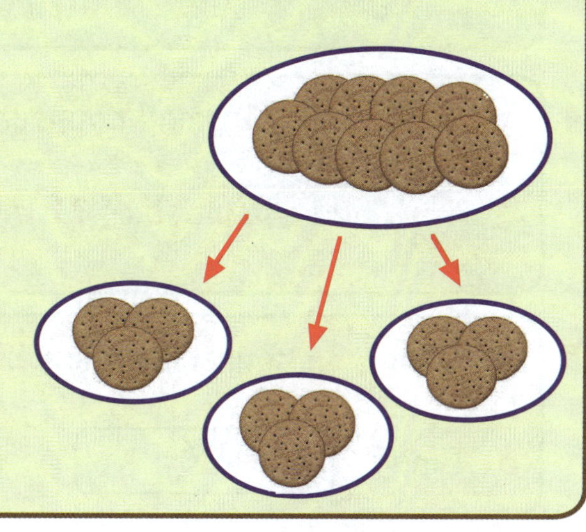

We say that **9 divided by 3 = 3**.

or **9 ÷ 3 = 3**

Exercise 4 You will need small counters here, or sweets, coins or cubes. Possibly work in **groups of 3** or on your own.

1. a **Count** out **12** small counters. (any colours).

b Share them **equally** among you and your 2 friends.

c How many did each of you get ?

d **Copy** and **complete** :- **12 divided by 3 = ...** => **12 ÷ 3 = ...**

2. a This time **count** out **15** small counters.

b Share them **equally** between you **and** your **2** friends.

c How many did each of you get ?

d **Copy** and **complete** :- **15 divided by 3 = ...** => **15 ÷ 3 = ...**

3. a This time **count** out **18** small counters.

b Share them **equally** again. How many did each of you get ?

c **Copy** and **complete** :- **18 divided by 3 = ...** => **18 ÷ 3 = ...**

4. a **Count** out **21** small counters and share them **equally** between you.

b **Copy** and **complete** :- **21 divided by 3 = ...** => **21 ÷ 3 = ...**

5. a Share **24** counters, then **27** , then **30** between 3 people.

b Find :- **24 ÷ 3 = ...** **27 ÷ 3 = ...** **30 ÷ 3 = ...**

Exercise 5

1. **Copy** each of these and **complete** :-

a 9 ÷ 3 = ...   b 6 ÷ 3 = ...   c 15 ÷ 3 = ...

d 12 ÷ 3 = ...   e 18 ÷ 3 = ...   f 24 ÷ 3 = ...

g 21 ÷ 3 = ...   h 27 ÷ 3 = ...   i 30 ÷ 3 = ...

2. Find the missing numbers :-

a ■ ÷ 3 = 7   b ● ÷ 3 = 3   c ▲ ÷ 3 = 6

d ▲ ÷ 3 = 5   e ■ ÷ 3 = 8   f ● ÷ 3 = 10.

3. Do these questions **mentally**.

a **6** allergy pills were shared equally between **3** gardeners.

How many pills did each gardener get ?

b Dad ate the fish, but the **27** chips went to the **3** children.

If they got the same amount, how many did each get ?

c A farmer put **18** scarecrows into **3** fields.
Each field had the same number of scarecrows.

How many were in each field ?

d I put **3** fruit sticks on to each melon.

If I have **12** fruit sticks, how many melons will I need ?

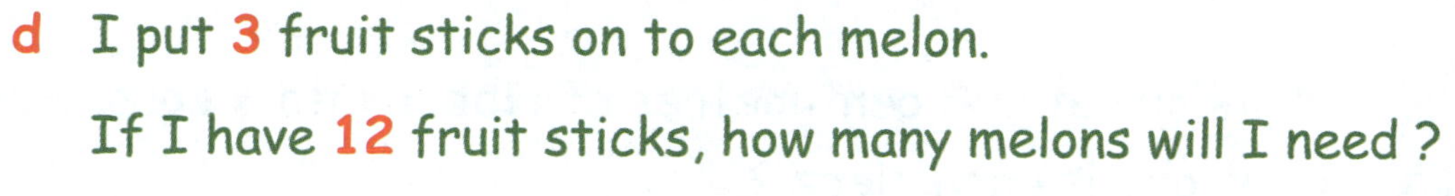

e A menu gives a choice of **30** items of food.
There are an equal number of starters, mains and desserts.

How many of each are there ?

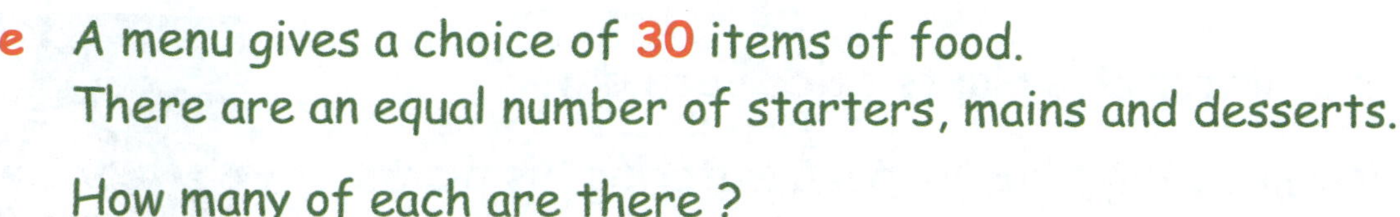

When **dividing** into **larger numbers** you have to do so in 2 steps.

Example What is 9 6 ÷ 3 ?

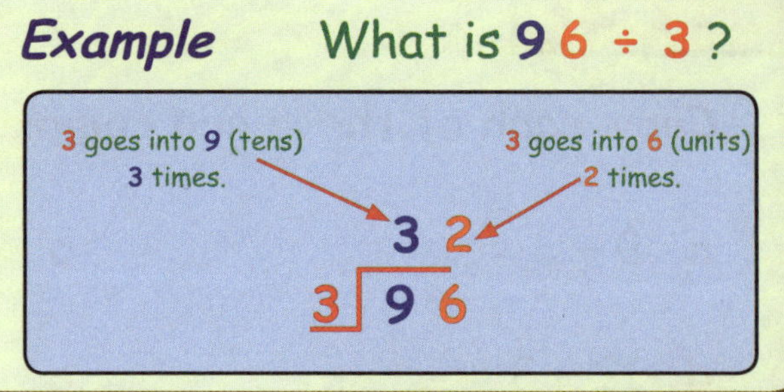

3 goes into 9 (tens) 3 times.
3 goes into 6 (units) 2 times.
3 2
3 | 9 6

4. **Copy** and **complete** :-

Worksheet 14·2

a.	3 ⟌ 39	b	3 ⟌ 66	c	3 ⟌ 30	d	3 ⟌ 69
e	2 ⟌ 28	f	3 ⟌ 36	g	2 ⟌ 60	h	3 ⟌ 90
i	2 ⟌ 86	j	3 ⟌ 93	k	2 ⟌ 64	l	3 ⟌ 99.

5. a **36** strawberries were spread equally amongst **3** ice-creams.

How many strawberries were in each bowl of ice-cream ?

b

3 pots had a total of **99** gold coins.
Each pot had the same number of coins.

How many were in each pot ?

c A potato grower has only **46** Ayrshire potatoes left.

She puts them equally into **2** bags.

How many are in each bag ?

d

A tailor cuts **90** centimetres of ribbon into **3** equal pieces.
How long is each piece ?

e Brian waters his plants **twice** each day.

How many days has he been watering his plants, if up till now he has watered them **26** times ?

The 3 ЯR's

Revisit - Review - Revise

1. **Work out :-**

a $6 \div 2$ b $18 \div 2$ c $12 \div 3$ d $9 \div 3$

e $14 \div 2$ f $15 \div 3$ g $16 \div 2$ h $24 \div 3$.

2. **Find :-**

a $2\overline{)24}$ b $3\overline{)63}$ c $2\overline{)82}$ d $3\overline{)33}$

e $2\overline{)60}$ f $2\overline{)40}$ g $3\overline{)39}$ h $3\overline{)90}$.

3. 

These cabinets each have **2** drawers in them.

If **22** drawers have been made, how many cabinets can be built ?

4. **60** bits of fish were shared equally amongst **3** penguins.

How many bits did each penguin get ?

5. 

Grandpa had **26** sweets, which he shared equally with his grandson, Rabbie.

How many did the two of them get each ?

6. A roll of ribbon is **36** cm long.

a Alex cuts it in **half**. How long will each piece be ?

b Alex then cuts each half into **3** equal pieces.

What will the length of one piece be ?

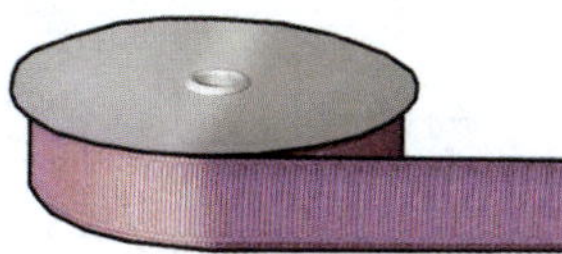

Chapter 15

The Missing Number

Algebra

Be able to find a missing value in a maths sentence.

Example 1

4 + □ = 9

"4 add what gives 9"

Answer 5. □ = 5.

Example 2

8 - □ = 2
"8 take what gives 2"
Answer 6. □ = 6.

Exercise 1 — Worksheet 15·1

1. What **number** does □ stand for ?

a 1 + □ = 6 b 3 + □ = 7 c 4 + □ = 8

d 6 + □ = 9 e 2 + □ = 10 f 0 + □ = 9

g 5 + □ = 8 h 8 + □ = 8 i 6 + □ = 13

j 4 + □ = 15 k 7 + □ = 16 l 9 + □ = 18.

2. Work out what **number** □ stands for in each of these :-

a 5 - □ = 4 b 6 - □ = 2 c 8 - □ = 5

d 9 - □ = 7 e 8 - □ = 8 f 6 - □ = 0

g 11 - □ = 6 h 10 - □ = 1 i 12 - □ = 3

j 15 - □ = 7 k 19 - □ = 7 l 18 - □ = 8

m 19 - □ = 3 n 20 - □ = 15 o 25 - □ = 18.

Simple Equations with + and –

Be able to solve simple equations involving adding and subtracting.

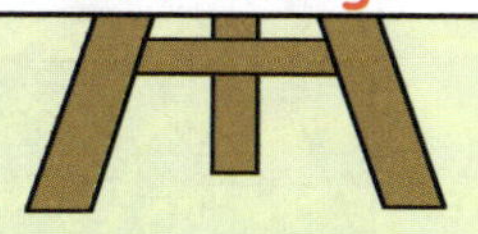

Example 1

Example 2

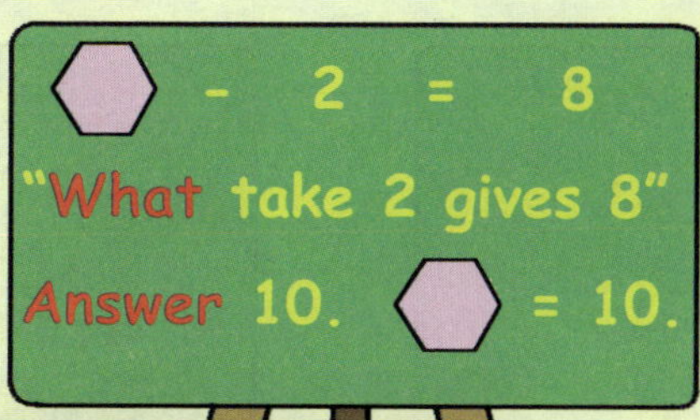

⬡ – 2 = 8
"What take 2 gives 8"
Answer 10. ⬡ = 10.

These are called **equations**.

The answer to an **equation** is called the **solution**.

Exercise 2

1. What **number** does ☆ stand for in these ?

a ☆ + 2 = 7	b ☆ + 4 = 9	c ☆ + 1 = 10
d ☆ + 9 = 12	e ☆ + 0 = 6	f ☆ + 11 = 18
g ☆ + 19 = 23	h ☆ + 13 = 25	i ☆ + 17 = 26
j ☆ + 18 = 30	k ☆ + 21 = 35	l ☆ + 25 = 40
m ☆ – 6 = 8	n ☆ – 7 = 9	o ☆ – 9 = 11.

2. Work out what **number** ⬡ stands for in each of these :-

a 3 + ⬡ = 8	b 6 + ⬡ = 16	c 4 + ⬡ = 12
d 9 – ⬡ = 4	e 8 – ⬡ = 1	f 11 – ⬡ = 8
g ⬡ + 8 = 20	h ⬡ + 9 = 17	i ⬡ + 14 = 21
j 13 + ⬡ = 19	k ⬡ – 6 = 13	l 12 + ⬡ = 21.

Simple Equations with x and ÷

Be able to solve simple equations involving multiplying and dividing.

Example 1

What times 3 gives 18
Answer 6. ⏢ = 6.

Example 2

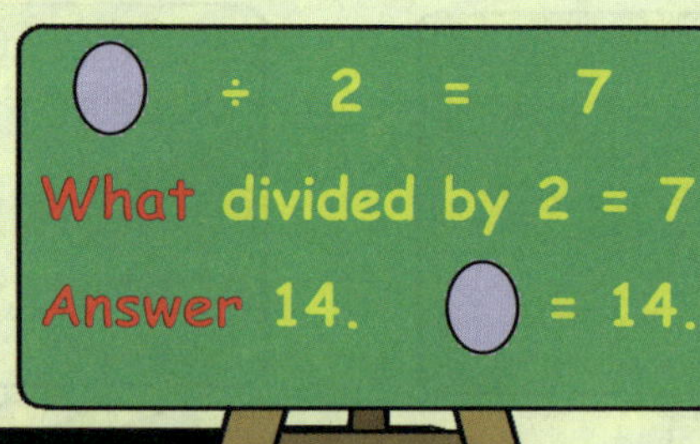

⬭ ÷ 2 = 7
What divided by 2 = 7
Answer 14. ⬭ = 14.

Worksheet 15·3

Exercise 3

1. What **number** does ⏢ stand for in these ?

a ⏢ x 2 = 8	b ⏢ x 3 = 15	c ⏢ x 2 = 20
d ⏢ x 3 = 30	e ⏢ ÷ 3 = 6	f ⏢ ÷ 2 = 9
g ⏢ x 3 = 27	h ⏢ x 2 = 16	i ⏢ ÷ 3 = 10
j ⏢ ÷ 2 = 7	k ⏢ ÷ 3 = 4	l ⏢ x 3 = 12.

2. Work out what **number** ● stands for in each of these :-

a 3 x ● = 6	b 2 x ● = 20	c 3 x ● = 27
d 16 ÷ ● = 8	e 3 ÷ ● = 1	f 24 ÷ ● = 8
g ● x 2 = 6	h ● x 3 = 21	i ● x 2 = 14
j ● ÷ 3 = 5	k ● ÷ 2 = 10	l ● ÷ 3 = 3.

Which Signs are Missing ?

Be able to put in +, −, x and ÷ to make an equation correct.

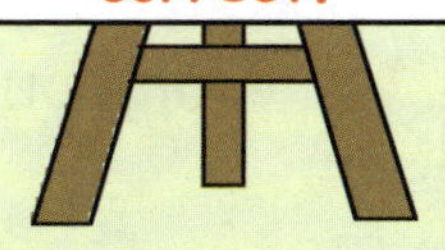

The circle 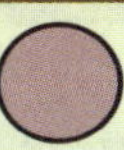 is covering up a mathematical sign.

Choose from +, −, x or ÷

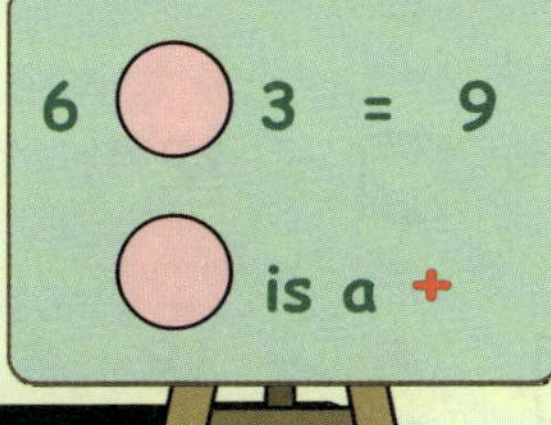

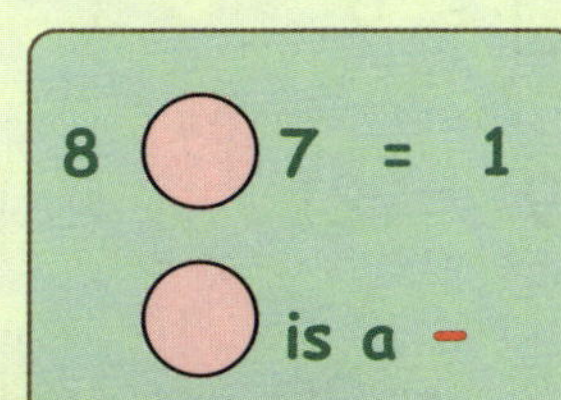

8 ● 2 = 4

● is a ÷

Exercise 4

1. What **sign** does ● stand for here ? Choose from +, −, x or ÷.

a 5 ● 5 = 10	b 8 ● 8 = 0	c 2 ● 7 = 14
d 6 ● 3 = 2	e 5 ● 3 = 15	f 9 ● 2 = 7
g 16 ● 2 = 8	h 9 ● 7 = 16	i 10 ● 2 = 20.

2. **Copy** the following and put in a +, −, x or ÷ to make the sum work.

a 3 ...... 3 = 0	b 7 ...... 3 = 10	c 3 ...... 4 = 12
d 21 ...... 3 = 7	e 50 ...... 5 = 45	f 7 ...... 8 = 15
g 3 ...... 9 = 27	h 15 ...... 9 = 6	i 3 ...... 3 = 1
j 3 ...... 3 = 6	k 3 ...... 3 = 9	l 3 ...... 3 = 0.

The 3 R's

Revisit - Review - Revise

1. Work out what **number** ☐ stands for in each of these :-

a 5 + ☐ = 11	b 9 − ☐ = 5	c 15 + ☐ = 21
d 18 − ☐ = 10	e 2 × ☐ = 6	f 3 × ☐ = 12
g ☐ + 7 = 13	h ☐ + 9 = 21	i ☐ − 5 = 18
j ☐ − 9 = 21	k ☐ × 2 = 20	l ☐ × 3 = 27
m 17 + ☐ = 29	n ☐ − 12 = 28	o ☐ ÷ 2 = 6
p 27 ÷ 3 = ☐	q ☐ ÷ 3 = 10	r ☐ ÷ 2 = 50.

2. **Copy** the following and put in a +, −, × or ÷ to make the sum work.

a 8 ... 8 = 0	b 5 ... 3 = 8	c 2 ... 5 = 10
d 15 ... 3 = 5	e 17 ... 8 = 25	f 19 ... 11 = 8
g 7 ... 2 = 14	h 8 ... 3 = 24	i 3 ... 3 = 1
j 18 ... 2 = 9	k 23 ... 12 = 35	l 50 ... 20 = 30
m 2 ... 11 = 22	n 20 ... 3 = 60	o 50 ... 2 = 25
p 90 ... 3 = 30	q 77 ... 23 = 100	r 50 ... 3 = 150.

3. Here are 6 calculations.

   Put them into the correct **3 pairs** with an = sign between them.

   8 × 2   24 − 14   10 + 11   13 + 3   30 ÷ 3   3 × 7

Chapter 16

Fractions 1

Half of Something

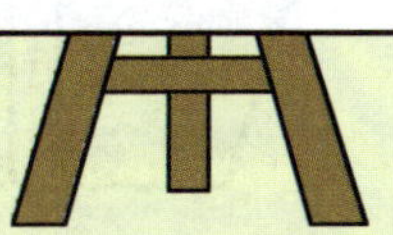

Recognise what is meant by a half.

If you cut a shape into **2 equal** bits, each bit is called a **half**.

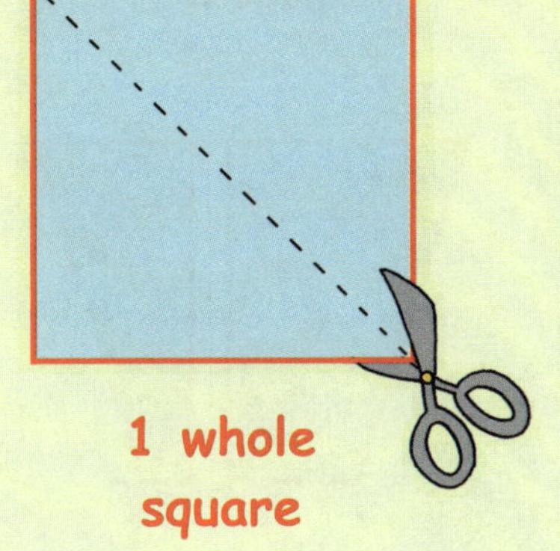

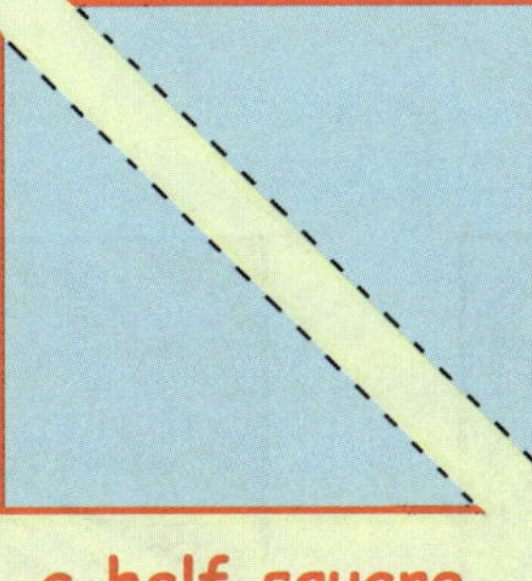

A **half** is written like this :- $\frac{1}{2}$ (one "bit" out of two "bits")

Two **halves** put back together make one **whole**.

Exercise 1

1. Practice writing the **half** symbol (10 times) - $\frac{1}{2}$.

2. a Has this triangle been cut in **half** ?

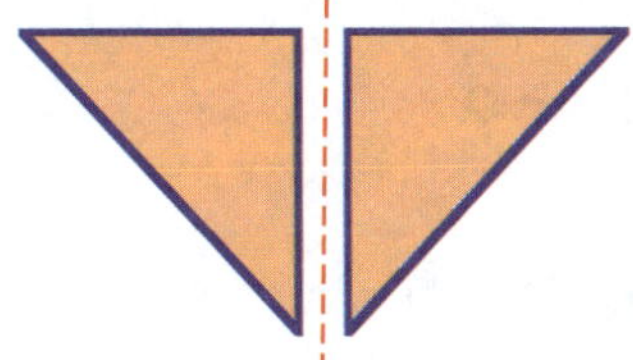

b Has this circle been cut in **half** ?

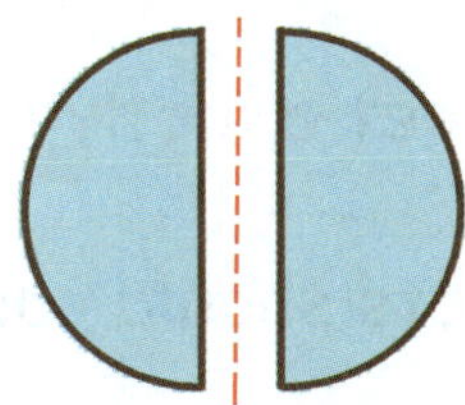

c Has this rectangle been cut in **half** ?

3. Which of these shapes have been cut **exactly** in **half** ? (**Yes** or **No**).

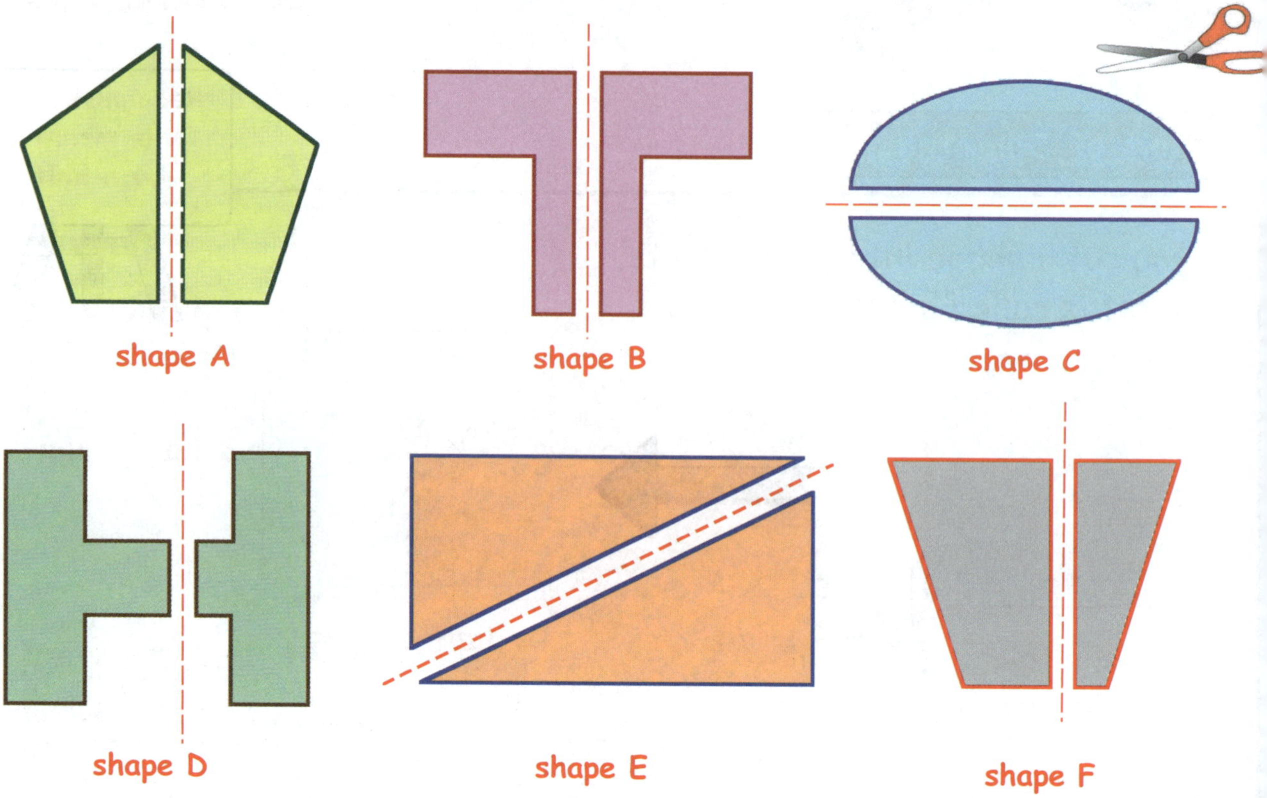

shape A

shape B

shape C

shape D

shape E

shape F

Worksheet 16·1

4. Tim and Lorna had **10** sweets. They tried to share them equally.

Tim's sweets

Lorna's sweets

a Did they each get **exactly half** of the sweets ?

b How many sweets should each of them have ?

c How many should Lorna give to Tim so they do have $\frac{1}{2}$ each ?

5. Andy shared these **20** yellow counters with his friend James.

Andy

James

a Did both of them get exactly **half** the counters each ?

b How many **more** did James get than Andy ?

6. Ari and Bree broke a bar of chocolate into 2 pieces.

a Did both Ari and Bree get **exactly half** each ?

b How many **more** squares did Bree get than Ari ?

7. Julie and Janice have a bag of 12 balloons. They each get exactly **half** of the balloons.

How many balloons did each of them get ?

8. Bob and Bill have a box of 14 toy cars. They each get **half** of the cars.

How many cars does Bill have ?

9. A bag has sixteen marbles. Sadie is given **half** of them.

How many marbles are left in the box ?

Worksheet 16·2

Quarter of Something

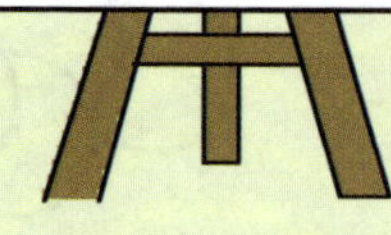

Recognise what is meant by a quarter.

If you cut a shape into **4 equal** bits, each bit is called a **quarter**.

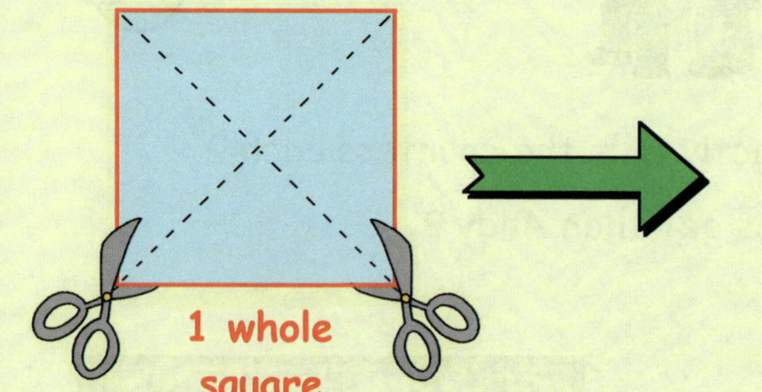

quarter

quarter quarter

quarter

A **quarter** is written like this :-

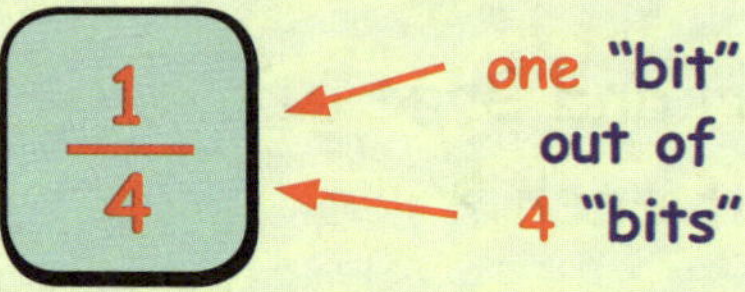

Four **quarters** put back together make a **whole**.

Two **quarters** put together make a **half**.

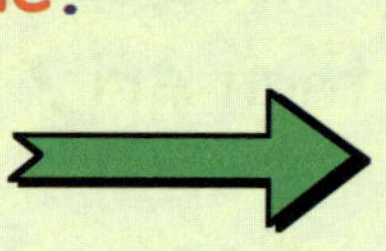

Exercise 2

1. Practice writing the **quarter** symbol (10 times) - $\frac{1}{4}$.

2. Has this circle been cut into **quarters** ?

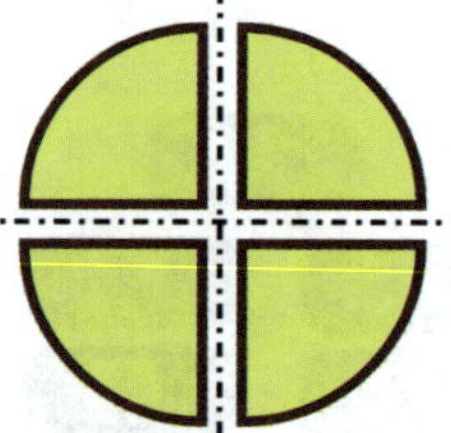

3. Has this rectangle been cut into $\frac{1}{4}$'s ?

4. Has this square been cut into $\frac{1}{4}$'s ?

5. Which of these have been cut **exactly** into **quarters** ? (**Yes** or **No**).

shape A

shape B

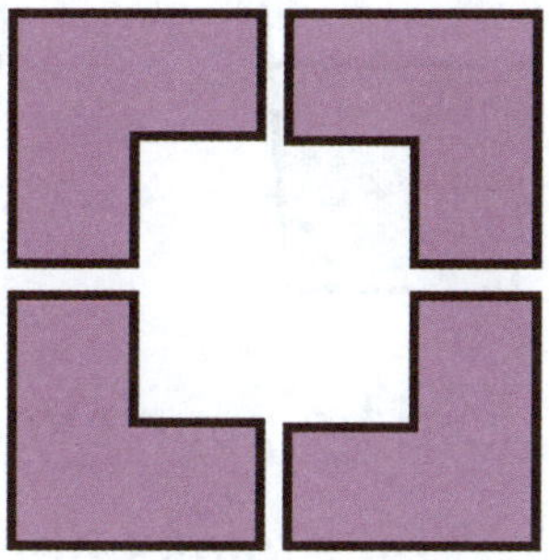

shape C

shape D

shape E

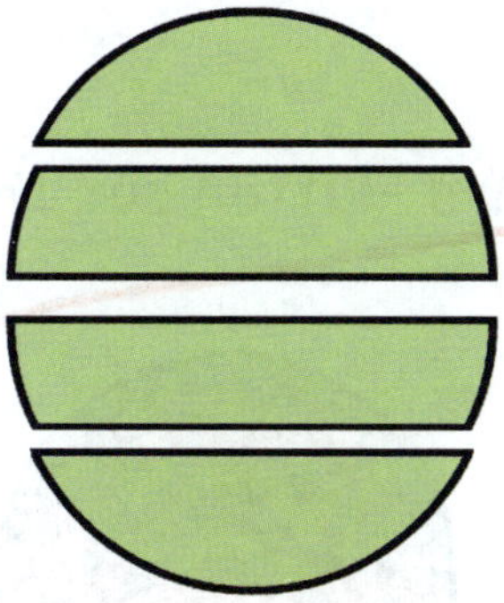

shape F

Worksheet 16·3

6. Jenny cut her birthday cake into 4 equal slices.

   Timmy ate one of the slices.

   What **fraction** did Timmy eat ?

7. Bobby, Jane, Nick and Wei share some tennis balls.

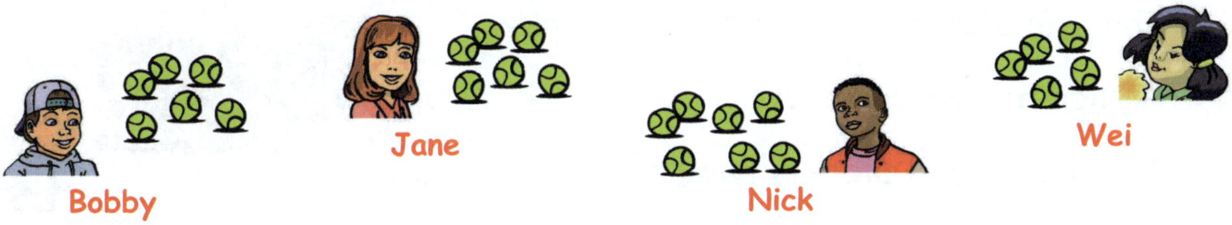

Bobby

Jane

Nick

Wei

   a Did each of them get a **quarter** of the balls ?

   b Who got **most** ?

   c Who got **least** ?

8. Mr Doak emptied a carton of limeade into 4 glasses.

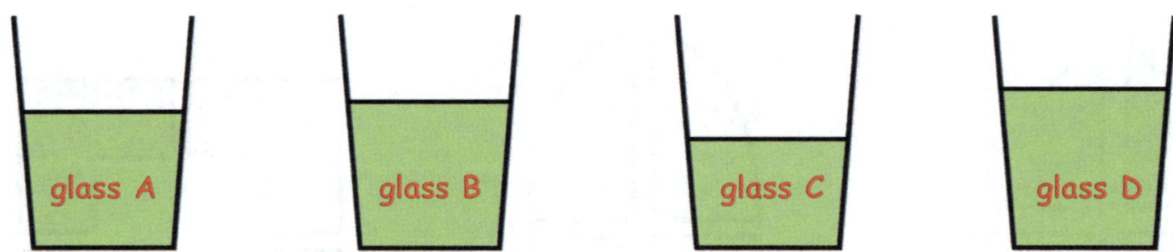

a Did he pour exactly a **quarter** of the limeade into each glass ?

b Which glass held **most** ?

c Which glass held **least** ?

9. Mrs Hutton cut this pizza into **exactly** four equal slices.

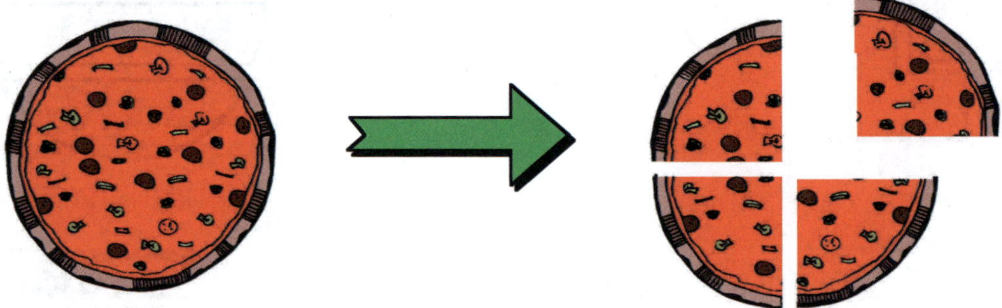

a What **fraction** is each slice called ?

Tommy ate **two** of the pizza slices.

b What **fraction** had Tommy eaten ?

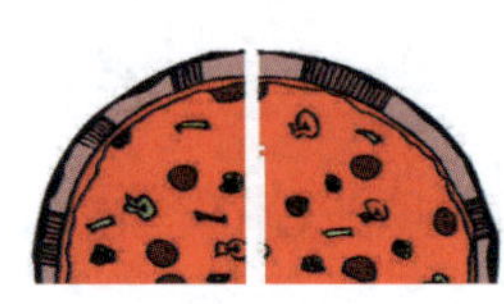

Tommy

10. This is a picture of a Battenburg Cake.

A slice has been cut off.

The slice has 4 pieces, two **pink** and 2 **yellow**.

slice

a What **fraction** of the slice is **1 pink** piece ?

b What fraction of the slice is **two pink** pieces ?

Worksheet 16·4

Exercise 3 Mixed Exercise on a half and a quarter.

1. There are 12 pencils in a packet.

a How many pencils would I have if I took **half** of them ?

b How many pencils would I have if I took a **quarter** of them ?

2.

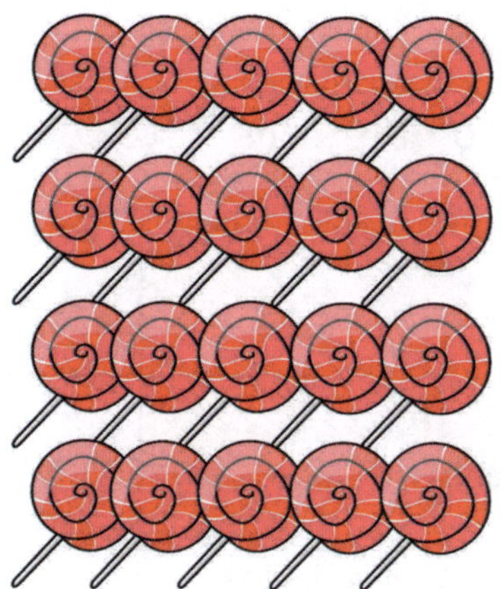

There are twenty lollipops in a box.

a How many lollipops would I have if I took **half** of them ?

b How many lollipops would I have if I took a **quarter** of them ?

3. There are 16 golf balls in a bucket.

a How many balls would I have if I took **half** of them ?

b How many balls would I have if I took a **quarter** of them ?

4. a What is a **half** of 6 ?

b What is a **half** of 14 ?

c What is a **half** of 40 ?

d What is a **half** of 100 ?

5. a What is a **quarter** of 8 ?

b What is a **quarter** of 12 ?

c What is a **quarter** of 40 ?

d What is a **quarter** of 100 ?

Revisit - Review - Revise

1. Which of these shapes have been split in **half** ? (**Yes** or **No**).

a 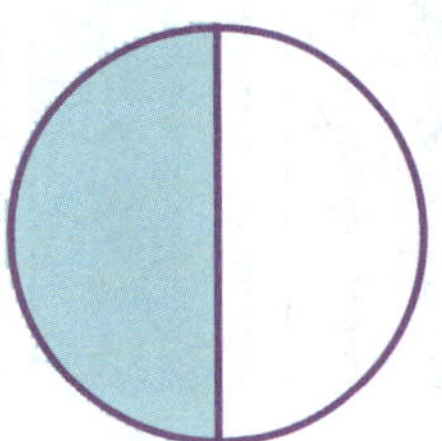

b 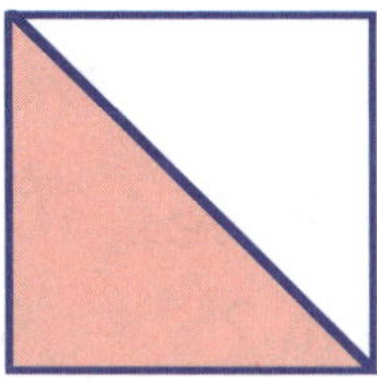

c 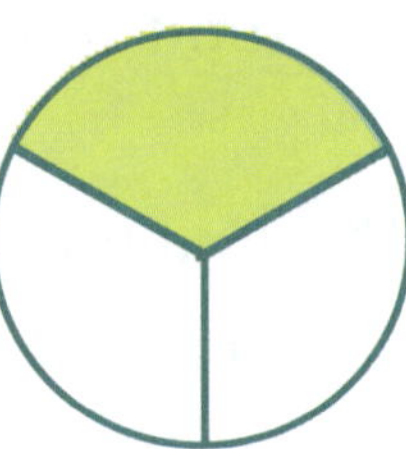

2. Which of these shapes have been split into **quarters** ? (**Yes** or **No**).

a 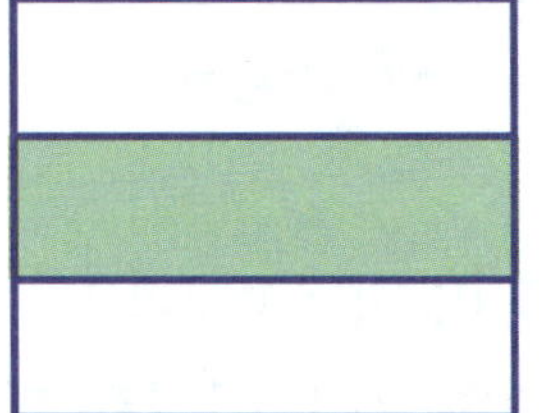

b 

c 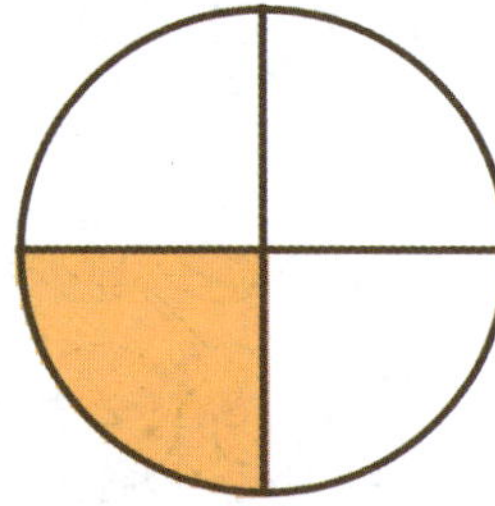

3. There are 10 pins in a box.
Mr. Darcy took **half** of the pins.

How many pins did he take ?

4. Pete has 16 one pence coins.
He gives a **quarter** of them to Simon.

How many coins does Pete **now have** ?

5. 

Addison has 20 sports tops.
A **quarter** of them are football tops.

How many are **NOT** football tops ?

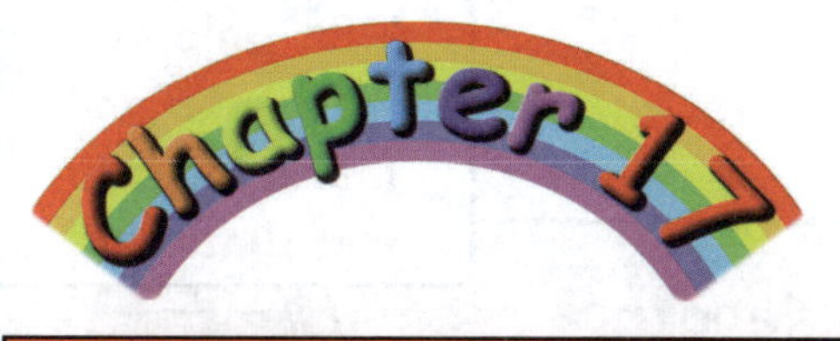

Length

Be able to estimate and measure length using old methods.

Length (A long time ago)

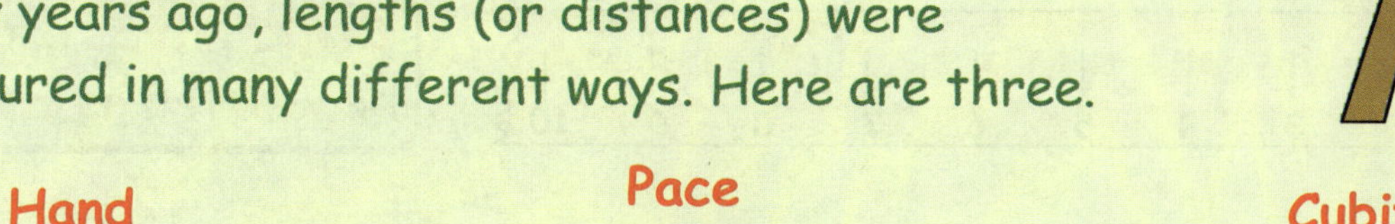

Many years ago, lengths (or distances) were measured in many different ways. Here are three.

Hand

hand-span

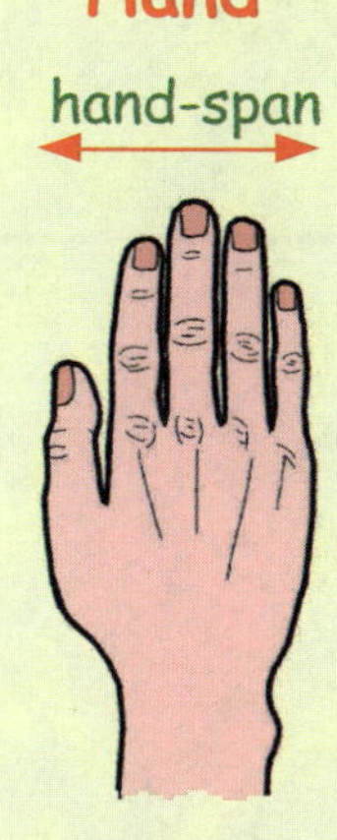

Pace

one step

Cubit

elbow to fingertips

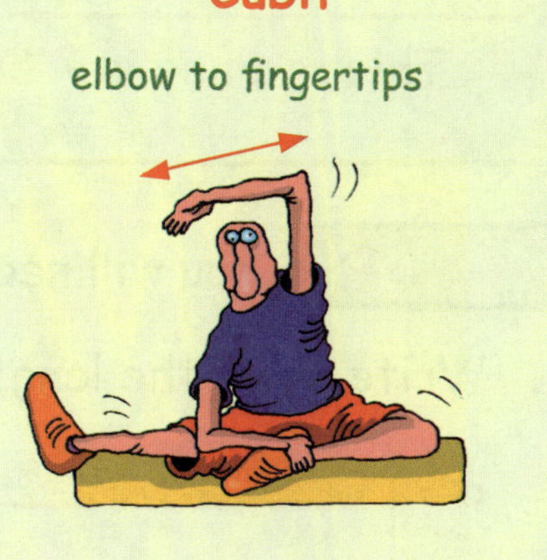

Exercise 1

1. a **Guess** (estimate) how many **hands** high your desk is.

   b **Guess** (estimate) how many **hands** high your teacher is.

   c **Guess** (estimate) how many **paces** from the door to the back wall.

   d **Estimate** how many **paces** the length of the corridor is.

   e **Estimate** how many **cubits** it is from your desk to the door.

   f **Estimate** how many **paces** it is from the floor to the ceiling.

2. a **Measure** some of the lengths in question **1** using these units.

   b Find **more old** units used to measure lengths.

3. The above methods are **NOT** good ways of measuring length.

   Discuss why not.

Metric Length - Centimetres

Be able to estimate and measure using centimetres.

Today most lengths are measured using ***metric*** length.

A **ruler** measures small lengths in **centimetres**.

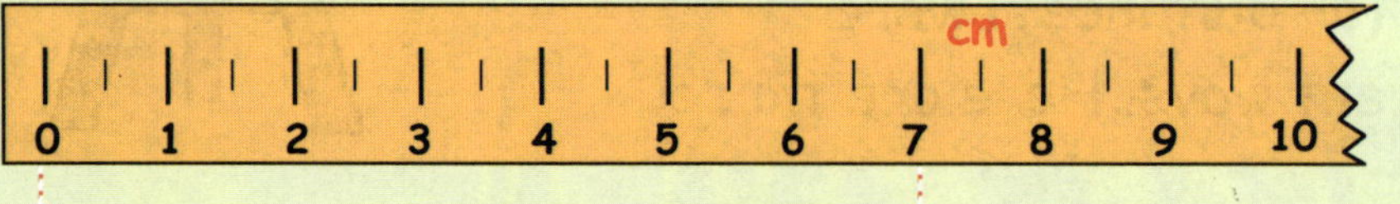

This red line is **7 cm** long.

Centimetres can be written as **cm**.

Exercise 2 You will need a ruler here.

1. Write down the lengths of these lines in centimetres (**cm**) :-

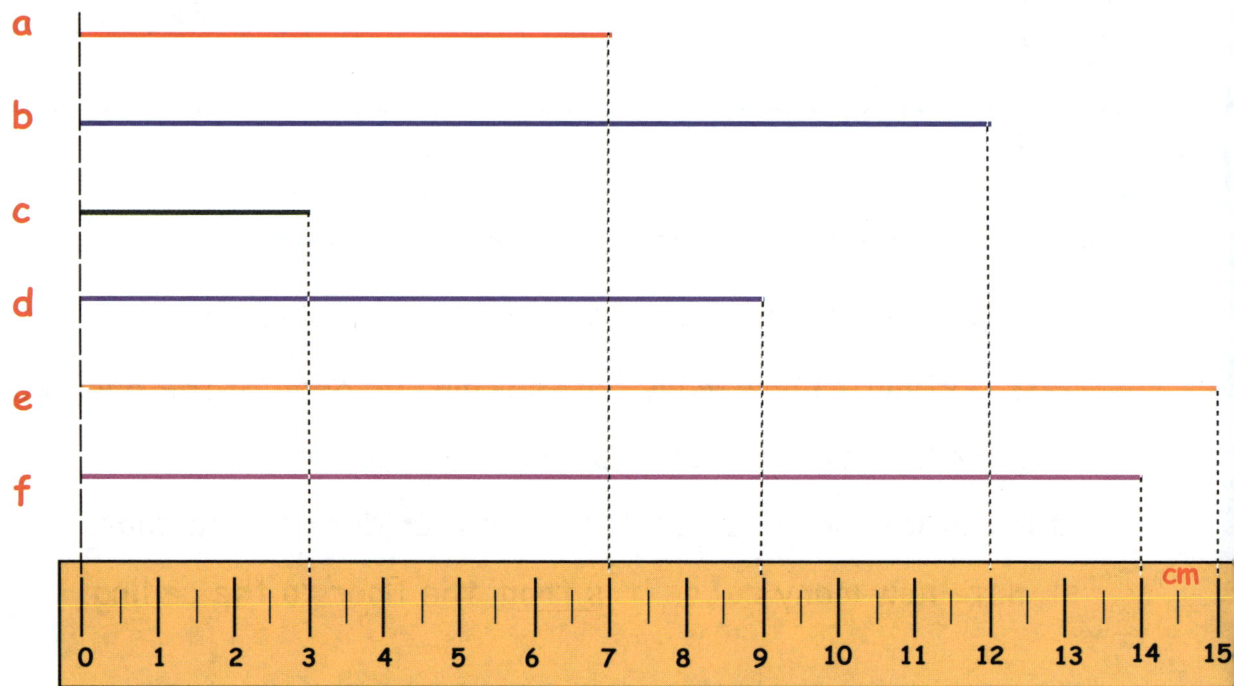

2. Use your **ruler** to measure these lines and write down your answer :-

a

b

2. c

d

e

f

3. Measure and write down the size of :-

a

b

c

d

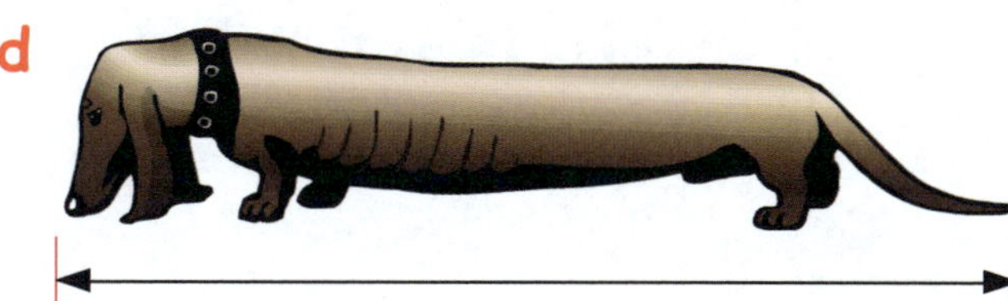

e

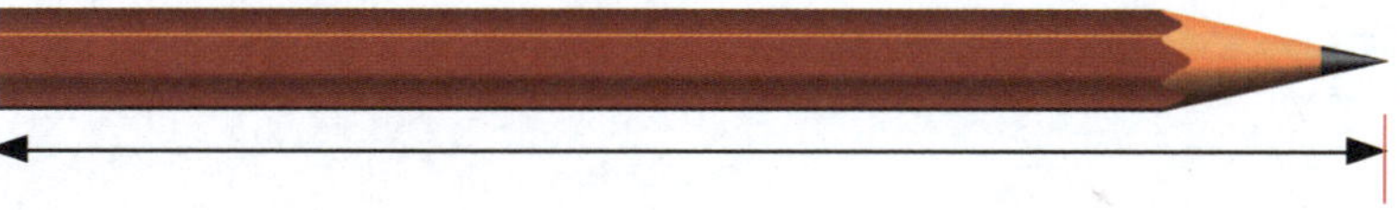

f

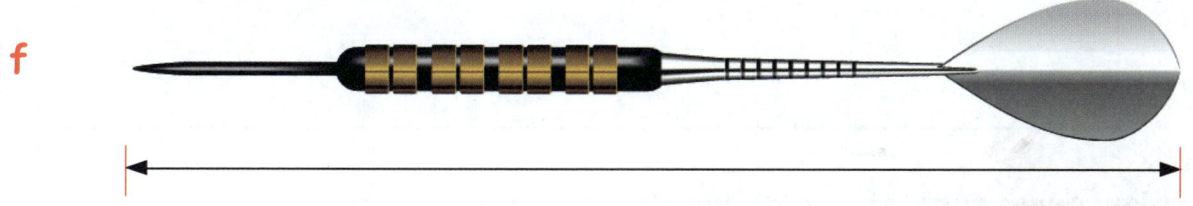

Worksheet 17·1

4. **Estimate** (guess) the length of each of these (in **cm**) :-

a The **width** of this book. (*Across the page*).

b The **length** of this book. (*Up and down the page*).

c The **length** of your longest finger.

d The **height** of your desk.

5. Use your ruler to **measure** each of the above (in question **4**) and write down your answers.

6. Use your ruler to **draw** and label lines which measure :-

a 3 cm	b 9 cm	c 14 cm	d 1 cm
e 16 cm	f 7 cm	g 4 cm	h 23 cm.

7. Measure the **length** and the **breadth** of each of these and write down your answers.

a

b

c

8. Now **draw** each of the shapes **carefully** and **accurately**.

9. Use your ruler to draw each of the following :-

a A **rectangle** measuring **6 cm** long and **2 cm** wide.

b A **rectangle** measuring **8 cm** long and **5 cm** wide.

c A **square** with all its sides **5 cm**.

10. a Which insect is **smaller** ?

1

2

b Which tyre is **narrower** ?

1 2

c Which flower is **taller** ?

1

2

d Which door is **wider** ?

e Which handle is **longer** ?

1 2

11. a Measure each coloured line below and write down each length.

b Which is the **longest** line ?

c Which is the **shortest** line ?

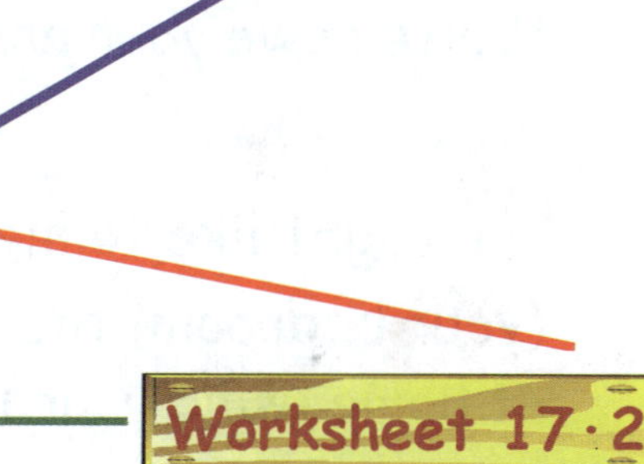

Measuring in Metres

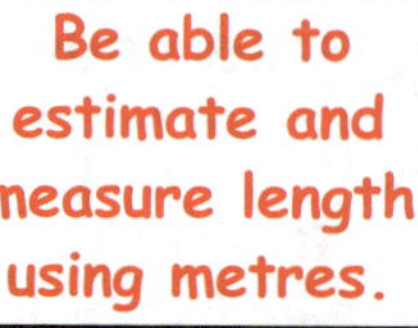

Be able to estimate and measure length using metres.

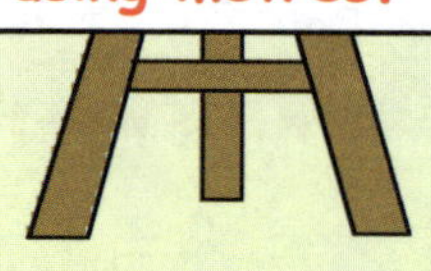

Sometimes for longer lengths, it is better to measure in **metres** (**m**).

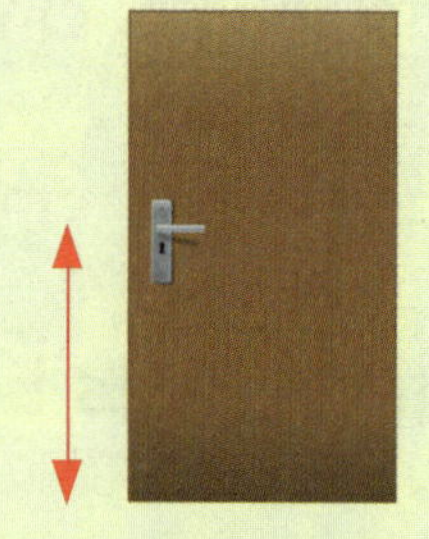

A metre is **about** the distance from the ground to a door handle.

A **metre** is exactly **100 centimetres**.

1 m = 100 cm

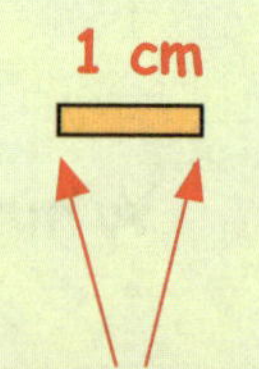

10 20 30 40 50 60 70 80 90 100

1 metre

Exercise 3 *Ask your teacher for a 1 metre strip.*

1. Without measuring, **guess** (*to the nearest metre*) :-

   a the **height** of your desk

   b the **height** of the ceiling

   c the **length** of your classroom

   d the **width** of your classroom

   e the **length** of the corridor

   f the **width** of the school gate

   g the **height** of the school building.

2. Use your metre strip to measure **some** of the above. Write down your answers.

3. You might like to measure some other objects (your bedroom, the length of your bath ....) at home using your metre measure.

4. Fold your metre strip in half. Now fold it again. You now have a metre strip split into **quarters**.

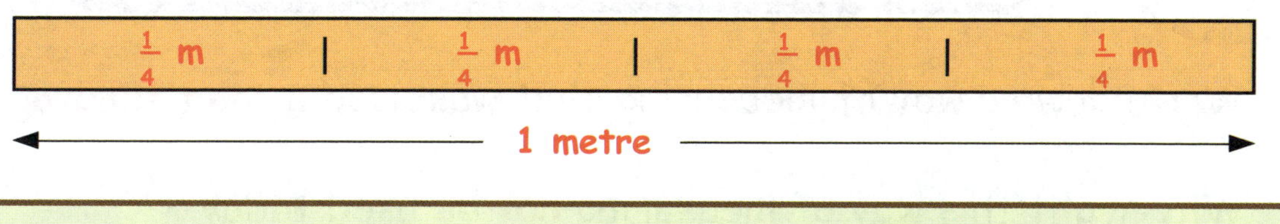

This picture shows a table which is **one** and **1 quarter metres** long.

$1\frac{1}{4}$ metres.

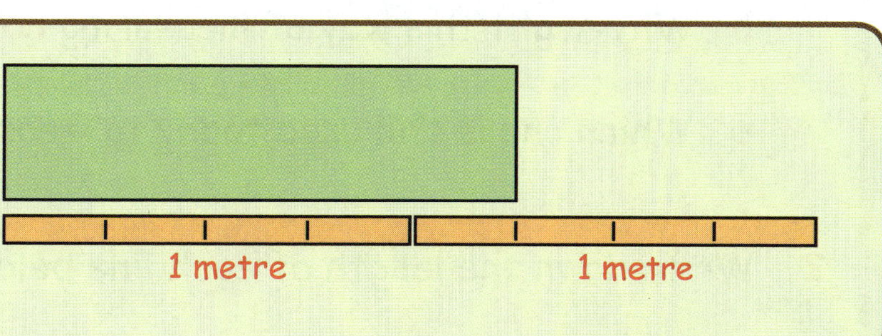

5. Without measuring, **guess** (to the nearest **quarter** metre) :-

   a the **height** of your teachers desk

   b the **height** of the classroom door

   c the **length** of the teacher's board

   d the **height** of your teacher.

6. Use your metre strip to measure all of the above in question 5.

7. Remember :- **1 metre = 100 cm.** How many **cm** in :-

a 1 m	b 5 m	c 8 m	d 3 m
e 9 m	f 7 m	g 6 m	h 10 m
i 4 m	j $\frac{1}{2}$ m	k $\frac{1}{4}$ m	l $1\frac{1}{2}$ m ?

8. **100 cm = 1 metre.** How many **metres** are in :-

a 400 cm	b 800 cm	c 200 cm	d 500 cm
e 700 cm	f 900 cm	g 250 cm	h 1000 cm ?

Revisit - Review - Revise

1. a Write down a way of measuring that was used **a long time ago**.

   b Why might this way of measuring **not** be used today ?

   c Which one is still used today to measure the height of a horse ?

2. Write down the length of each line below :-

   a

   b

   c

   d

3. What you would use (a **ruler** or a **metre strip**) to measure :-

   a the length of the classroom

   b the length of this page

   c the length of a **toy** bus

   d the length of a **real** bus ?

4. Write down how many **centimetres** there are in one **metre**.

5. a Draw a **rectangle** with length 6 **cm** and width 3 **cm**.

   b Draw a **square** with side length **4 cm**.

   c Draw a **rectangle** with length **7 cm** and width $3\frac{1}{2}$ **cm**.

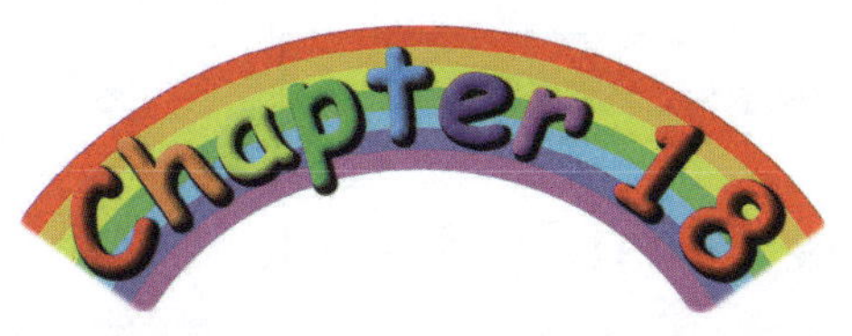

Dividing by 2 - Remainders

Be able to divide by 2 when there is a remainder.

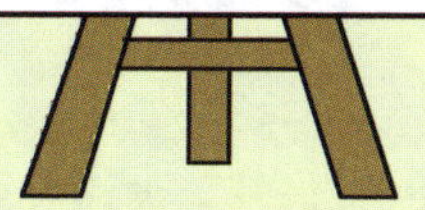

Quite often when you divide or share objects there are some left over - these are called **remainders**.

Example Share 9 bananas between 2 monkeys.

4 bananas to one monkey.

4 bananas to the other monkey.

But there is 1 banana left over.

We say that 9 (bananas) shared by 2 gives 4 each, **remainder 1**.

9 ÷ 2 = 4 **remainder 1** or

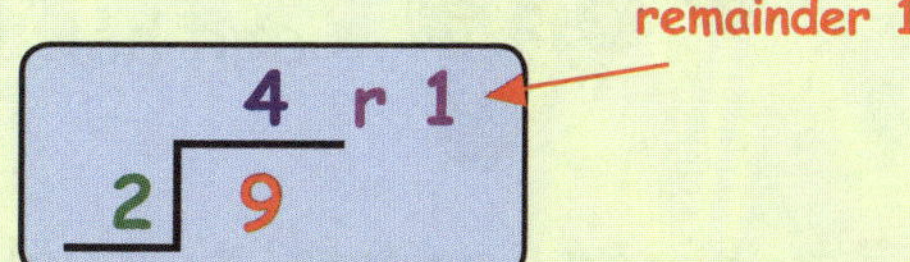

When **dividing** into **larger numbers** you may also get **remainders**.

Example 1 What is 2 7 ÷ 2 ?

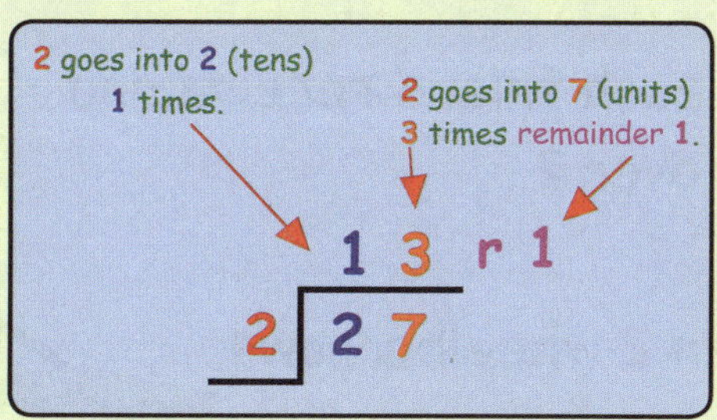

2 goes into 2 (tens) 1 times.
2 goes into 7 (units) 3 times remainder 1.
1 3 r 1
2 | 2 7

Example 2 What is 6 3 ÷ 2 ?

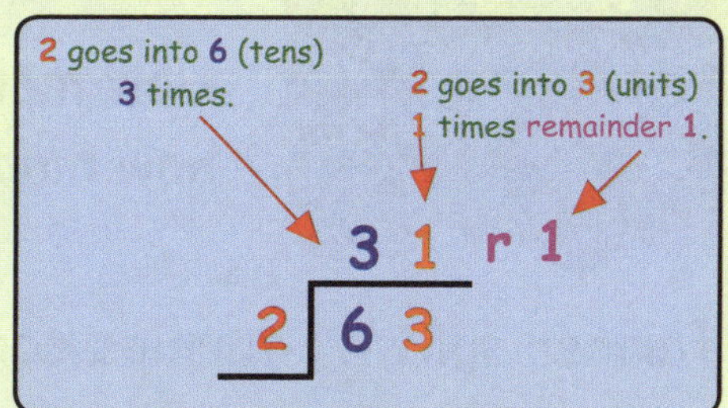

2 goes into 6 (tens) 3 times.

Exercise 1

Worksheet 18 · 1

1. **Copy** each of these and **complete**. You can use counters to help.

a 5 ÷ 2 = ... b 9 ÷ 2 = ... c 7 ÷ 2 = ... d 11 ÷ 2 = ...

e 15 ÷ 2 = ... f 13 ÷ 2 = ... g 17 ÷ 2 = ... h 19 ÷ 2 = ...

2. **Copy** and **complete** these :-

a 21 ÷ 2 = ... b 49 ÷ 2 = ... c 67 ÷ 2 = ... d 85 ÷ 2 = ...

e $2\overline{)27}$ f $2\overline{)61}$ g $2\overline{)43}$ h $2\overline{)89}$.

Set down as division sums and work them out to answer each question.

3. **2** squirrels share **25** nuts equally between them.

How many nuts does each one get and how many will be left over ?

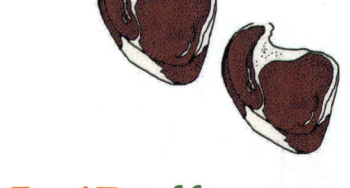

4. A butcher cut **41** steaks and put them in **2** equal bundles

How many steaks were in each bundle and how many were left over ?

5. **67** toffees were split equally between John and Candy.

How many did each get and how many toffees were left over ?

6. **83** one pence coins were shared between **2** frienc

How many coins did each friend receive and how many were left over ?

7. A farmer split **47** turnips equally between **2** wheelbarrows.

How many turnips were placed in each wheelbarrow and how many did not go into a barrow ?

Dividing by 2 - More on Remainders

Be able to divide any number by 2 when there are remainders.

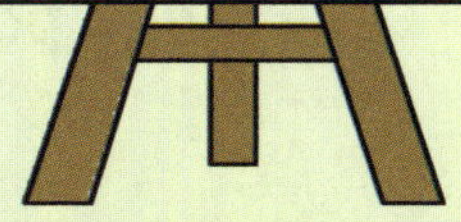

Sometimes, dividing the **first digit** gives a **remainder**.

Example 1 What is 5 4 ÷ 2 ?

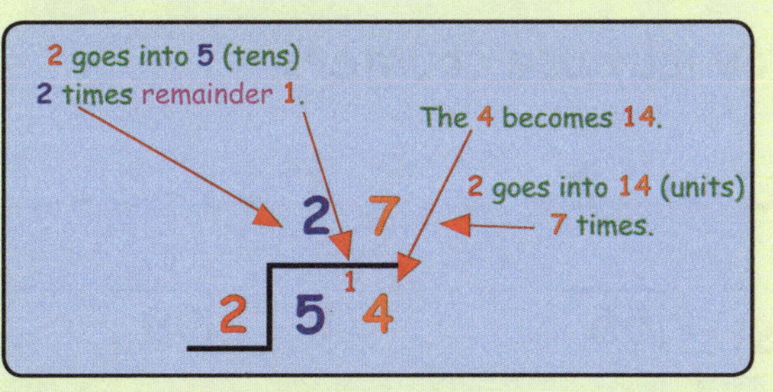

2 goes into 5 (tens)
2 times remainder 1.
The 4 becomes 14.
2 goes into 14 (units)
7 times.
2 7
2 | 5 ¹4

5 4 ÷ 2 = 2 7 remainder 1

Example 2 What is 7 3 ÷ 2 ?

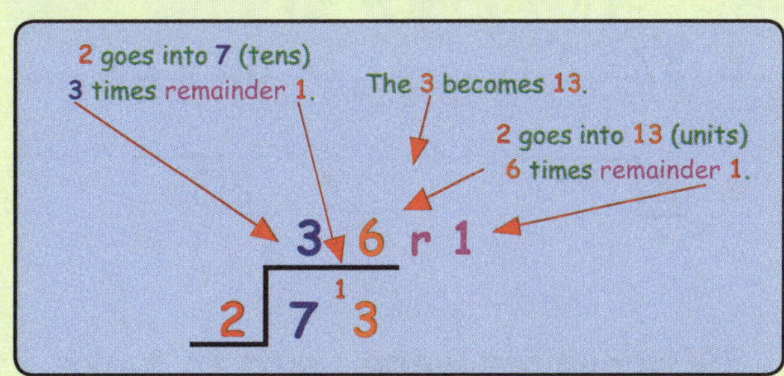

2 goes into 7 (tens)
3 times remainder 1.
The 3 becomes 13.
2 goes into 13 (units)
6 times remainder 1.
3 6 r 1
2 | 7 ¹3

7 3 ÷ 2 = 3 6 remainder 1

Exercise 2

Worksheet 18·2

1. **Copy** each of these and **complete**. You can use counters to help.

a 34 ÷ 2 = ... b 70 ÷ 2 = ... c 76 ÷ 2 = ... d 98 ÷ 2 = ...

e $2\overline{)38}$ f $2\overline{)90}$ g $2\overline{)72}$ h $2\overline{)54}$

Set down as division sums and work them out to answer each question.

2. a **50** tropical fish were split equally between **2** tanks.

   How many fish were put in each tank ?

b

The total number of horses in **two** races is **32**.

If each race has the same number of horses, how many are there in each race ?

3. The total number of newspapers in **2** bundles is **74**.

   If each bundle has the same number of papers, how many are in the bundle ?

4. Twins Al and Joe have to deliver a total of **96** newspapers.

   They each have to deliver the same amount.

   How many papers will each deliver ?

5. **Copy** and **complete** these divisions. You may use counters.

   a $37 \div 2 = ...$ b $59 \div 2 = ...$ c $91 \div 2 = ...$ d $73 \div 2 = ...$.

   e $2\overline{)17}$ f $2\overline{)33}$ g $2\overline{)55}$ h $2\overline{)99}$.

6. **39** brownies were used to make **2** wedding cakes.

   How many brownies went in each cake and
   how many brownies were left over ?

7. A cook used **57** apples to make **2** identical pies.

   How many apples were put in each pie
   and how many were left over ?

8. **Copy** and **complete** :-

   a $16 \div 2 = ...$ b $28 \div 2 = ...$ c $45 \div 2 = ...$ d $97 \div 2 = ...$

   e $2\overline{)51}$ f $2\overline{)84}$ g $2\overline{)27}$ h $2\overline{)93}$.

9. Chocolate eggs are put in boxes of **2**.

   How many boxes are needed for **87** eggs
   and how many eggs will be left without a box ?

10. **23** people go into a restaurant where each table
    seats only **2** people.

    How many tables for two did they use up and how
    many had to sit on their own ?

Dividing by 3 - Remainders

Be able to divide by 3 when there is a remainder.

3 boys were sharing out 8 chocolate coins.

The first boy got 2 coins.

The second boy got 2 coins.

The third boy got 2 coins.

This uses up 6 coins, so there are 2 coins left over.

We say that 8 (chocolate coins) shared by 3 gives 2 each, **remainder 2**.

$8 \div 3 = 2$ remainder 2

or

$$\begin{array}{r|l} & 2 \text{ r } 2 \\ \hline 3 & 8 \end{array}$$

remainder 2

Example 1 What is $95 \div 3$?

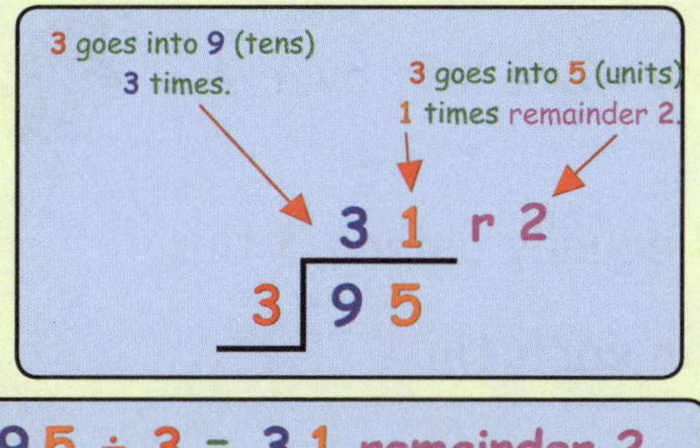

$95 \div 3 = 31$ remainder 2

Example 2 What is $72 \div 3$?

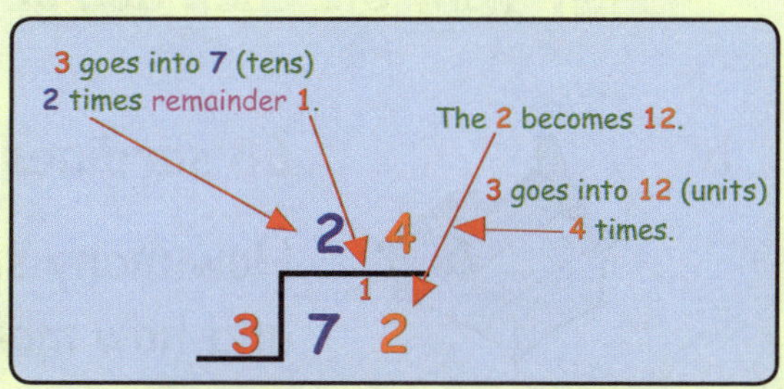

3 goes into 7 (tens) 2 times remainder 1.
The 2 becomes 12.
3 goes into 12 (units) 4 times.
2 4
3 | 7 12

$72 \div 3 = 24$

Example 3 What is $46 \div 3$?

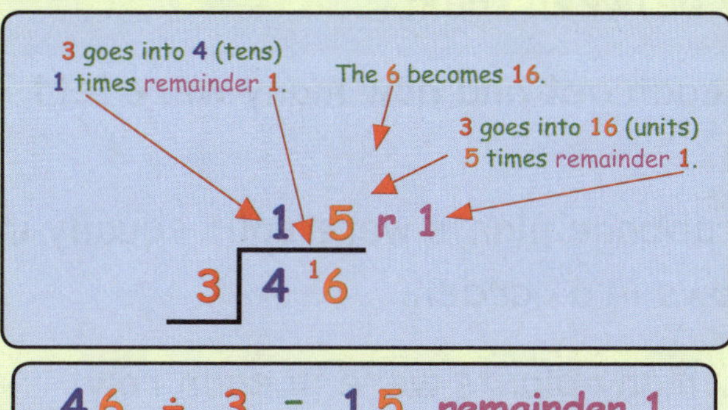

$46 \div 3 = 15$ remainder 1

Exercise 3

Worksheet 18·4

1. **Copy** and **complete** :-

a $11 \div 3 = ...$ b $16 \div 3 = ...$ c $20 \div 3 = ...$

d $7 \div 3 = ...$ e $14 \div 3 = ...$ f $19 \div 3 = ...$

g $22 \div 3 = ...$ h $25 \div 3 = ...$ i $29 \div 3 = ...$.

2. **Copy** and **complete** these divisions :-

a $3\overline{)32}$ b $3\overline{)34}$ c $3\overline{)61}$ d $3\overline{)35}$

e $3\overline{)67}$ f $3\overline{)62}$ g $3\overline{)94}$ h $3\overline{)47}$

i $3\overline{)73}$ j $3\overline{)83}$ k $3\overline{)88}$ l $3\overline{)92}$.

Set down as division sums and work them out to answer each question.

3. a **17** biscuits are shared equally between **three** dogs.

How many did each dog get and how many were left over ?

b 

68 sardines were divided equally among **3** tins.

How many sardines went in each tin and how many were left ?

c Joyce, Paula and May were given **49** £1 coins to be shared equally between them.

How many coins did each get and how many were left ?

d 

74 cabbage plants were split equally into **3** rows in a garden.

How many plants were in each row and how many were not in the rows ?

4. **Copy** and **complete** :-

a $3\overline{)27}$ b $3\overline{)36}$ c $3\overline{)42}$ d $3\overline{)48}$

e $3\overline{)51}$ f $3\overline{)57}$ g $3\overline{)72}$ h $3\overline{)78}$

i $3\overline{)84}$ j $3\overline{)87}$ k $3\overline{)93}$ l $3\overline{)102}$

5. a In a garden centre, **54** watering cans were laid out equally along **3** shelves.

How many watering cans were on each shelf ?

b **81** textbooks were bought for **3** classes.

How many books did each class get ?

c **18** pieces of meat were fed to **3** lions in a zoo.

How many pieces did each lion get ?

d 

72 parrots are kept in **3** aviaries, in equal numbers.

How many parrots are in each aviary ?

6. **Copy** and **complete** :-

a $3\overline{)43}$ b $3\overline{)53}$ c $3\overline{)20}$ d $3\overline{)10}$

e $3\overline{)17}$ f $3\overline{)29}$ g $3\overline{)46}$ h $3\overline{)73}$

i $3\overline{)76}$ j $3\overline{)88}$ k $3\overline{)98}$ l $3\overline{)103}$.

Worksheet 18·5

* *Remember - set down the following as division sums and work them out.*

7. a 77 crayfish were placed in 3 baskets.

   Each basket had the same number of crayfish in it.

   How many was that and how many extra fish were there ?

b 

   Ted made 23 sandwiches to take with him on his fishing trip. He shared them equally amongst himself and his 2 friends.

   How many sandwiches did each receive ?

   The remainder went to the seagulls.

   How many did the seagulls get to eat ?

c 52 windows in an office block have to be washed. Bob, Bill and Ben decide to wash the same number of windows.

   What is the most they each can wash and how many would that leave unwashed ?

d 13 children turned up for swimming lessons. They were split into 3 equal groups.

   How many were in each group and how many children were left out ?

e Claire's mum bought 38 bags of crisps for a party.

   If everyone ate 3 bags each, how many people were at the party and how many extra bags of crisps were there ?

f A total of 86 fish were shared equally between 3 seals.

   How many fish did each seal get and how many were left over ?

8. **Copy** these divisions and work them out :-

a	$2\overline{)27}$	b	$3\overline{)51}$	c	$2\overline{)28}$	d	$3\overline{)31}$
e	$2\overline{)45}$	f	$3\overline{)38}$	g	$2\overline{)40}$	h	$3\overline{)45}$
i	$3\overline{)59}$	j	$2\overline{)52}$	k	$3\overline{)61}$	l	$2\overline{)63}$
m	$3\overline{)67}$	n	$2\overline{)69}$	o	$3\overline{)81}$	p	$2\overline{)76}$

9. The recipe says I need **40 ml** of milk and the only measuring spoon I have holds **3 ml**.

   How many **3 ml** spoonfuls will I have to use and how much milk will be left over ?

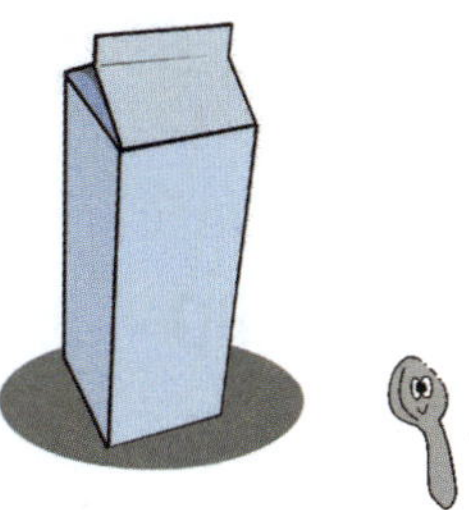

10. Jack buys **51** metres of rope to make skipping ropes for his gym class.

    If each rope has to be **2** metres long, how many can he make and what length of rope is unused ?

11. Last night, it took Cheryl's brother **twice** as long as her to do his homework.

    It took him **40** minutes. How long did it take Cheryl ?

12. 

    Joe is out to spend his **£79** birthday money. After buying the top **2** computer games (both at the same price) he still has £1 to spend.

    a How much was each game ?

    b He buys **3** lollies with the £1 and still has 1p left.

    How much was each lolly ?

The 3 Я's

Revisit - Review - Revise

1. **Work out :-**

   a $2\overline{)26}$ b $3\overline{)36}$ c $2\overline{)31}$ d $3\overline{)46}$

   e $3\overline{)65}$ f $2\overline{)51}$ g $2\overline{)99}$ h $3\overline{)74}$.

2. **Find :-**

   a $37 \div 2$ b $55 \div 3$ c $51 \div 2$ d $85 \div 3$

   e $80 \div 3$ f $69 \div 2$ g $83 \div 2$ h $83 \div 3$.

3. A parent buys **20** toy cars to be shared among **3** children.
   How many will each child get and how many will be left over ?

4. 

   The canoes at the boating pond hold **3** people.

   What is the least number of canoes that will be needed to carry **40** people and how many canoes will have less than 3 in them ?

5. **61** pupils in Primary 3 have to be split equally into **2** classes.

   a How many children should there be in each class.

   b The head teacher now has a problem. What is it ?

6. Charlie decides to buy cinema tickets for her and her friends.

   The tickets are **£2** each and she has **£25** with her.

   a How many tickets will she be able to buy ?

   b How much money will she have left ?

Statistics 1

Reading from a Table

Interpreting information from a table.

Information which appears in a **table** or a **chart** should be easy to read.

This table shows the number of pupils from a Primary 3 class who were absent from school during one week last winter.

Day	Number Absent
Monday	4
Tuesday	6
Wednesday	7
Thursday	9
Friday	10

- there were **6** absent on Tuesday.
- there were 3 more absent on Friday than on Wednesday.
- the longer the week went on, the more absences there were.

Many more pieces of information can be taken from the table !

Exercise 1

1. Use the table above to answer these questions :-
   - a How many pupils were absent on Monday ?
   - b How many pupils were absent on Wednesday ?
   - c How many **more** were absent on Thursday than Monday ?
   - d How many **less** were absent on Tuesday than Wednesday ?
   - e How many absences were there **altogether** that week ?

2. Siobhan has set her TV box to record her favourite programmes while she is at work.

Start Times	Programme
7·00	Emmerdake
7.30	Corrie Road
8·00	CSI Ayr
9·00	Our Family

a What time is **CSI Ayr** on at ?

b When does **Emmerdake** start ?

c How long **after** Corrie Road starts does CSI Ayr come on ?

3.

	S1	S2	S3
Gerry	21	16	25
Tanya	17	19	25

Gerry and Tanya counted the number of goals they had scored over the past 3 seasons.

Gerry scored **16** in **season 2**.

a How many goals did Tanya score in season 2 ?

b How many goals did Gerry score in season 1 ?

c Who scored more goals **altogether** ? How many was that ?

4. Every 3 months Tom and Betty saved some money in their bank.

	March	June	Sept.	Dec.
Tom	£6	£12	£3	£13
Betty	£10	£8	£3	£8

a How much did Tom save in March ?

b How much did Betty save in June ?

c Who saved **more** in December and **how much** more ?

5. The table shows the cost of boxes of flavoured luxury chocolates.

a What is the cost of a box of **milk** chocolates ?

b What is the cost of a box of coffee flavoured chocolates ?

c If I buy a box of each flavour, what is the **total** cost ?

Flavour	Cost
Milk	£6
Dark	£9
Coffee	£10
Orange	£8
Hazelnut	£12

6. Two friends treated themselves to a meal out.

The table shows what both of them ate.

a Who had **Chat** for starter ?

b What did Dave have for his **main course** ?

	Starter	Main	Extra
Dave	Pakora	Bhoona	Spicy Onion
Donna	Chat	Curry	Chapati

c What did each of them have as an **extra** ?

7. The table shows the number of cars sold by two local garages last weekend.

	Fri	Sat	Sun
Melville's	14	15	20
Phoenix	17	22	21

a How many cars did **Melville's** sell on Friday

b How many cars did **Phoenix Cars** sell each day ?

c What was the **total** number sold on the Friday ?

d How many cars **altogether** were sold by Phoenix at the weekend ?

8. A holiday hotel has posted a list of activities for the day.

Starting Times	Activity	Where ?
1.00	Archery	Football Field
1.30	Table Tennis	Games Room
3.00	Water Polo	Swimming Pool
4.00	Bingo	Lounge Bar

a What time does the **table tennis** start ?

b Where does the **water polo** take place ?

c Sandra is in the **lounge bar** at ten past four.

What is she playing ?

9. OD2 have 3 cinemas in Scotland. Here is one of their adverts.

	5.00	7.00	9.00
Glasgow	Duty Call	Luv Me 2	Tiny Tom
Edinburgh	Duty Call	B Team	Luv Me 2
Aberdeen	Tiny Tom	Duty Call	Luv Me 2

a What film is showing in **Glasgow** at 5.00 ?

b What film is showing in **Edinburgh** at 7.00 ?

c What film is showing in **Aberdeen** at 9.00 ?

d List where and at what times I could see the **Tiny Tom**.

10. The table shows the prices of short stay hotel breaks from Perth.

	2 nights	3 nights	4 nights	1 week
York	£70	£90	£110	£150
Blackpool	£100	£120	£140	£180
London	£150	£190	£230	£300

a How much would it cost to go to **York** for 2 nights ?

b How much would it cost to go to **LONDON** for a week ?

c Tom spent £140 on a break.

Where did he go and **for how long** ?

Reading from a Pictograph

Interpreting information from a pictograph.

A **pictograph** is a graph which uses **pictures** to show information.

Each picture in the graph stands for a **number** which can be found in a **key**.

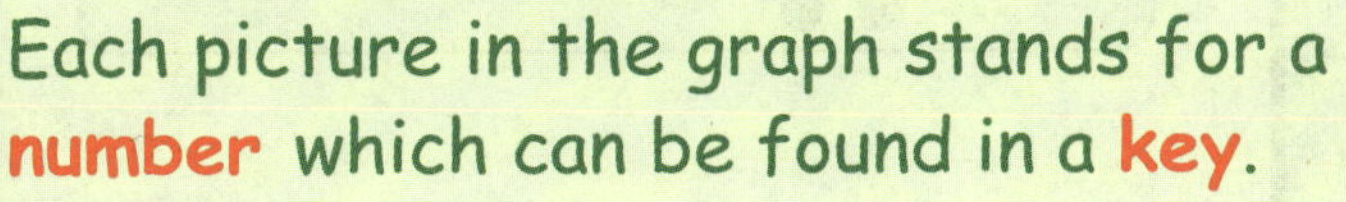

Key: 🯅 stands for 2 children.

Example

The pictograph here shows the number of primary 2 children who bring a packed lunch to school.

On Wednesday **5** children bring a packed lunch to school. (**not** two and a half !)

Exercise 2

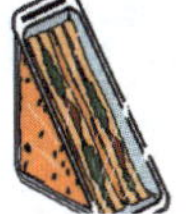

1. Look at the **pictograph above**.

   a How many pupils bring packed lunches on Monday ? *(not 5).*

   b How many pupils bring packed lunches on Tuesday ?

   c How many packed lunches **in total** were brought to school ?

   d One day each week, the lunch room offers special 50p lunches.
   Which day do you think it is ? Give a reason.

2. This pictograph shows the number of people waiting in a queue for the dodgems at the shows one evening.

5.00	●
6.00	● ● ●
7.00	● ● ● ◐
8.00	● ● ● ● ◐
9.00	● ● ● ● ●

How many were in the queue at :-

a 5.00   b 6.00   c 7.00

d 8.00   e 9.00 ?

3. This pictograph shows the number of flights to Spain which Ryanjet make during the winter months.

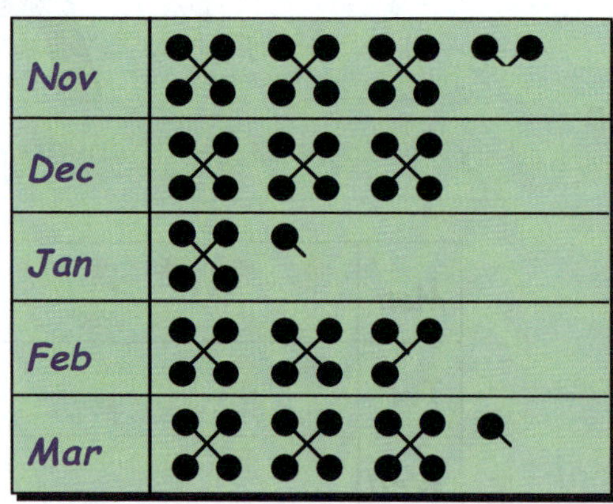

a Write down how many flights there are **each month**.

b Which month has the **most** flights ?

c Which month has the **fewest** flights .... and **why** ?

d What's the **total** number of flights in **February** and **March** ?

4. The number of police officers who were on duty outside a football park is shown.

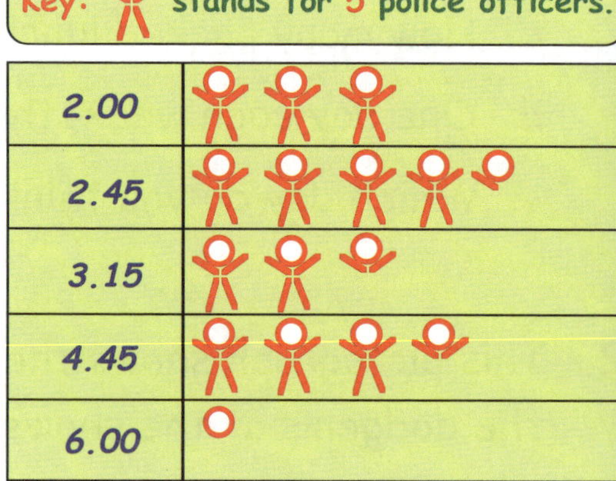

a Look at the key.

How many officers does this symbol stand for ?

b How many were on duty at 2.00, one hour before kick off ?

c How many were on duty at 2.45, just before kick off ?

d Just as the match started, at 3.15, how many police officers were on duty ?

Reading from a Bar Graph

Be able to interpret information from a bar graph.

This bar graph shows what a number of people like to do in their leisure time.

Notice that **3** people like to go bowling.

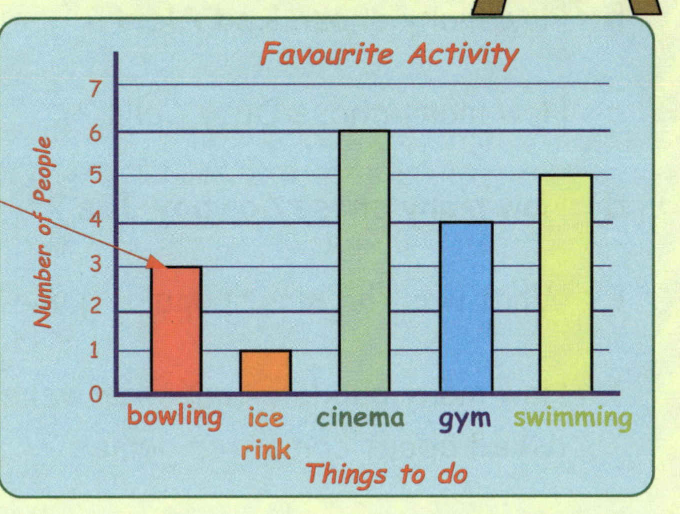

Exercise 3

1. From the **bar graph** above :-

a How many people like to go to to the ice rink ?

b How many people like to go to the cinema ?

c How many people like to go swimming ?

d How many people like to go to the gym ?

e What is the **most** popular thing to do ?

f Where is the **least** popular place to go ?

g How many **more** people chose the cinema than the ice rink ?

h How many people were asked in **total** ?

i How many people did **not** choose to go to the cinema ?

2. The bar graph shows the favourite computer games of a Primary 2 class.

a How many pupils chose Blue Rain ?

b How many chose Red Alert ?

c How many chose Duty Calls ?

d How many chose Cowboy Joe ?

e What was the **most** popular game ?

f How many pupils **altogether** were asked about computer games ?

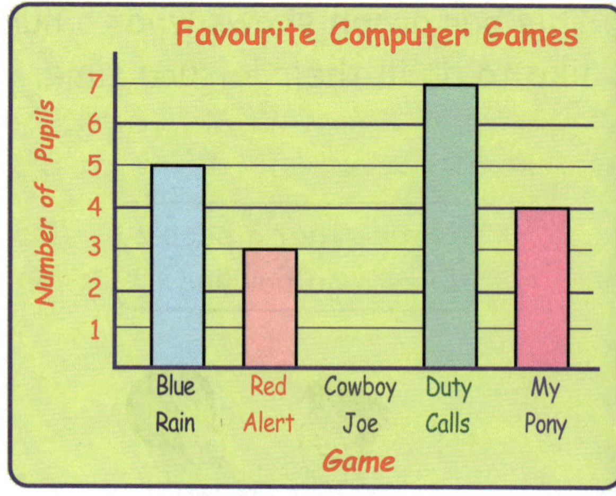

3. This bar graph shows the number of boxes of crisps eaten at the school disco.

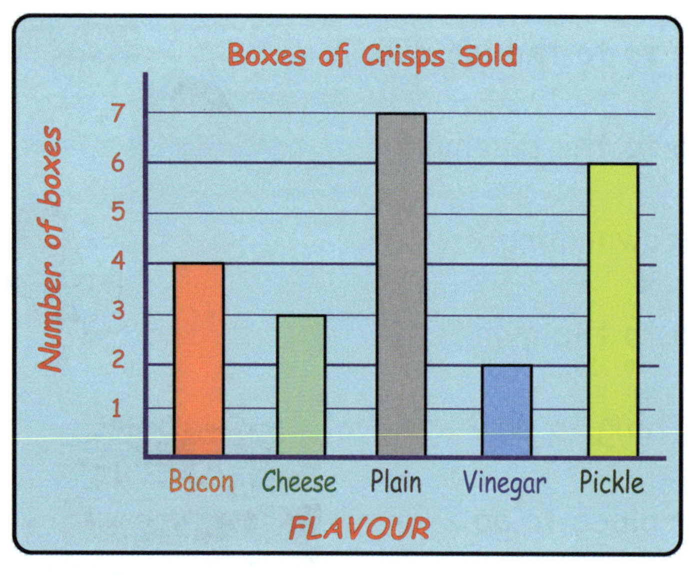

a How many boxes of **each** were eaten ?

b What was the **most** popular flavour of crisp ?

c What was the **least** popular flavour ?

d How many **more** boxes of **pickle** than **bacon** crisps were eaten ?

e How many **fewer** boxes of **vinegar** than **plain** crisps were eaten ?

f How many boxes of crisps were eaten **altogether** ?

4. The bar graph shows the number of items sold in an electrical store one Friday evening.

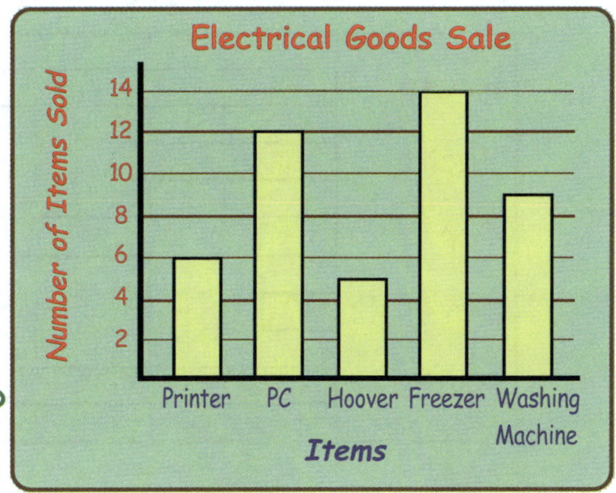

a Write down the number of printers sold. (not 3 !)

b Write down the number of hoovers sold.

c Which item sold most - how many ?

d How many **more** washing machines than hoovers were sold ?

5. The bar graph here shows what kind of home baking people prefer with their cup of tea.

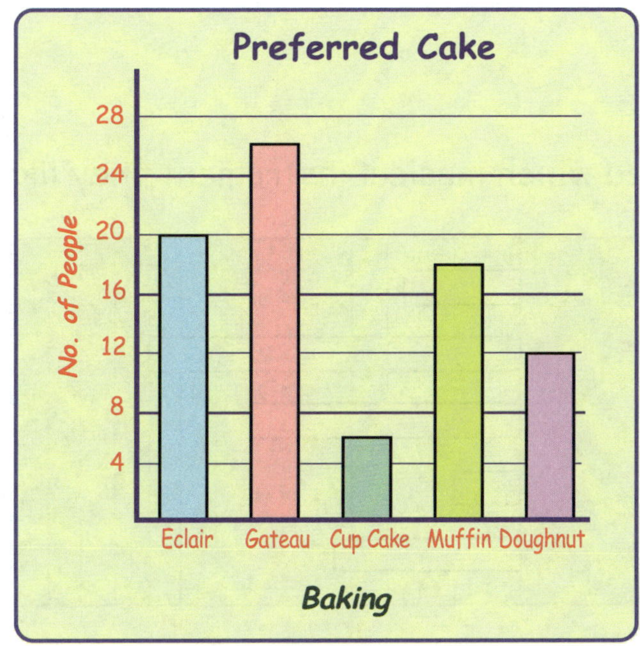

a Does the scale on the left of the graph go up in 1's, 2's, 3's, 4's or 5's ?

b What was the **least** popular cake ?

c How many preferred an eclair ?

d How many said cup cake ?

e How many said doughnut ?

f How many **altogether** said muffin or doughnut ?

g How many **more** preferred gateau to eclair ?

6. Some people were asked what they would buy if they won a lot of money.

Their answers are shown in a **horizontal bar graph**.

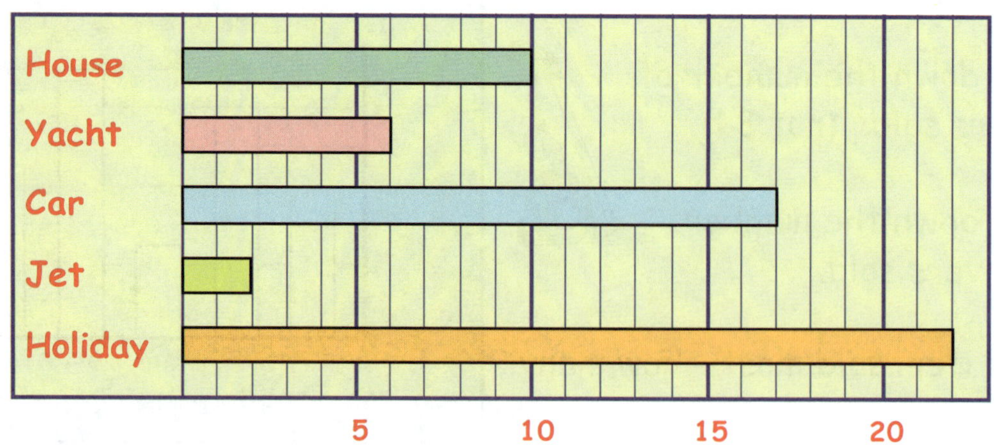

a How many people would buy a house ?

b How many would spend the money on a car ?

c What was the **most** popular answer ? .... How many voted for that ?

d How many **more** preferred their own yacht to a private jet ?

e How many people were asked ?

7. Some pupils in Scotland were asked which musical instrument they liked.

Here are their answers :-

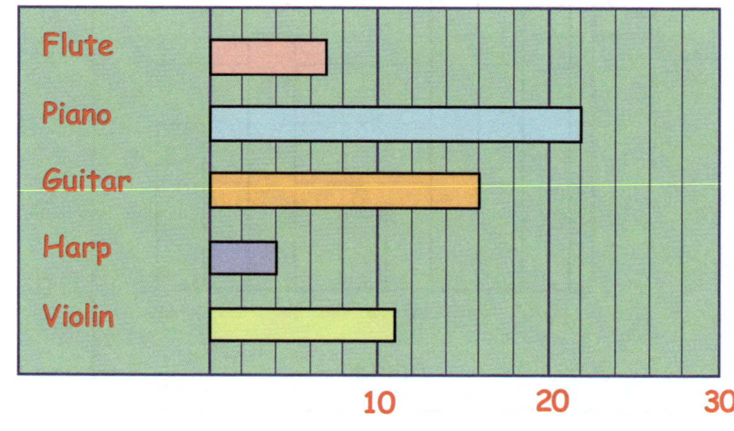

a How many said harp ?
(*not 2*).

b How many said piano ?

c How many said flute ?

d How many **more** liked

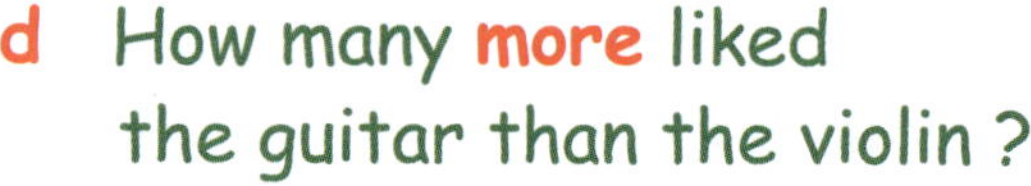

the guitar than the violin ?

e How many pupils **altogether** were asked ?

The 3 R's

Revisit - Review - Revise

1. The bar graph shows the number of patients who visited their dentist one week.

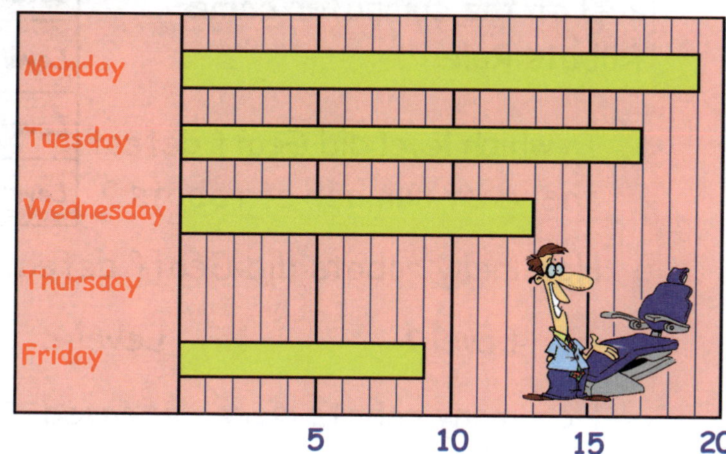

   a How many of his patients did the dentist see on Monday ?

   b How many patients did he see **in total** that week ?

   c How many **more** patients did he see on Tuesday than Friday ?

   d The dentist had a day off. Which day was that ?

2. The prices (per kg) of three types of meat sold in two food stores are shown in the table.

	TUSCOS	AZDO
Roast	£6·50	£7·50
Chop	£5·00	£4·00
Mince	£6·00	£7·50

   a How much is the roast in Azdo ?

   b What does mince cost in Tuscos ?

   c How much **dearer** are chops in Tuscos compared to Azdo ?

   d Mary bought a roast in Tuscos and **2 lots** of mince in Azdo. What did she pay **in total** ?

3. At a special family dinner, there were two choices for each course.

	Starter	Main	Dessert
1.	Soup	Turkey	Trifle
2.	Prawns	Steak Pie	Fruit

   a What was the starter in choice 1 ?

   b What was the dessert in choice 2 ?

   c Write down the choice of main course.

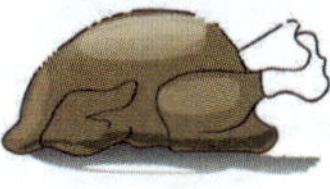

4. The pictograph shows how many robots Geoff defeated in each level of the computer game "Robots Rule !".

Key: stands for **4** robots

Level 1	
Level 2	
Level 3	
Level 4	

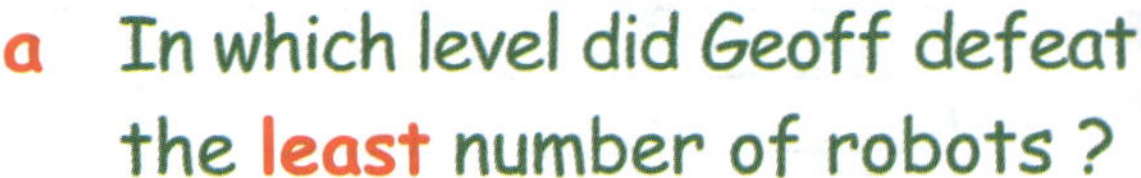

a In which level did Geoff defeat the **least** number of robots ?

b How many robots did Geoff defeat in :-

(i) Level 1 (ii) Level 2 (iii) Level 4 ?

c How many robots were defeated **altogether** ?

5. Some people were asked which room in the house they would renew if they had the money. Their answers are in the bar graph.

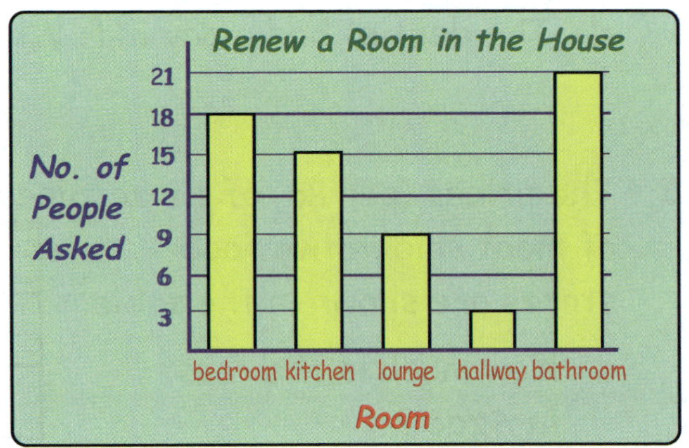

a Is the scale going up in 1's, 2's or 3's ?

b How many people said kitchen ?

c Which room was the least popular ?

d What is the **total** for bathroom and bedroom ?

e How many **more** preferred kitchen to lounge ?

6. Cinema ticket prices are shown.

	Mon - Fri		Weekend	
	Adult	Child	Adult	Child
Muffets II	£8	£3	£10	£5
Attack !!	£9	£4	£12	£6
GoldenEar	£10	£5	£14	£7

a How much for 1 adult at GoldenEar on Thursday ?

b How much for 2 children at Muffets II on Sunday ?

c Mrs Ross paid £18 for herself and her son.

Which film did they see and when did they go ?

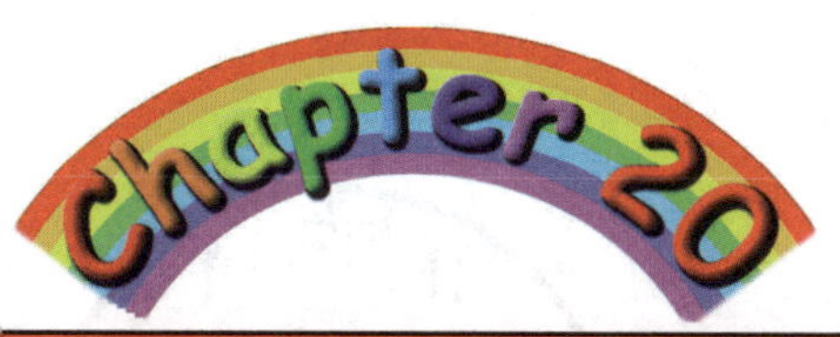

Position & Movement

A Right Angle and Quarter Turn

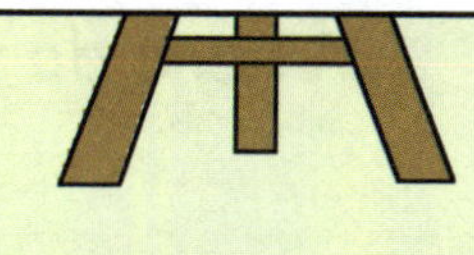

The hands of a clock move in a **clockwise** direction.

Anticlockwise is the opposite direction.

Do you remember what a **quarter** looks like ?

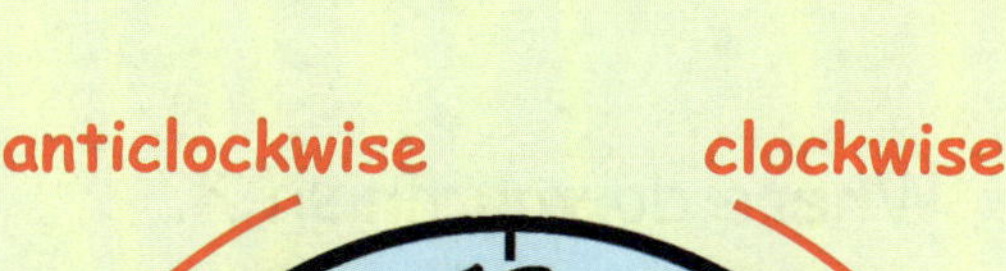

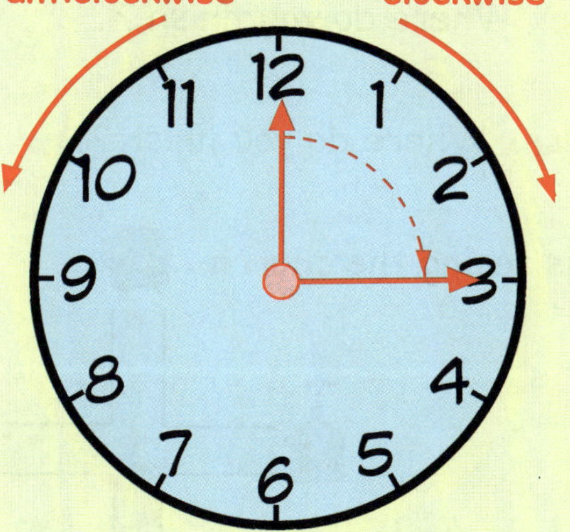

When the big hand moves **clockwise** from the **12** to the **3**, it has moved through a $\frac{1}{4}$ **turn clockwise** or a **quarter turn clockwise**.

A **quarter turn** is the same as a **right angle**.

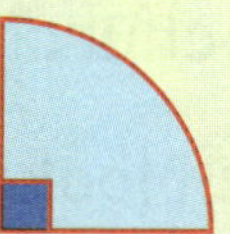

Exercise 1

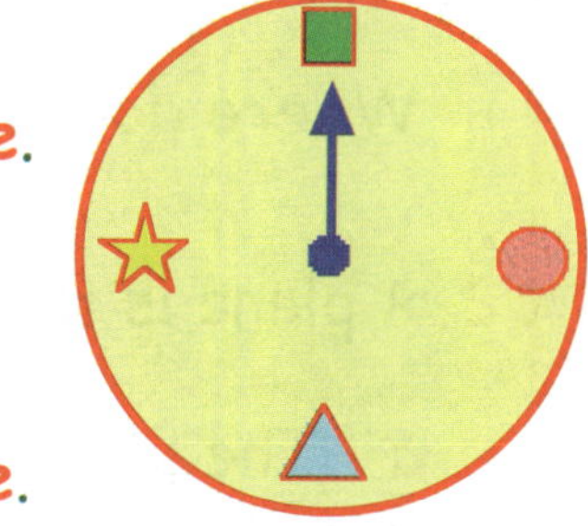

1. The blue arrow in the circle makes a $\frac{1}{4}$ turn **clockwise**.

   Which shape is it pointing to ?

2. Instead, the blue arrow makes a $\frac{1}{4}$ turn **anticlockwise**.

   Which shape is it pointing to now ?

3. The arrow points at the green square and makes a $\frac{1}{2}$ turn **clockwise**.

   Which shape is it pointing to now ?

4. This blue arrow starts at **12**. Make a $\frac{1}{4}$ turn **anticlockwise**.

Where do you finish ?

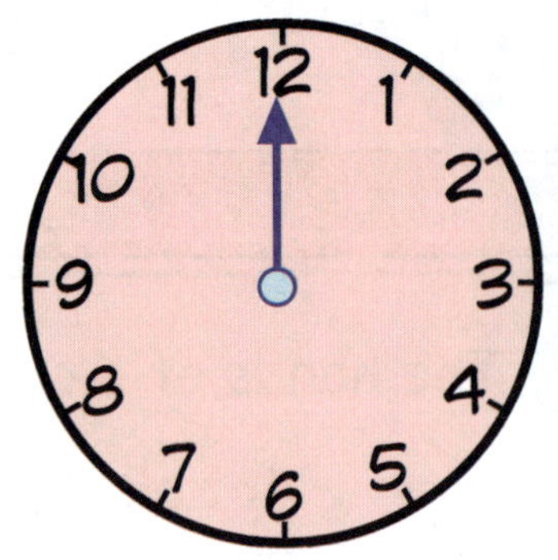

5. Set the arrow to **6**. Make a $\frac{1}{4}$ turn **clockwise**.

Where do you finish this time ?

6. The arrow points to **9**. Make a $\frac{1}{2}$ turn **clockwise**.

Where will the arrow then point to ?

7. Start at **2**. Make a **full turn clockwise**. Where do you finish ?

8. Start at **1**. Make a **half turn clockwise**. Where do you finish ?

9. Billy is standing at a crossroads. He is facing the **church**.

Billy makes a $\frac{1}{4}$ turn **anticlockwise**.

What is Billy then looking at ?

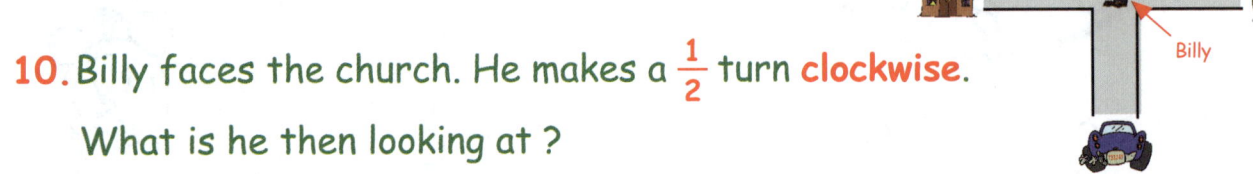

10. Billy faces the church. He makes a $\frac{1}{2}$ turn **clockwise**.

What is he then looking at ?

11. This time Billy is facing the **bus**. He makes a **right angle** turn **clockwise**.

Where does he end up facing ?

12. A plane is flying towards a mountain.

a The plane makes a $\frac{1}{4}$ turn **clockwise**.

Where is the plane flying towards now ?

b The pilot **then** makes a $\frac{1}{2}$ turn **anticlockwise**.

Where is the plane then flying towards ?

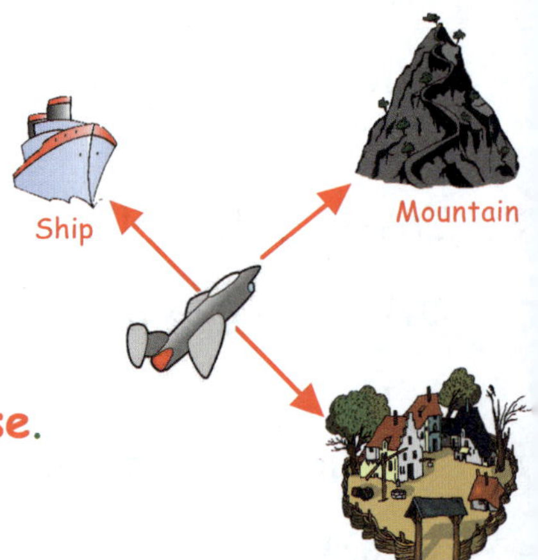

Describing a Journey

Be able to follow a journey using "forwards", "left" and "right".

Example

Davy follows a path over some paving slabs .

Lisa gives Davy these instructions to get from one side to the other.

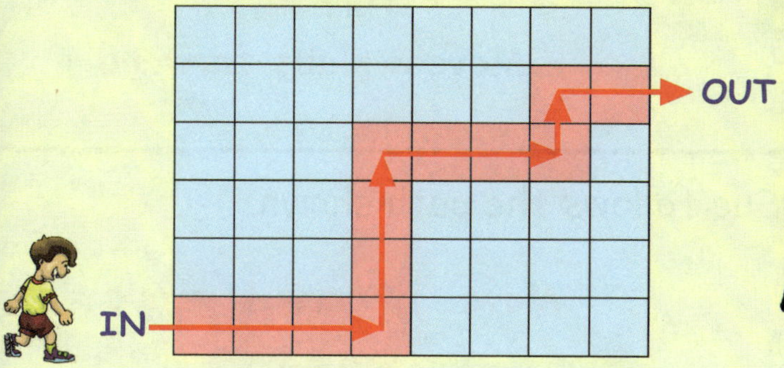

IN → OUT

Move 4 slabs forward
Turn left
Move 3 slabs forward
Turn right
Move 3 slabs forward
Turn left
Move 1 slab forward
Turn right
Move 2 slabs forward

Exercise 2

1. Write directions to show how Sara managed to get through the maze.

   Copy this and **complete** :-

   Move ... slabs forward
   Turn .....
   Move ... slabs forward
   Turn .....
   Move ... slabs forward

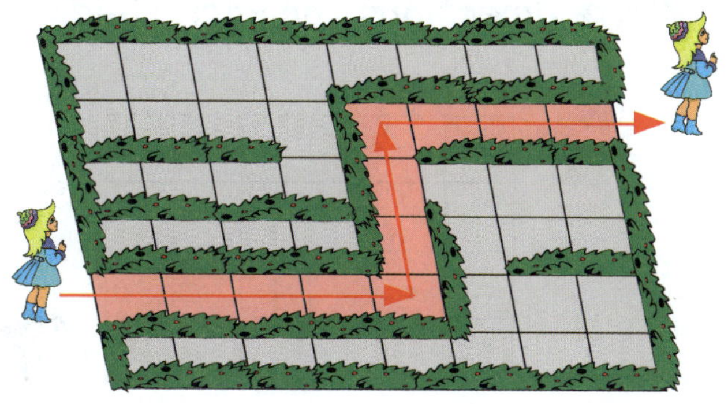

2. Write directions to get Jane and Nick through each maze.

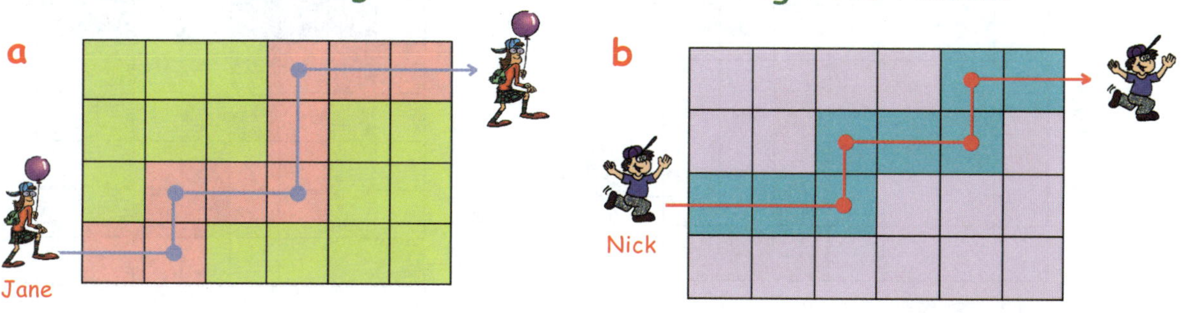

Worksheet 20 1

More Complicated Journeys

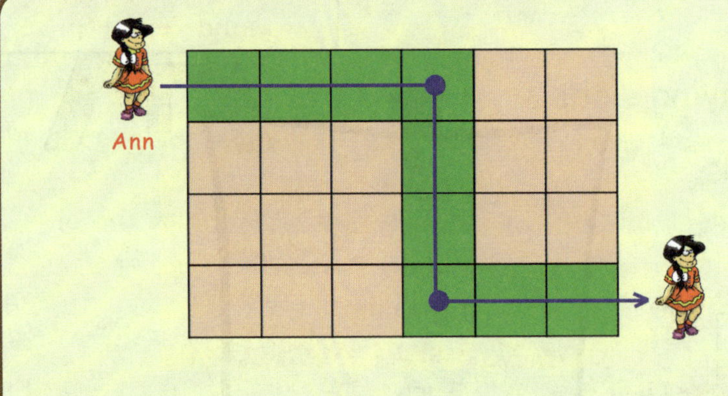

Move **4** slabs forward
Turn **right**
Move **3** slabs forward
*(Ann is facing **down** the page)*
Turn **left**
Move **3** slabs forward

3. Write directions to show how Sue follows the path shown.
Copy and **complete** :-

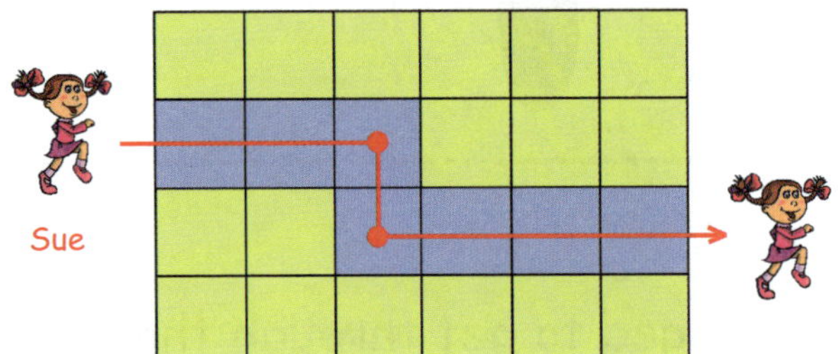

Move ... slabs forward
Turn .....
Move ... slabs forward
(Sue is facing down the page)
Turn ....
Move ... slabs forward

4. Write directions for each child to follow the chosen path.

a **b**

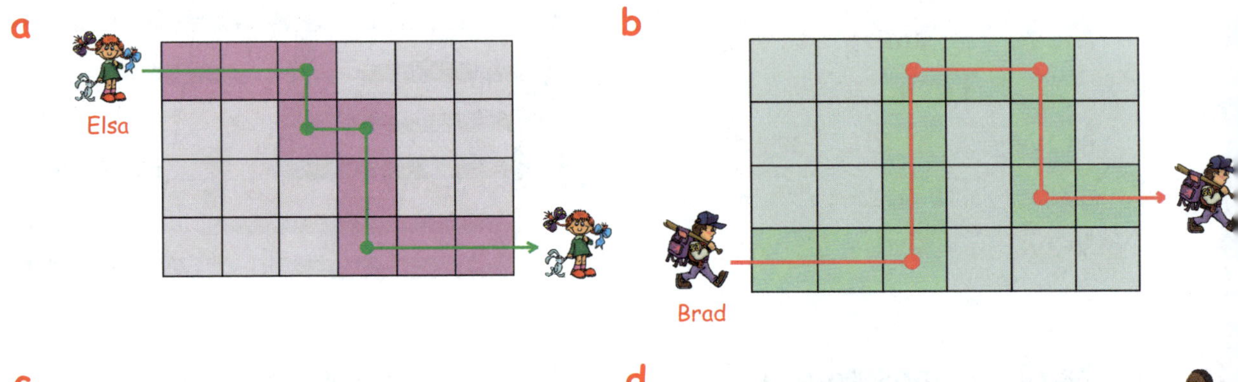

c **d**

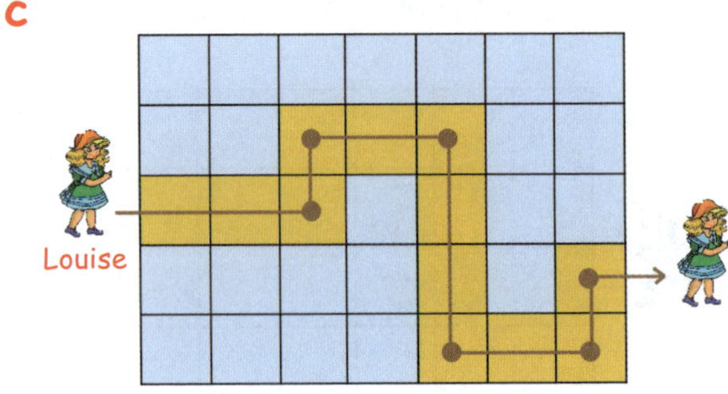

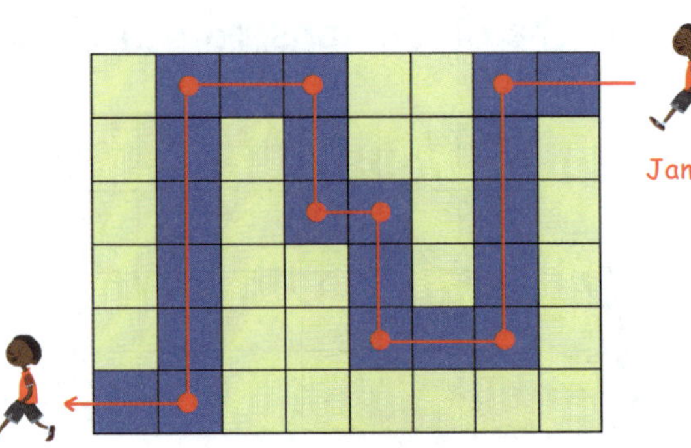

Worksheet 20·2

Shown is a map of Creely Island.

To drive from **BARNS** to the **Windmill** :-

> Drive along **Figgs Road**.
>
> Take the **2nd** on the **right** onto **Brads Road**.
>
> Take the **2nd** on the **left** onto **Gibbs Road**.
>
> The **Windmill** is at the end.

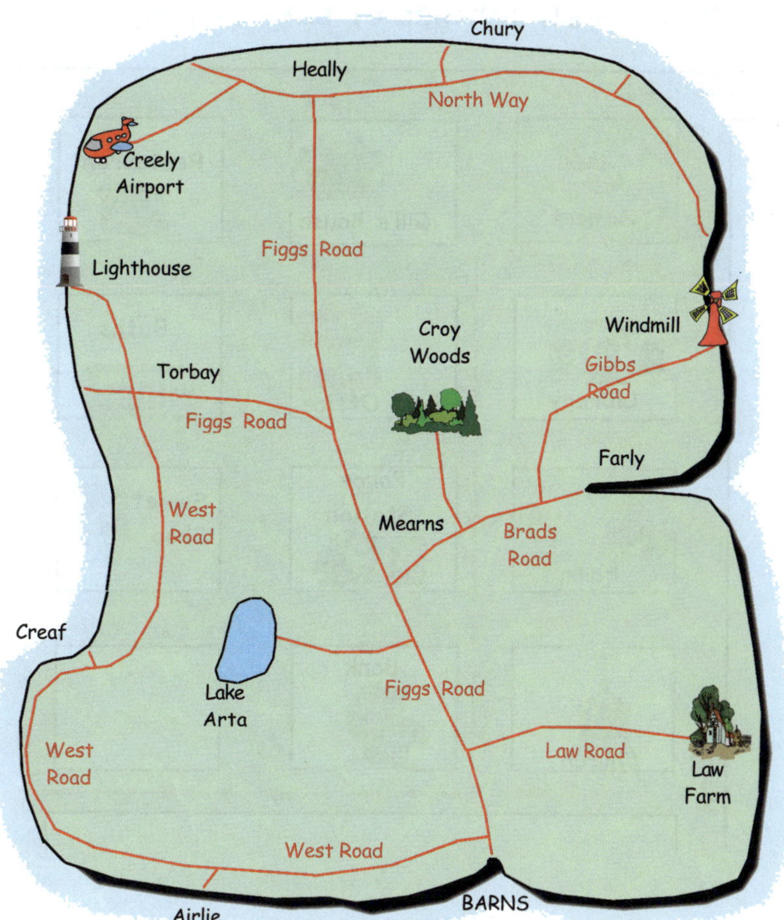

5. Say how you would drive from **BARNS** to **Law Farm**.

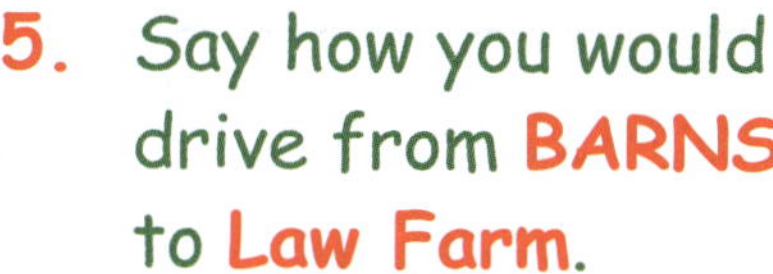

6. Give instructions as to how to drive from **BARNS** to **Lake Arta**.

7. How would you drive from **BARNS** to **Creaf** ?

8. George lives in **BARNS**.
   He needs to pick his friend up from Creely Airport.
   Describe how he would get there.

9. Jane lives in **Heally** and wants to drive to the **Lighthouse**.
   What route should she drive to get there ?

10. Jason lives in Farly and wants to drive to his friend's house in Chury.
    What route must he take ?

Shown is a street map of part of Drumly Village.

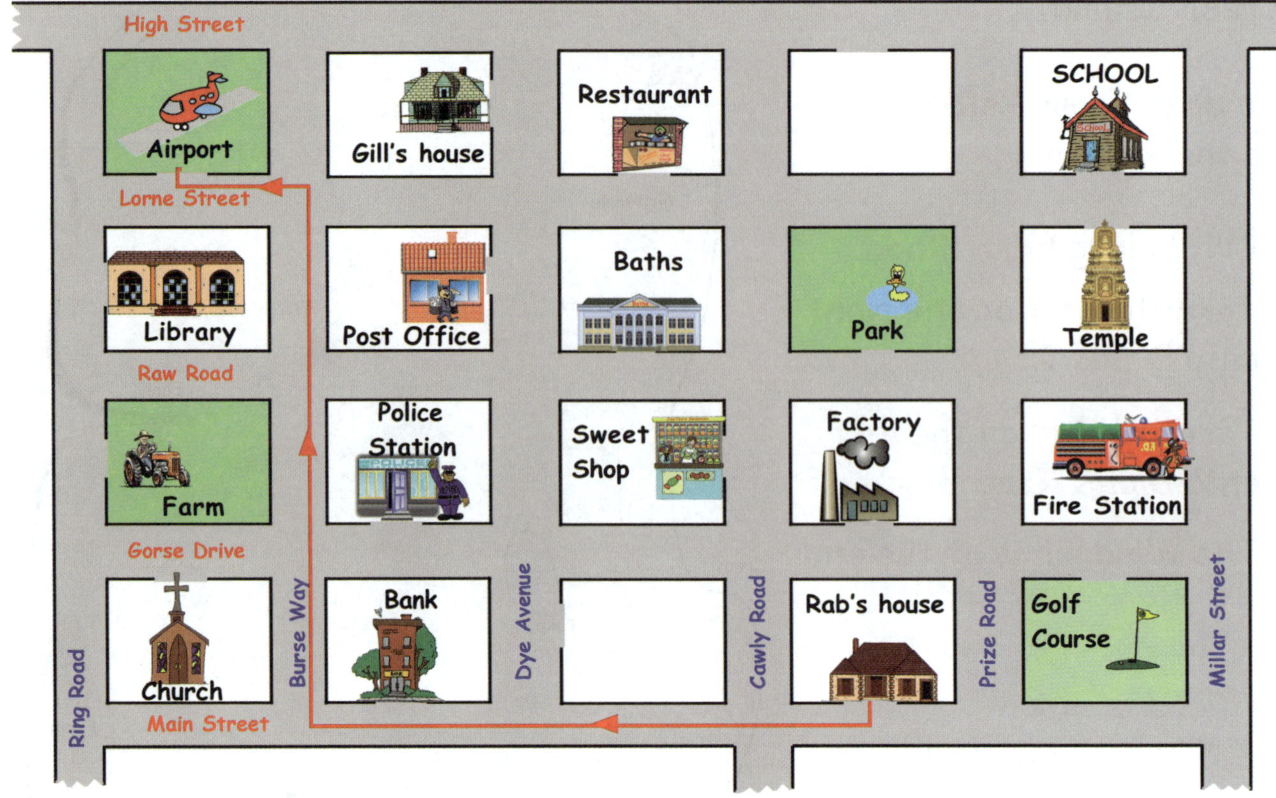

To get to the airport, Rab leaves his house, **turns right**, and walks along **Main Street**. He turns **3rd right** into **Burse Way** and takes the **3rd on his left** into **Lorne Street**. The airport is on his **right**.

11.a Rab wants to go to the **Post Office**. **Copy** and complete :-

Come out of Rab's house, turn .... Take the .... on the right into .... Avenue. The post office is the .... block on the ....

b Gill wants to go to the **Fire Station**. **Copy** and complete :-

Come out of Gill's house and turn .... Take the .... on the left into .... Then take the .... right into .... Street. The Fire Station is on her ....

c Give directions to walk from the **Police Station** to the **Park**.

d How would Stef get from the **School** to the **Sweet Shop** ?

Revisit - Review - Revise

1. Joe is in a field walking towards the farm.

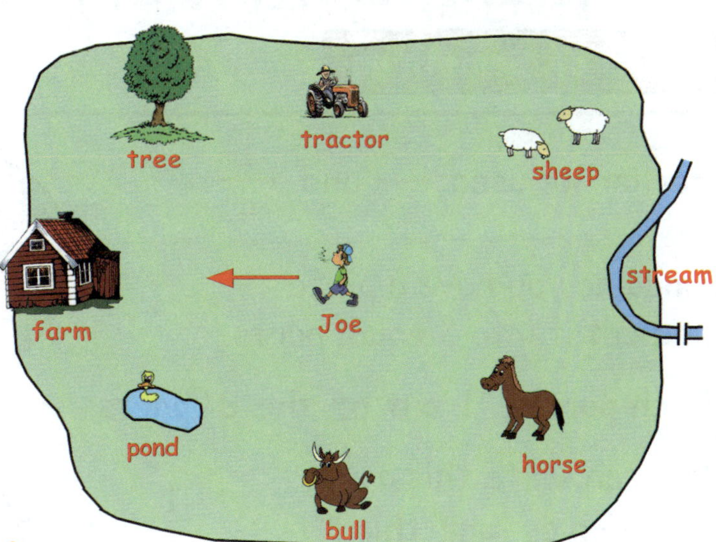

a What is the **first** thing Joe sees if he turns his head **clockwise** ?

b What will Joe be looking at if he makes a **quarter turn anticlockwise** ?

2.

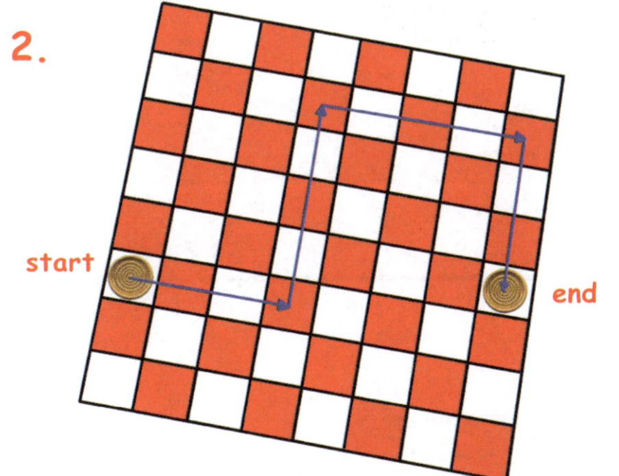

Jason moves a draughts piece around the table as shown.

Describe how he moved the piece.

Move ...... **squares forward**.
Turn ....

Move ...... **squares** ....
Turn ....

....

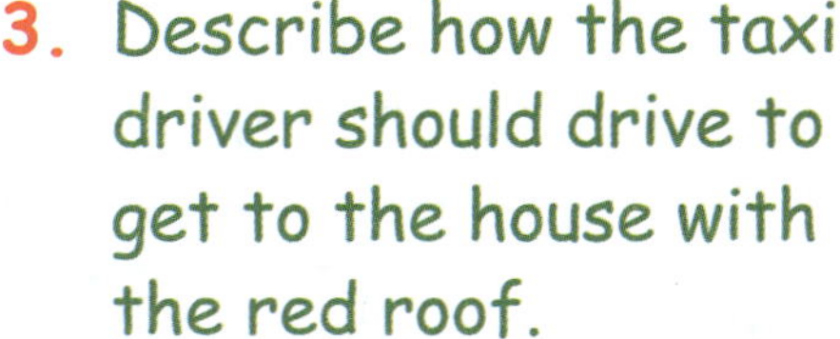

3. Describe how the taxi driver should drive to get to the house with the red roof.

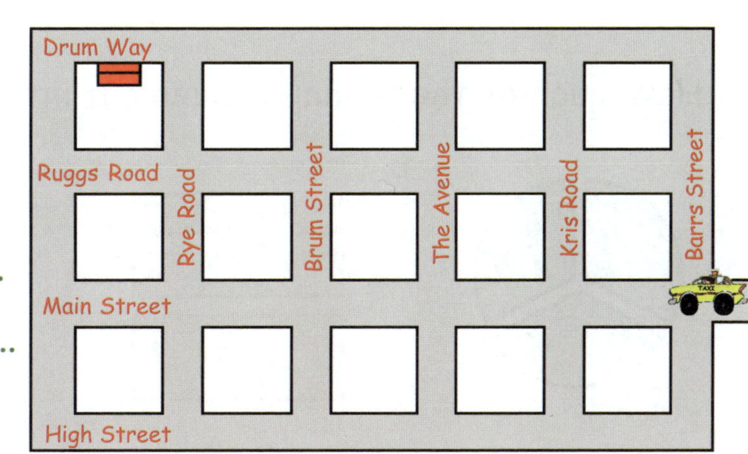

Drive along .... street.

Turn .... right into ....

....

Fractions 2

A Third of Something

Be able to recognise and shade a third of a shape.

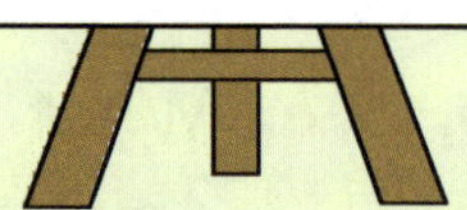

Earlier we used $\frac{1}{2}$ and $\frac{1}{4}$.

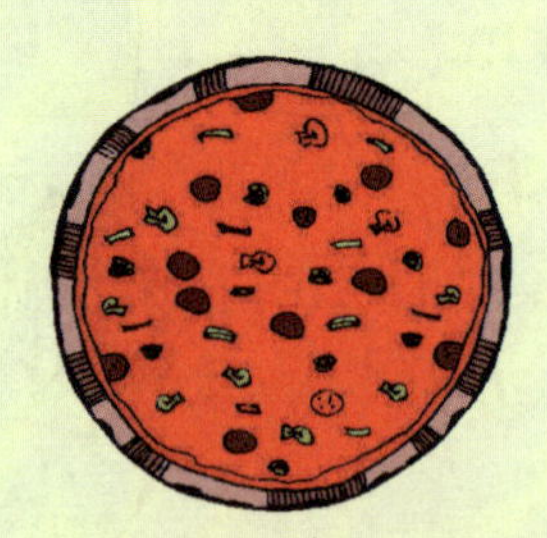

Imagine you have a pizza and cut it into **3 equal** parts.

Each **part** is "**1 out of the 3**" parts.

We can write this as a **fraction** as "**one third**" or :- $\frac{1}{3}$

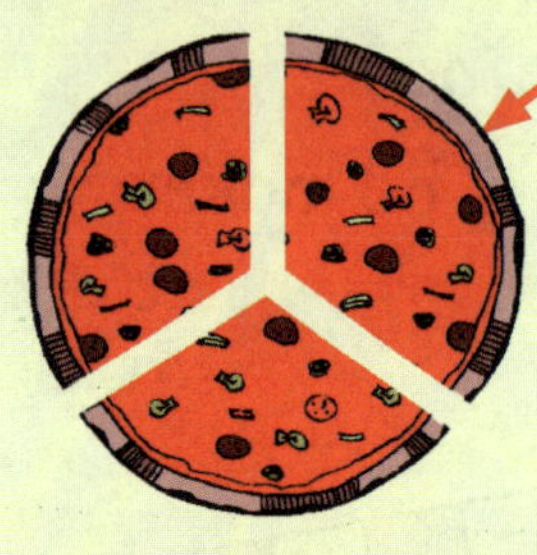

1 of the 3 parts was removed.

This tells you how many parts the shape was cut into. $\frac{1}{3}$ This tells you how many parts you are interested in.

Exercise 1

1. Has this shape been cut into **thirds** (3 **equal** parts) ?

   Write **yes** or **no**.

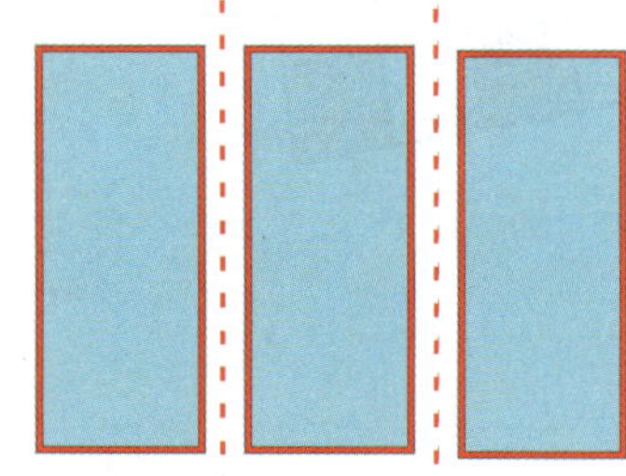

2. Have each of these shapes been cut into **thirds** ? (**Yes** or **No**).

a 

b 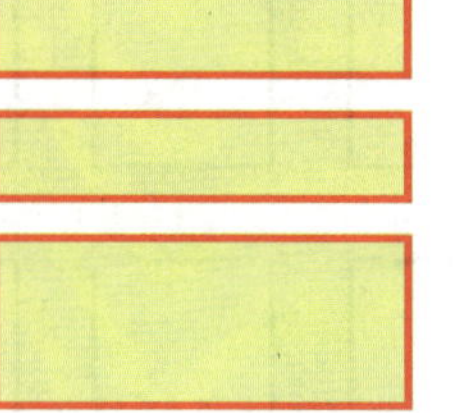

c 

d 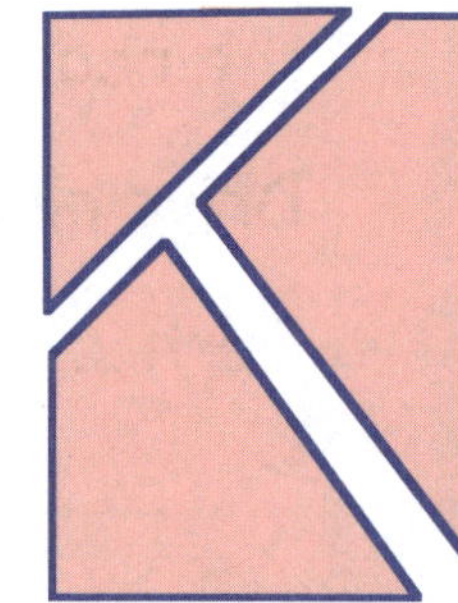

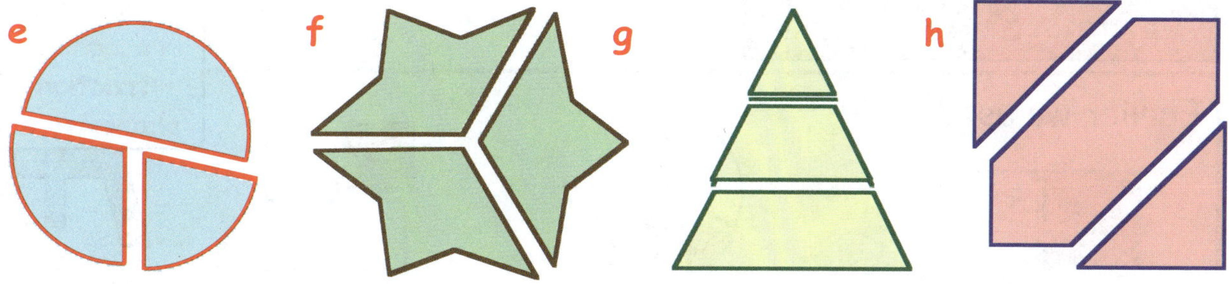

3. Kat, Paul and Gary share 18 sweets.

Do each of them have a **third** ? (Have they shared **equally** ?)

4. Bill, Ben and Pete share **£15**.

Bill

Ben

Pete

a Do each of them have a **third** ? (Have they shared **equally** ?)

b How much money should each of them have ?

5. There are 24 pencils in a box.

Zara, Zack and Zia share them equally.

a What **fraction** will they each get ?

b **How many** pencils should each of them get ?

A Fraction of Something

Be able to recognise what fraction of a shape is shaded.

Earlier we used

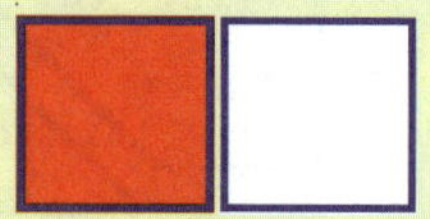

$\frac{1}{2}$ **one** part out of **2** bits.

$\frac{1}{3}$ **one** part out of **3** bits.

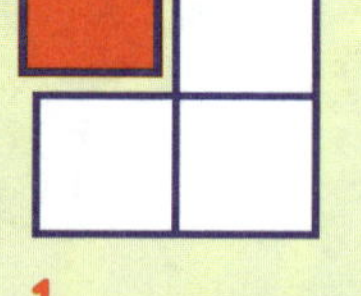

$\frac{1}{4}$ **one** part out of **4** bits.

This circle has split into 5 **equal** parts.

The **red** bit is "*one part out of 5*" parts.

This could be written as $\frac{1}{5}$.

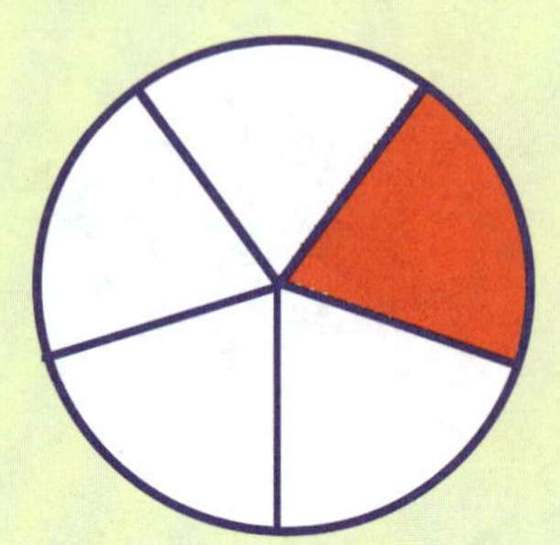

Exercise 2

Worksheet 21·1

1. This shape has six **equal** parts.

   What fraction is in **red**. $\frac{1}{?}$

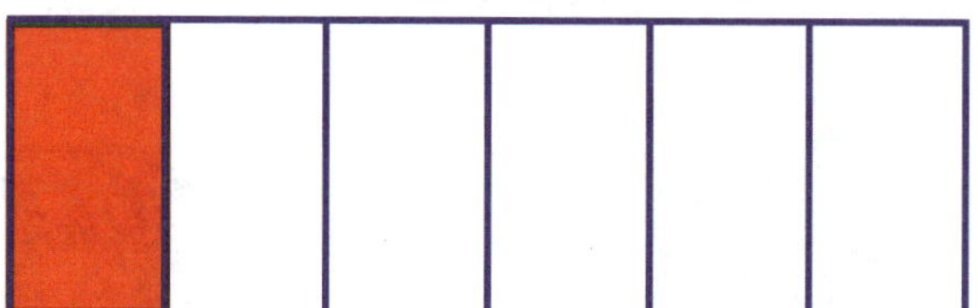

2. Each circle below is split into **equal** parts.

   Write down the fraction that is **red**.

a

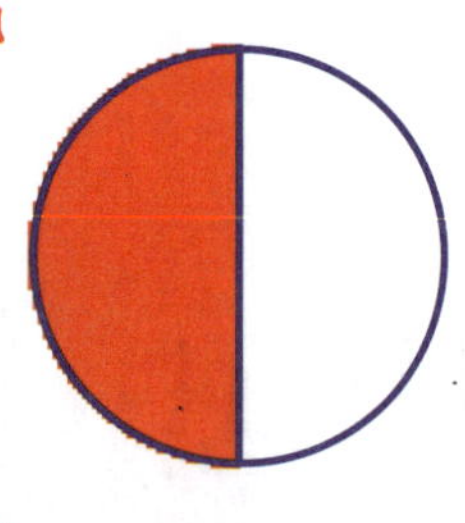

b

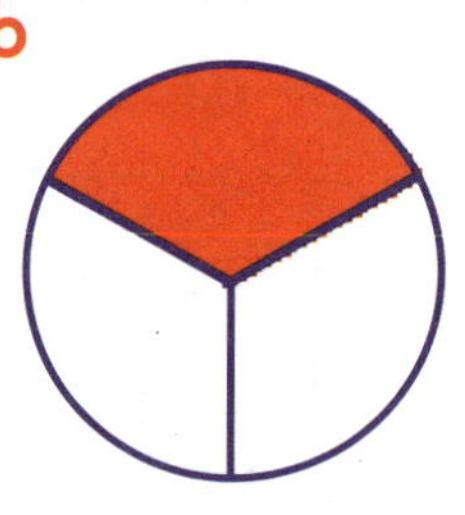

c

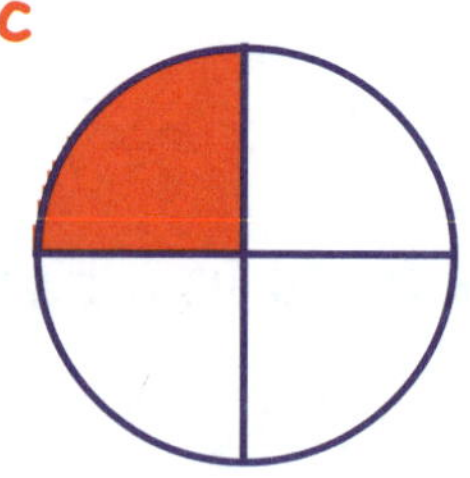

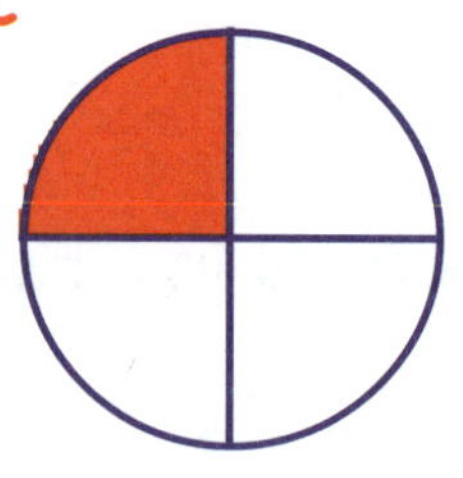

d

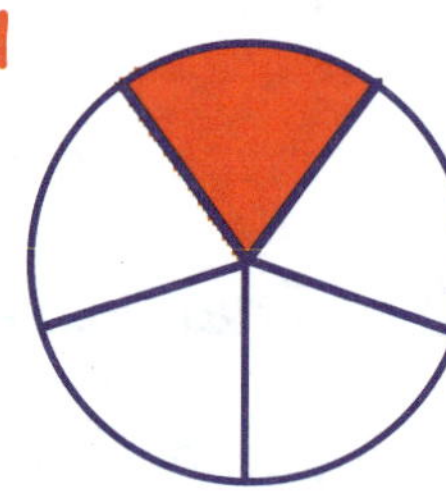

e

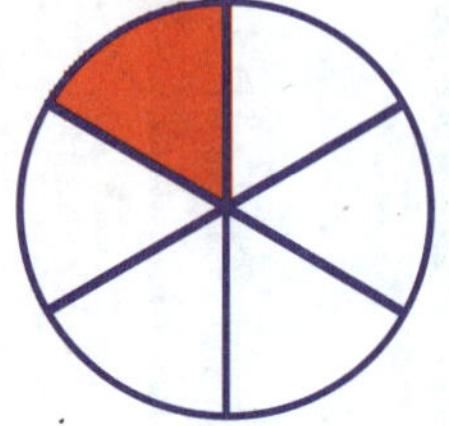

f

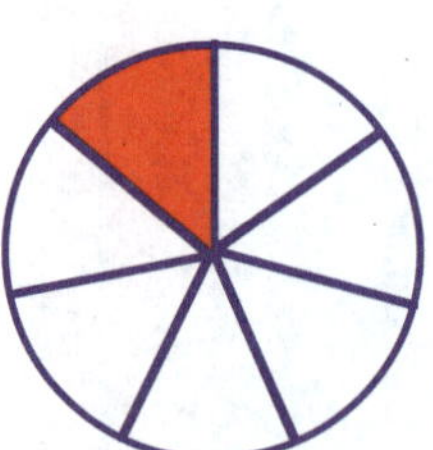

g

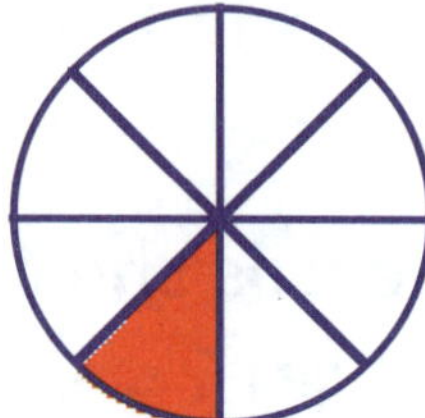

h

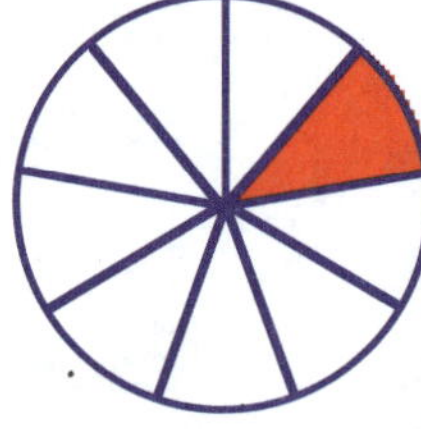

3. Each shape below is split into **equal** parts.

Write down the **fraction** of each shape that is **red**.

a

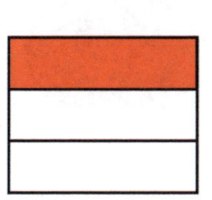

b

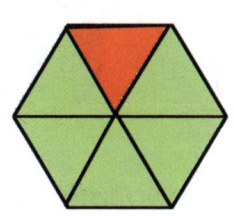

c

d

e

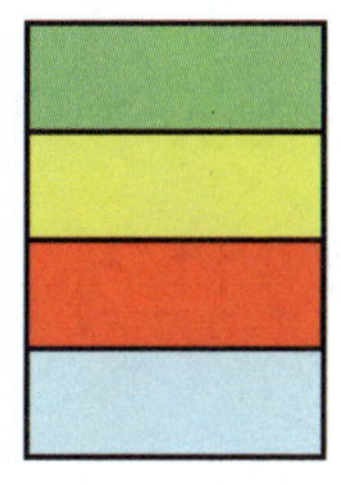

f

g

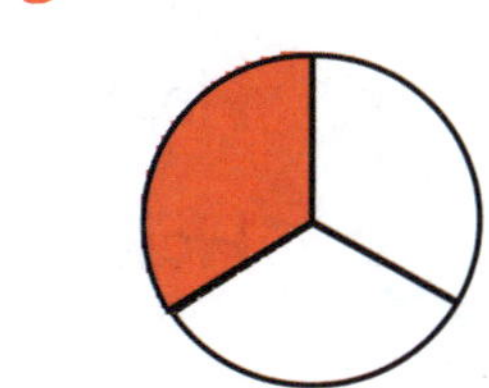

h

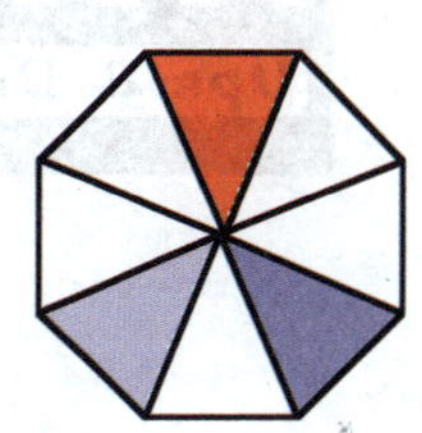

i

j

k

l

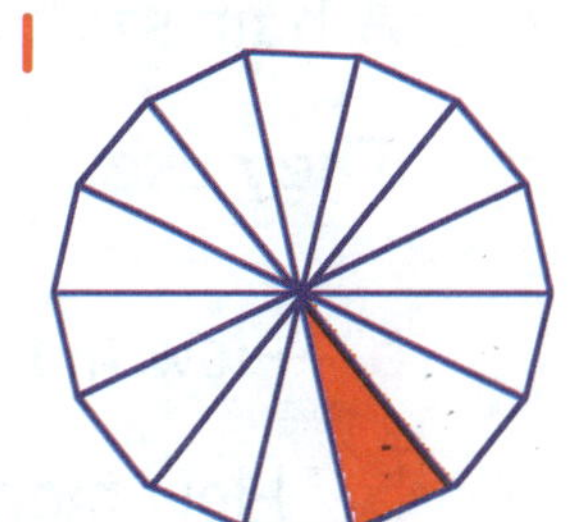

4. a How many **squares** has this grid been split into ?

b What fraction is **red** ?

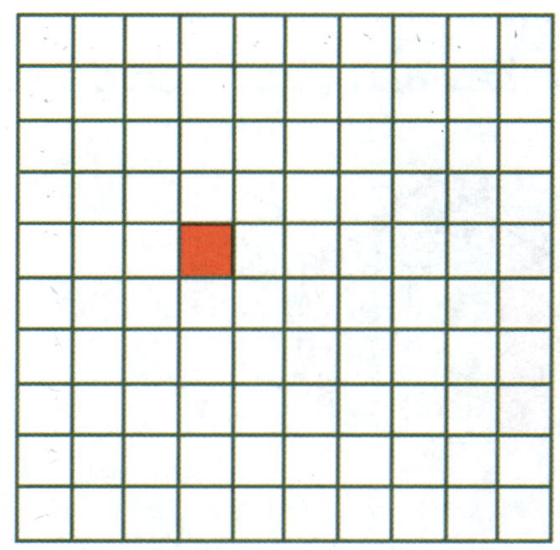

5. A **hexagon** is cut into 6 **equal** bits.

One bit of the hexagon is **red** ?

What **fraction** of the hexagon is **red** ?

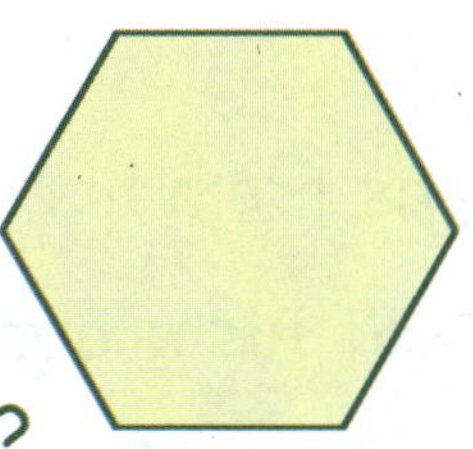

6. Ali has £15 in one pound coins.

He spends $\frac{1}{3}$ of the money

*(Split the coins into 3 **equal** piles).*

How much money did he spend ?

7. 

Paul has **20** "*Up's & Down's*" show tickets to sell.

His family buys $\frac{1}{2}$ of his tickets.

a How many tickets did his family buy ?

b How many tickets does he have left ?

8. A hair stylist has 12 hairclips in a box.

They use $\frac{1}{3}$ of them on a client.

a How many clips are used ?

b How many are left in the box ?

9. Jay, Kev and Chad decide to share the sweets in this box.

Jay takes $\frac{1}{3}$ of the sweets.

Kev takes $\frac{1}{4}$ of the sweets.

Chad takes $\frac{1}{5}$ of the sweets.

Who gets the **most** sweets ?

10. Lee eats **6** grapes from his lunch box.

He has eaten $\frac{1}{3}$ of his grapes.

How many grapes were in his lunch box ?

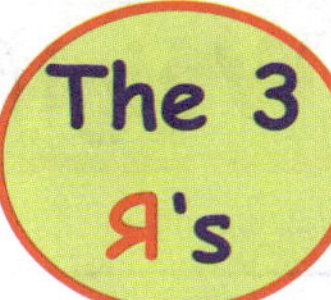

Revisit - Review - Revise

1. Write down what fraction of each is **coloured**.

a 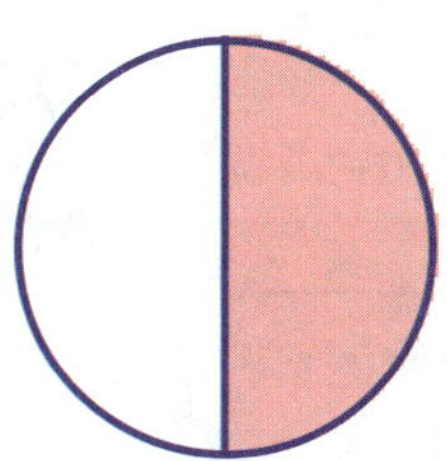

b 

c 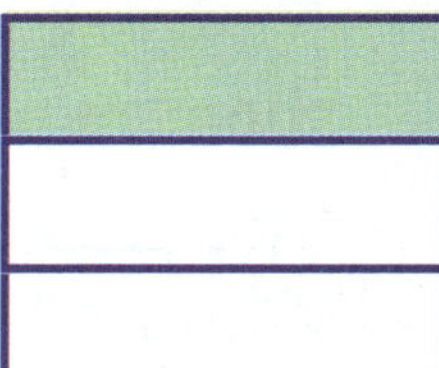

d 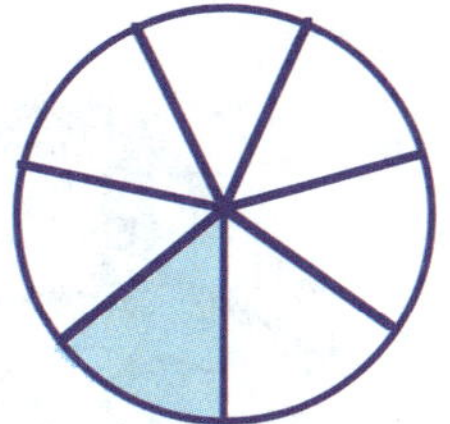

e 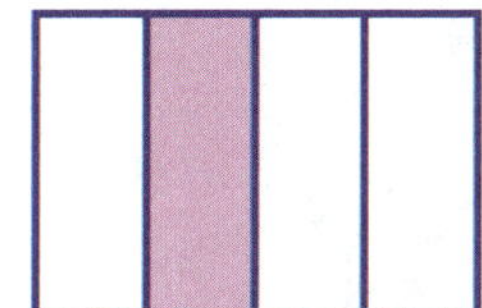

f 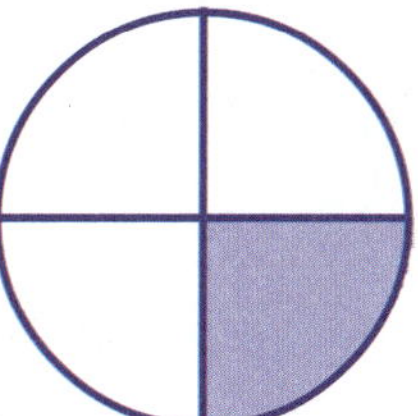

g 

h 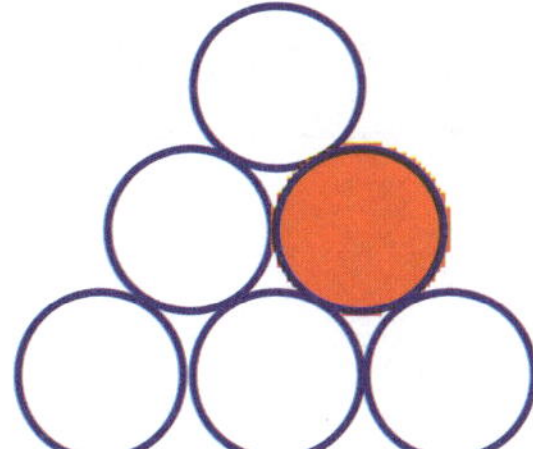

i 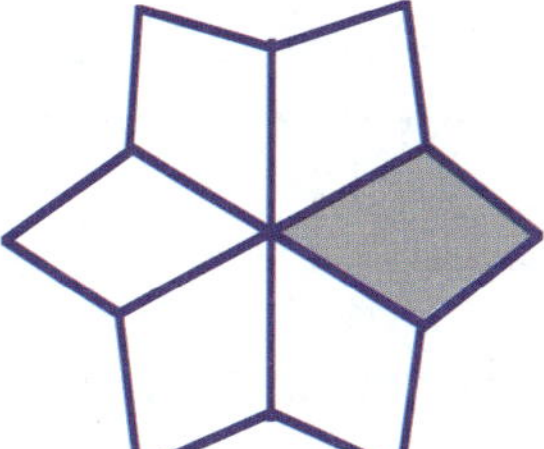

2. Ari has lots of five pence coins.

   He shared his coins amongst **himself and** his **2** friends.

   What **fraction** of the coins did Ari get ?

3. 

   Ollie has 12 comics.

   He gave $\frac{1}{3}$ of his comics to Tom.

   How many comics did he give to Tom ?

Weight

Words used in Weight

Understand and use appropriate vocabulary in weight.

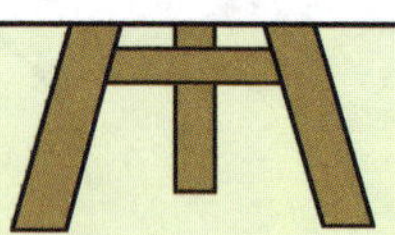

In **Length** (Chapter 17), we used words like :-

longer - **shorter** - **wider** - **narrower** - **taller** - **smaller**.

When measuring **weight** we will use the words **lighter** and **heavier**.

Examples

An elephant is **heavier** than a mouse.

A car is **lighter** than a bus.

Exercise 1

1. Which one is **lighter** :-

a a bush or a tree

b a tiger or a dog

c a chair or a sofa

d a jet plane or a balloon

e a desk or a chair

f a garden shed or a house

g a bed or a pillow

h a car engine or a jet engine

i a fish or a chip

j a carrot or a turnip ?

2. Which one is **heavier** :-

a a tennis ball or a football

b a robin or a cat

c a paper bag or a shopping trolley

d a beach ball or a bowling ball

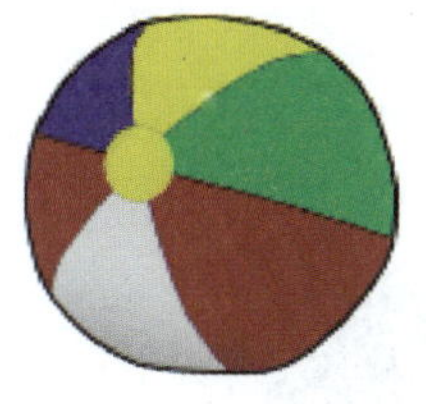

e a train or a bus

f a desk light or a street light

g a bath or a sink

h a flower or a bag of flour

i slippers or a pair of boots

j a pencil or a calculator ?

3. Put these animals in order of weight. Start with the **lightest**.

Frog

Goat

Bull

Dog

4. Put these in order of weight. Start with the **heaviest**.

Pencil

Desk

Chair

TJ Book

5. Which of these is **heavier** :-

a tomatoes or pineapple

b lemon or pepper

c kiwi or grapes

d watermelon or strawberry ?

6. Which of these is **lighter** :-

a chilli or mushroom

b red apple or green apple ?

7. If I placed a banana and a feather on the scales, which side would drop down - the left side or the right side ?

8.

What can you tell me about the two fruits on these scales ?

Measuring in Kilograms (kg)

Be able to estimate whether an object is lighter or heavier than 1 kg.

When we weigh objects we usually use kilograms.

We can write **kilograms** as **kg**.

A **litre** bottle of juice weighs **1 kilogram**. (**1 kg**)

A bag of sugar weighs **1 kg**.

Would an apple weigh **more** or **less** than 1 kilogram ?

If it is **lighter** it must weigh **less** than **1 kg**.

Exercise 2

1. Which is the **lighter** ?

a

2 kg

3 kg

b

15 kg

13 kg

c

86 kg

45 kg

d

207 kg

980 kg

2. Put each list in order. Start with the **heaviest**.

a 3 kg, 8 kg, 4 kg

b 9 kg, 11 kg, 14 kg, 10 kg

c 6 kg, 1 kg, 8 kg 20 kg

d 23 kg, 31 kg, 27 kg, 30 kg

e 147 kg, 131 kg, 211 kg

f 130 kg, 201 kg, 1000 kg, 99 kg.

3. a Make a list of **ten** things that would be **lighter** than **1 kg**.

   b Now make a list of **ten** things that would be **heavier** than **1 kg**.

4. a How many kilograms does your school bag weigh ?

   b Guess in kilograms the weight of your chair.

   c Guess in kilograms the weight of a cat.

5. How many 

are the same as 

?

6. Write down the **total** weight, in **kg**, of these :-

a 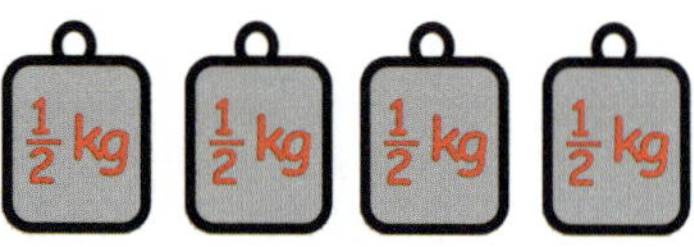

b 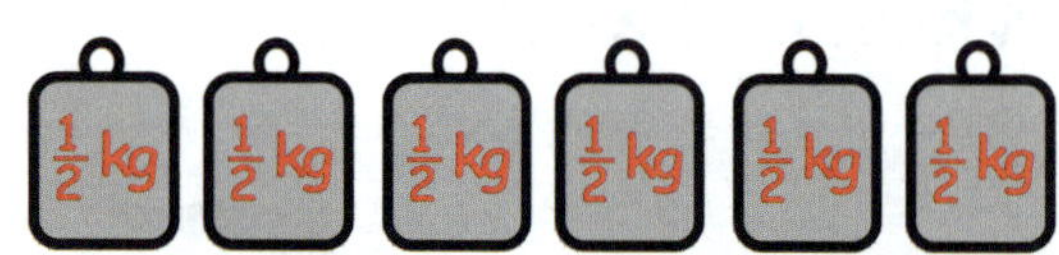

c 

d 

7. Ask your teacher for **five objects**, some **kilogram weights** and a **set of balancing scales**.

Weigh each object and put a tick in the correct box on the worksheet.

OBJECT	more than 1 kg	less than 1 kg	1 kg exactly
	fill in WORKSHEET 22·1		

Worksheet 22·1

Reading Scales

Be able to read the weight of an object on a set of scales.

Look at the scales below.

These pears weigh **2 kg**.

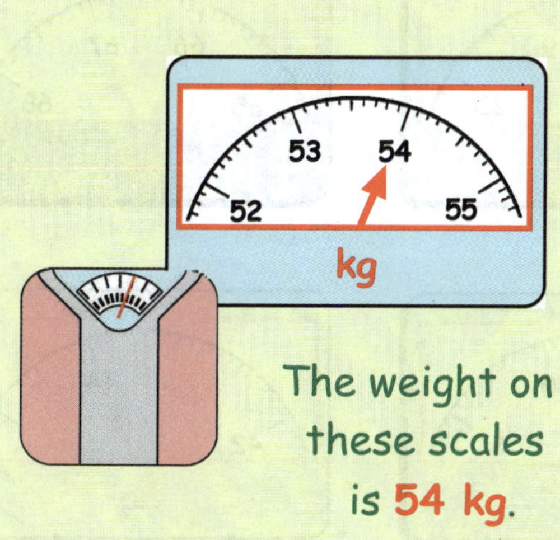

The weight on these scales is **54 kg**.

Exercise 3

Worksheet 22·2

Write down the weight on each of these scales :-

a

b

c

d

52 53 54 55

kg

e

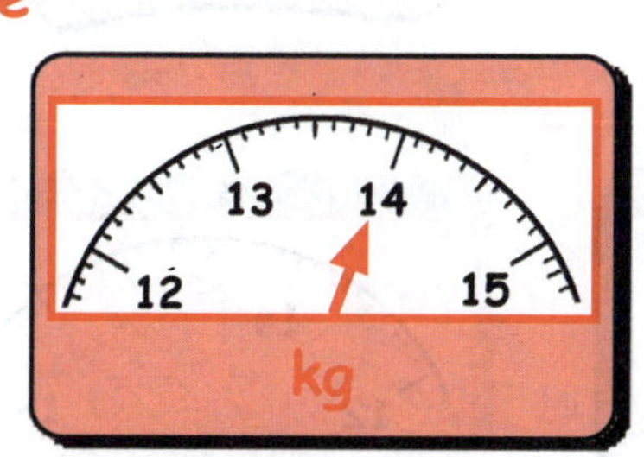

f

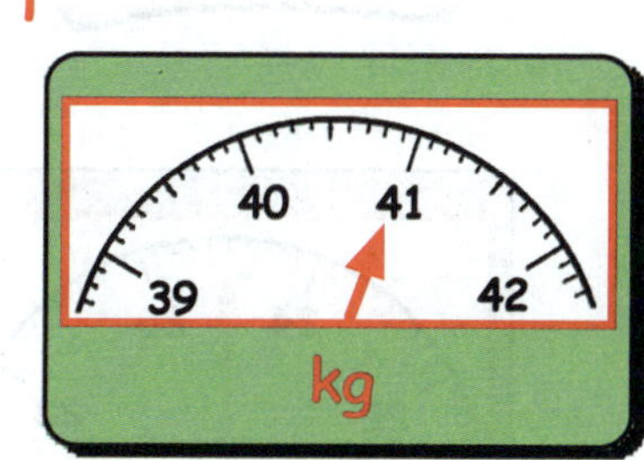

2. Write down the weight on each of these scales :-

3. These are much trickier ! Write down the weight on each scale :-

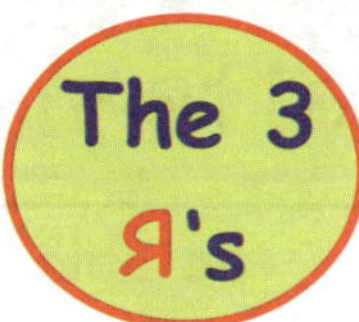

Revisit - Review - Revise

1. a Which one is **lighter** - a car or a truck ?

   b Which one is **heavier** - a teddy bear or a polar bear ?

2. Put these in order. Start with the **heaviest**.

T-shirt

socks

boots

coat

3. Which is **lighter** - the toy horse or the teddy ?

4. Write down **3** things in the classroom that are :-

   a **lighter** than 1 kilogram b **heavier** than 1 kilogram.

5. Write down the weight on each of these scales :-

a

b

c

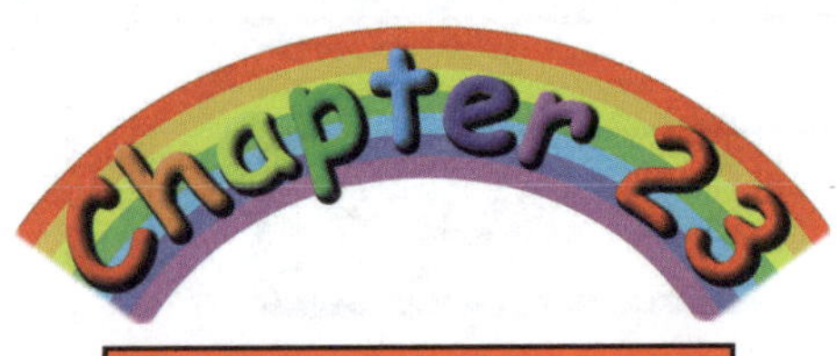

Coloured Pencils
will be needed

Patterns

Be able to recognise number patterns and continue them.

You can make **patterns** using shapes, colours and lines.

next shape →

next shapes →

next shapes →

Exercise 1

Worksheet 23·1

1. **Draw** and **colour** the next **2 shapes** in these patterns :-

a ....

b ....

c ....

d ....

2. Draw the next 3 patterns for each shape in your jotter :-

a ....

b ....

c ....

d ....

e ....

f ....

g ....

h ....

Worksheet 23·2

3. Using shapes and colours, make up a pattern of your own and show it to your teacher.

Patterns with Letters

Be able to recognise number patterns and continue them.

As well as using shapes, **patterns** can also be made up of **letters**. Can you spot the patterns in these ?

a b c d e f g The next letter in the pattern is **h**.

a c e g i k The next letter in the pattern is **m**.

F E D C B The next letter in the pattern is **A**.

Exercise 2

1. To help you with this exercise, write out all the **letters of the alphabet** in order.

2. Use your alphabet to help write the next **2 letters** in each pattern :-

   a m n o p q r ....
   b C D E F G H ....
   c L K J I H ....
   d b d f h j l ....
   e r q p o n ....
   f E H K N Q ....
   g ab cd ef gh ij ....
   h az by cx dw ....

3. **Copy** each list. **Put in** the missing letters.

   a P Q .... S T ....
   b q .... o n m ....
   c .... K .... M .... O ....
   d .... P R T V ....

4. Make up a **letter pattern** of your own and see if your neighbour and teacher can work out the next letter in your pattern. Make it hard !

Patterns with Numbers

Be able to recognise number patterns and continue them.

Patterns can also be made up using **numbers**.

1 3 5 7 9 11 — The next number in the pattern is **13**.

20 19 18 17 16 — The next number in the pattern is **15**.

5 10 15 20 25 — The next number in the pattern is **30**.

Exercise 3

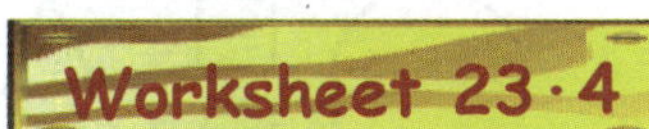

1. In each of the next number patterns below, write the next **2 numbers** :-

a	3 4 5 6 7	b	17 18 19 20 21 ....
c	27 26 25 24	d	2 4 6 8 10 ....
e	4 8 12 16 20	f	45 40 35 30 25 ....
g	80 70 60 50	h	27 24 21 18 15 ....

2. **Copy** these patterns and **put in** the missing numbers :-

a	10 15 .... 25	b	5 .... 9 11 13 ....
c	90 .... 60 50	d	.... 12 15 18 ....
e	28 .... 20 16	f	.... 33 44 66
g	31 .... 27 21	h	42 47 .... 57 62 ....
i	12 .... 34 45	j	0 50 .... 150 ....

The 3 R's

Revisit - Review - Revise

1. What **colours** should be used in the **next three** jelly beans for the pattern to continue ?

2. Draw the **next three** shapes in this pattern :-

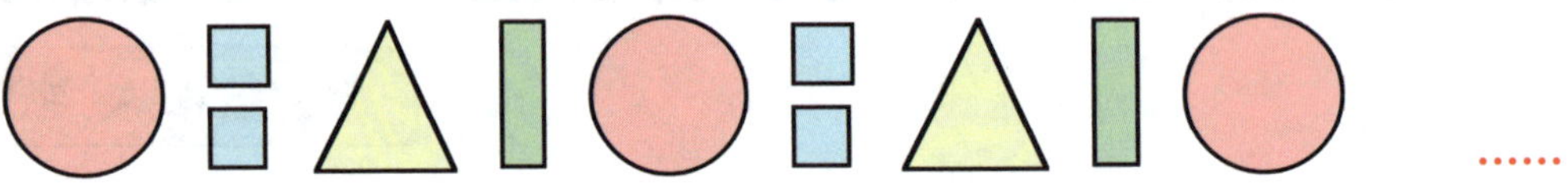

....

3. Draw **2 more** shapes in these patterns :-

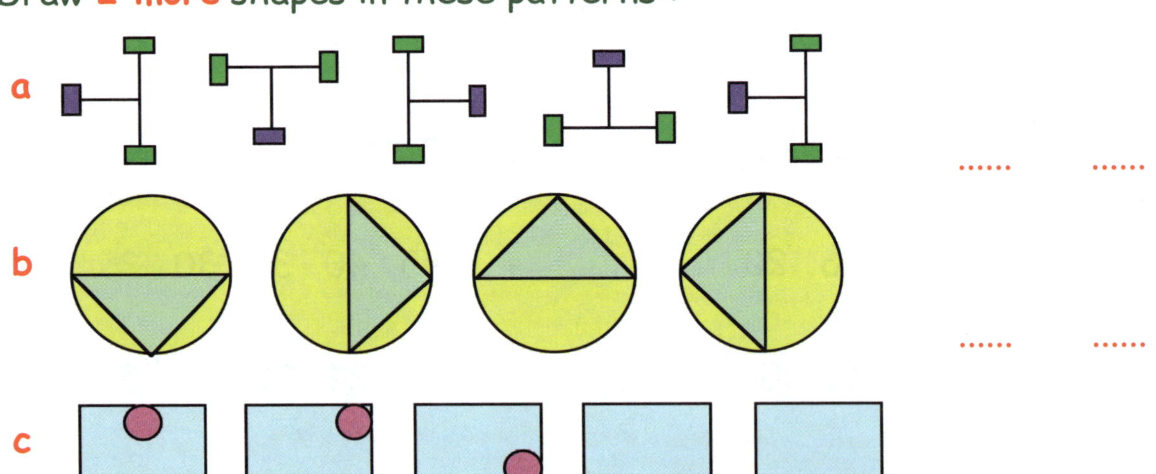

a ....

b ....

c ....

4. Write the next **2 numbers** or **letters** in each pattern :-

a 8, 9, 10, 11, ...

b 3, 5, 7, 9, ...

c a, c, e, g, i, ...

d Z, Y, X, W, ...

e 30, 26, 22, 18, ...

f 40, 50, 60, 70, ...

g abc, bcd, cde, def, ...

h 3, 7, 11, 15, ...

3D Shapes

3 Dimensions

Recognise and name common 3D (solid) shapes.

You have already met **2 dimensional (2D)** shapes.

These are the **flat** shapes -

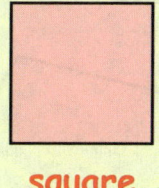

square

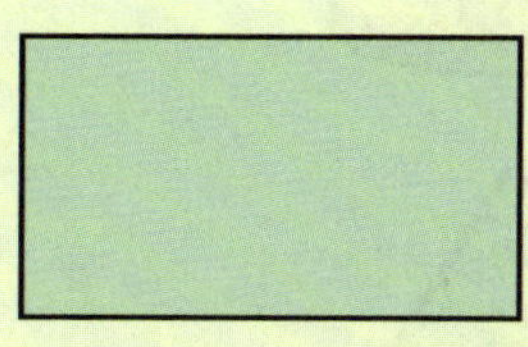
rectangle

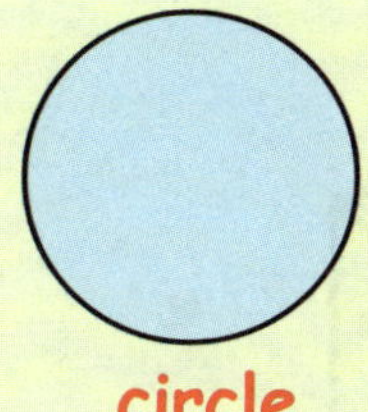
circle

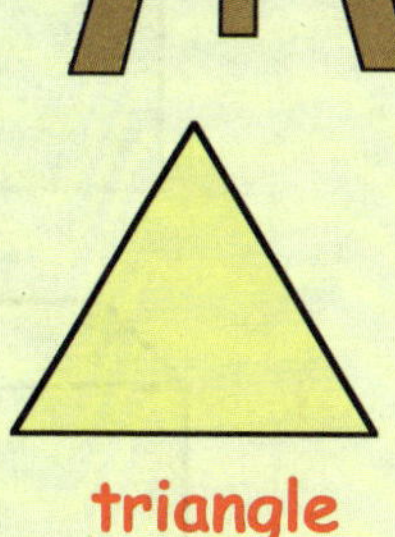
triangle

Now we look at the **solid** shapes - **3 Dimensional (3D)** shapes.

You should recognise these five **3D** shapes.

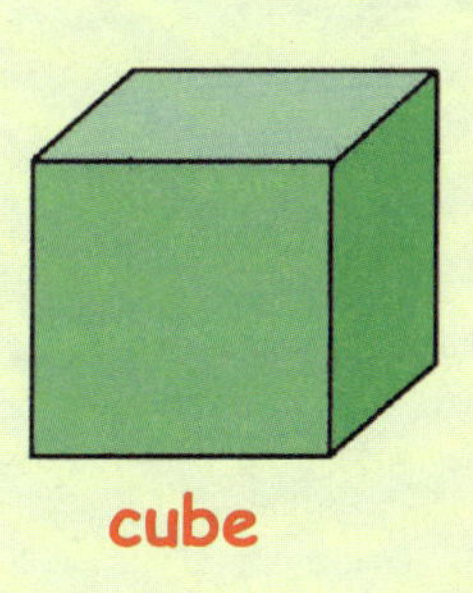
cube

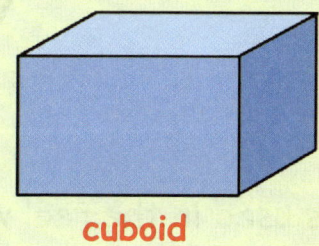

cuboid

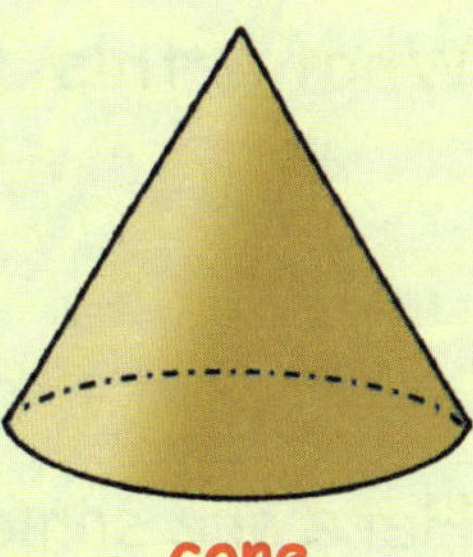
cone

cylinder

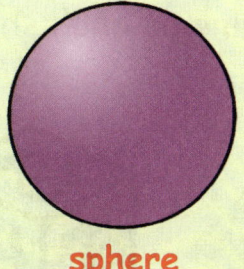

sphere

Here are three more **3D shapes** :-

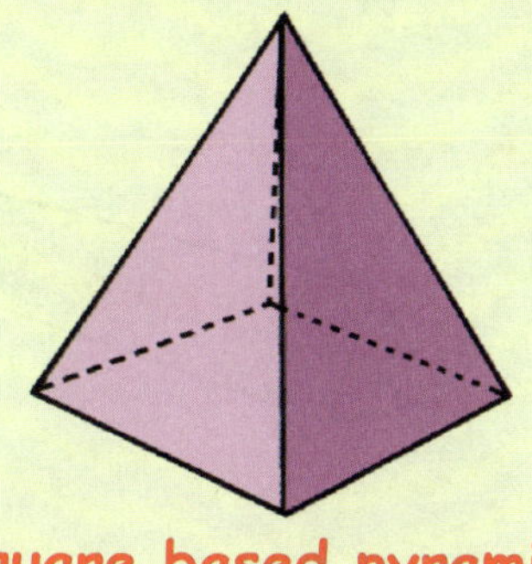
square based pyramid

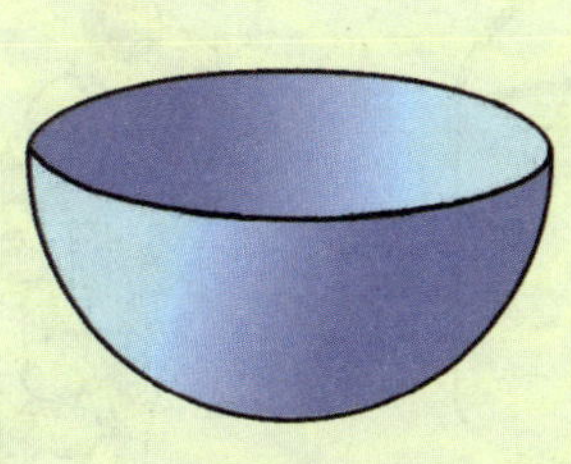
hemisphere

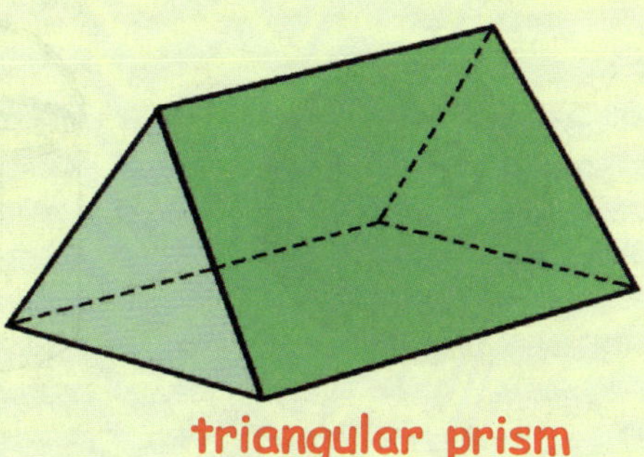
triangular prism

Exercise 1

1. Write the name of these 3 dimensional shapes :-

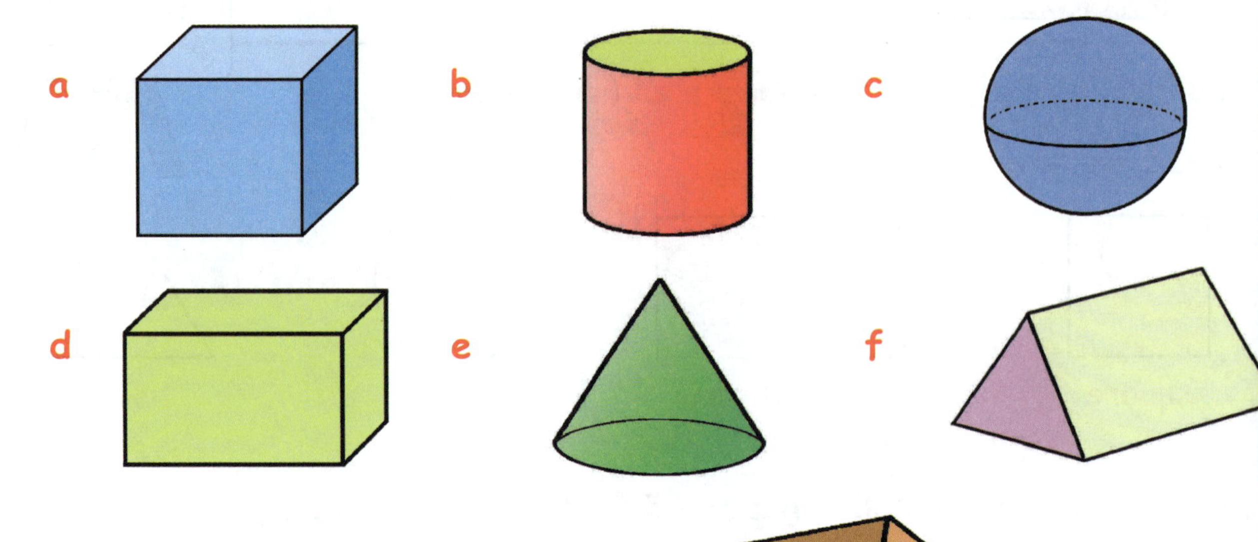

2. What is this 3D shape called ?

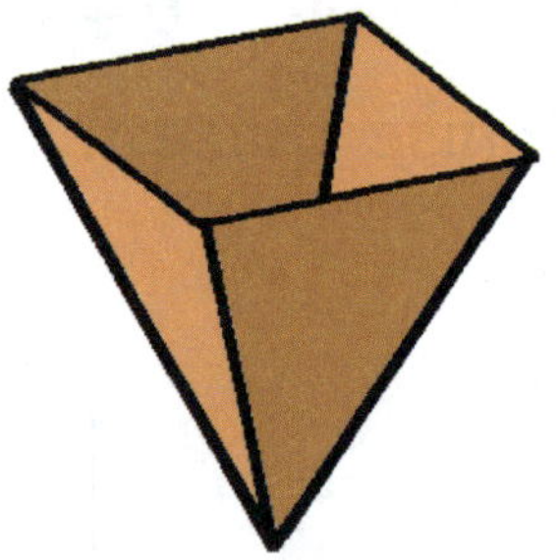

3. Here are some 3D items used in the real world.

   Write the **name** of each shape :-

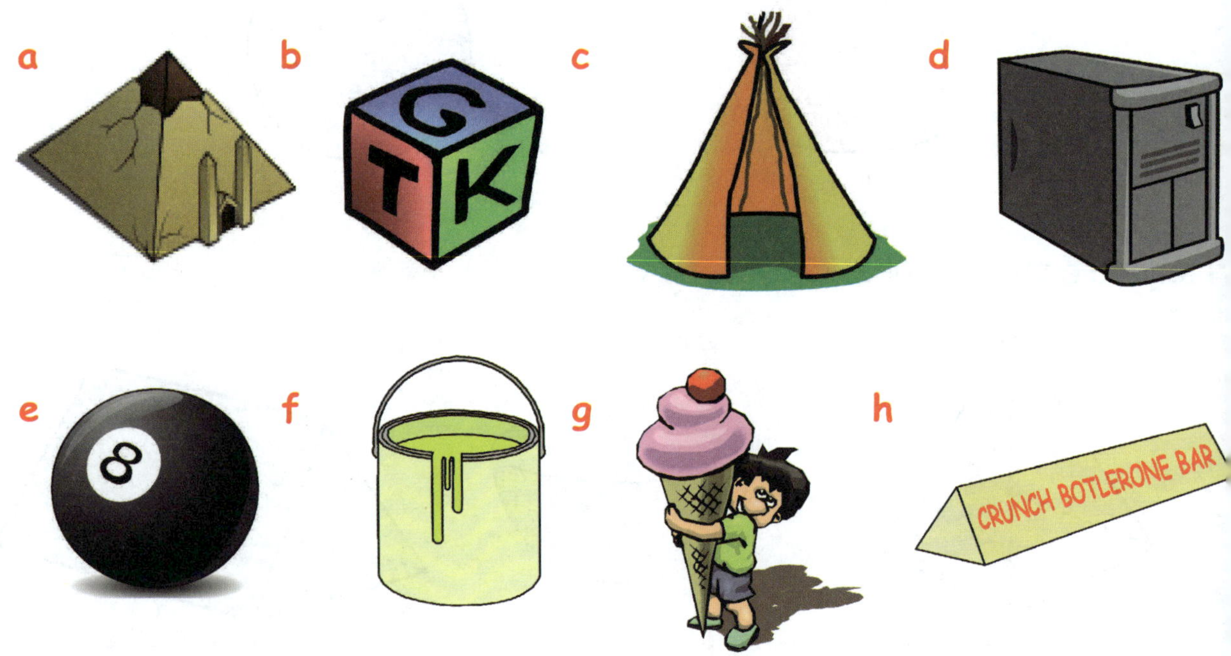

4. Make a list of the **3D shapes** used in each picture below.

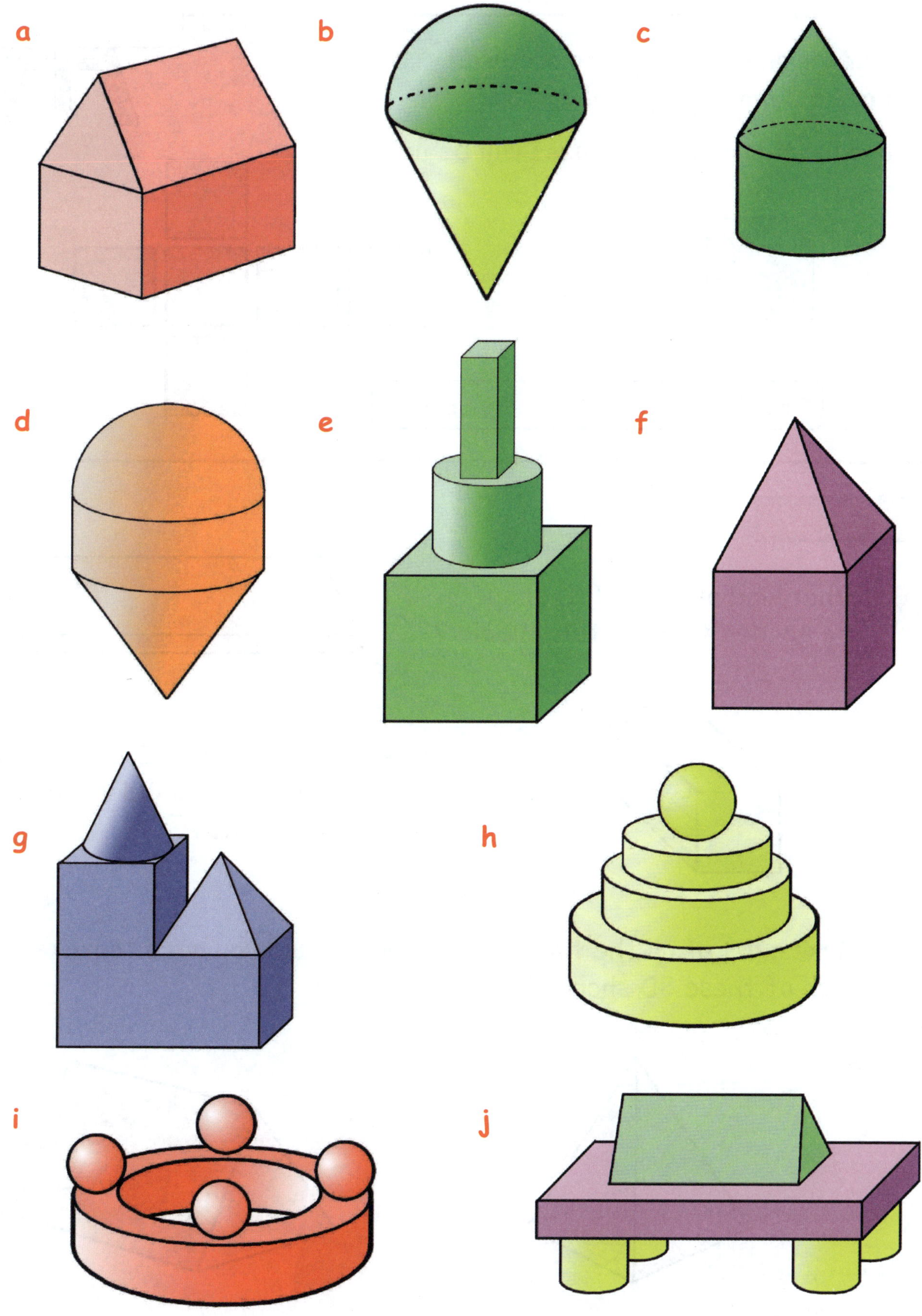

How to make a 3D Shape

Be able to make 3 dimensional shapes using 2 dimensional shapes.

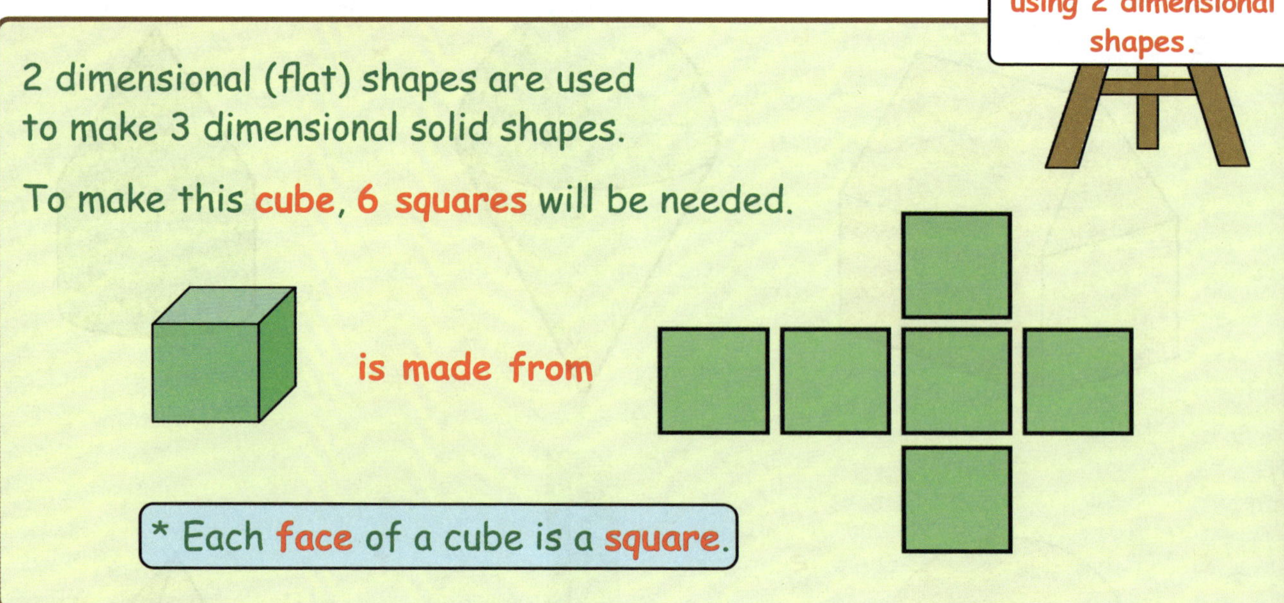

2 dimensional (flat) shapes are used to make 3 dimensional solid shapes.

To make this **cube**, **6 squares** will be needed.

is made from

* Each **face** of a cube is a **square**.

Exercise 2

1. What kind of **faces** (2D shapes) are needed to make this **cuboid** ?

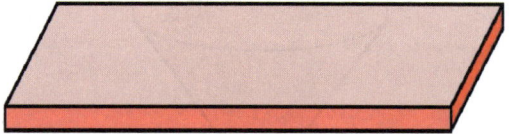

2. What kind of **faces** (2D shapes) are needed to make a **cuboid** with **two square faces** ?

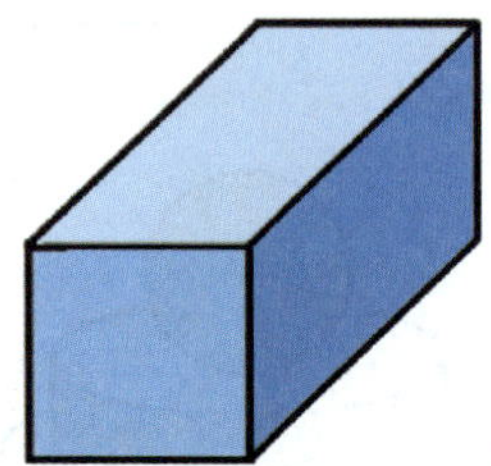

3. Make a list of all the **faces** (2D shapes) would you need to make each of these 3D shapes ?

a

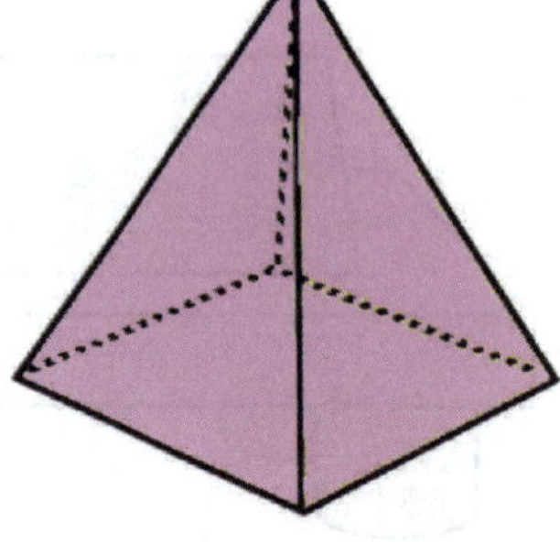

b

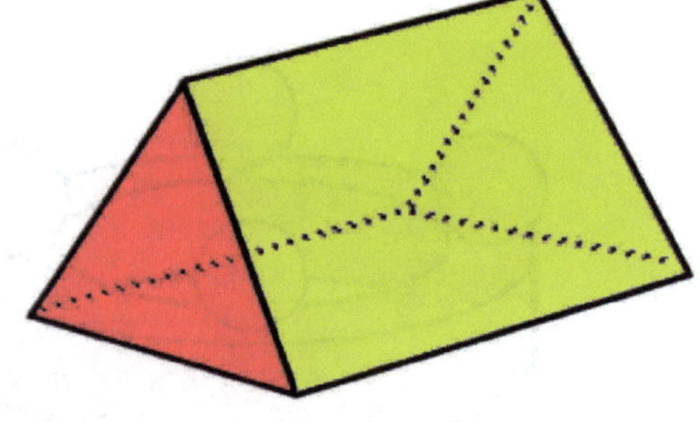

4. **Name the shape !**

What 3D shape is made from :-

a 6 squares

b 6 rectangles

c 2 triangles and 3 rectangles

d 4 triangles and 1 square

e 1 circle and 1 curved face

f 1 curved rectangle and 2 circles

5. Look at this **cube**.

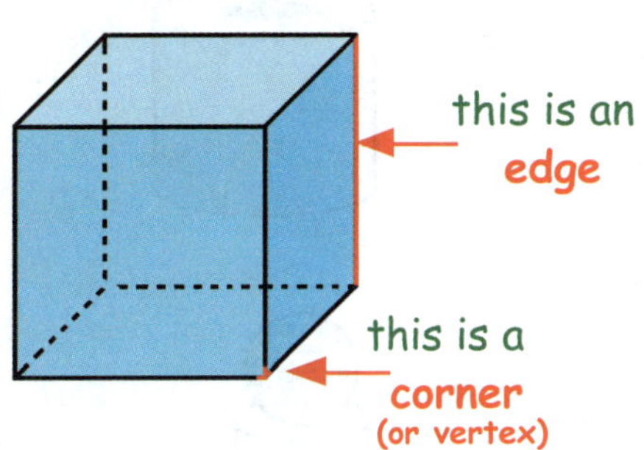

a How many **edges** does it have ?

b How many **corners** ?

6. The **cuboid**.

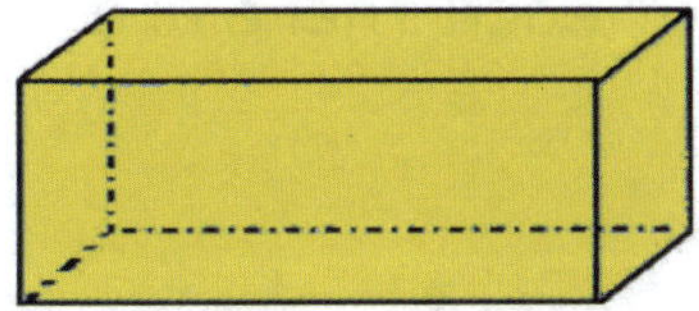

a How many **edges** does it have ?

b How many **corners** ?

7. The **square pyramid**.

a How many **edges** does it have ?

b How many **corners** ?

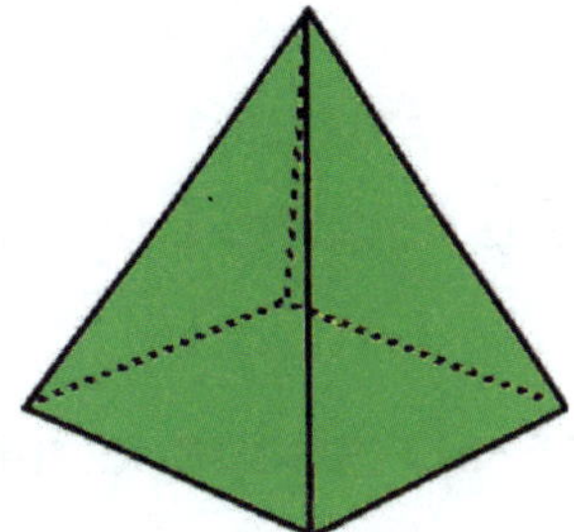

8. The **triangular prism**.

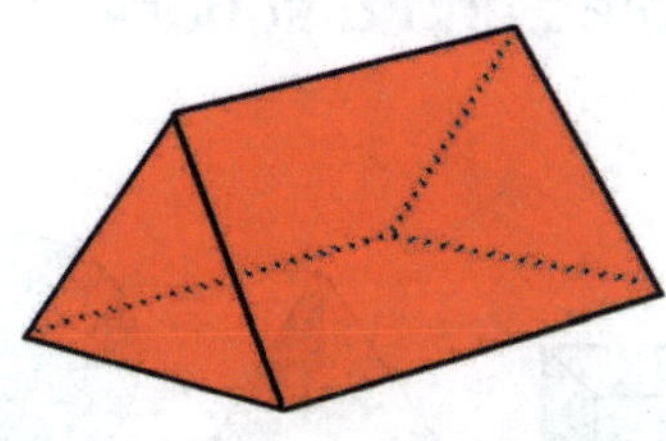

a How many **edges** does it have ?

b How many **corners** ?

9. What **2-D** shapes do you need to make a **cylinder** ?

The 3 Я's

Revisit - Review - Revise

1. What are the **names** of these 3 dimensional shapes ?

a 

b 

c 

d 

e 

f 

g 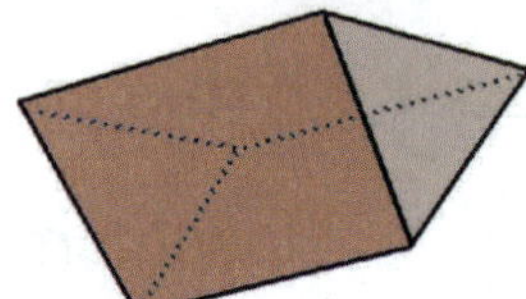

2. 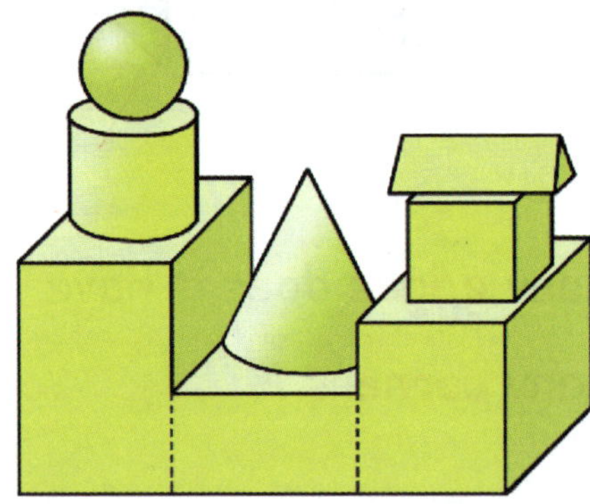

List the **3D shapes** shown in the picture and say how many of each there are.

3. List the **faces** that are needed to make a **square based pyramid**.

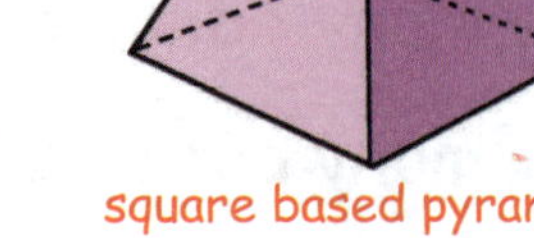
square based pyramid

4. What **3D shape** is made up of :-

a 6 squares

b 2 triangles and 3 rectangles

c 6 rectangles

d 4 triangles and a square ?

5. How many :-

a **edges** has a **cube**

b **corners** has a **cuboid**

c **edges** has a **square pyramid**

d **corners** has a **triangular prism** ?

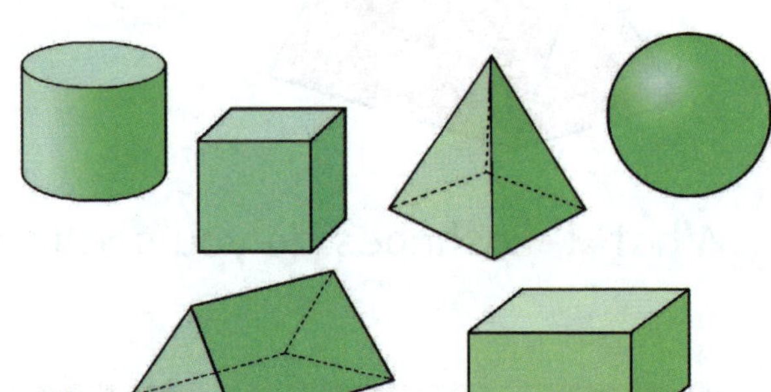

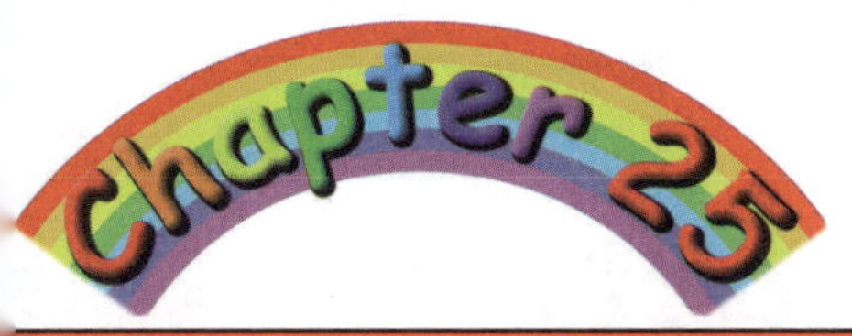

Statistics 2

Be able to draw a pictograph or a bar graph.

Drawing Pictographs and Bar Graphs

Example Drawing a Pictograph

Use the **key** shown to draw a **pictograph** which shows the pets owned by a P3 class.

Cat	Hamster	Dog	Goldfish	Rabbit
6	4	9	3	7

This means that :- (half face) stands for 1 child

Cat	☺ ☺ ☺
Hamster	☺ ☺
Dog	☺ ☺ ☺ ☺ ◐
Goldfish	☺ ◐
Rabbit	☺ ☺ ☺ ◐

Example Drawing a Bar Graph

The table opposite shows the favourite curry of twenty people who came out of a Chinese restaurant.

Prawn	-	5
Veg	-	3
Chicken	-	7
Beef	-	1
Mixed	-	4

This information can be displayed in a **bar chart**.

A **bar graph** needs :-

- a title
- a grid of lines
- headings
- labels
- and bars.

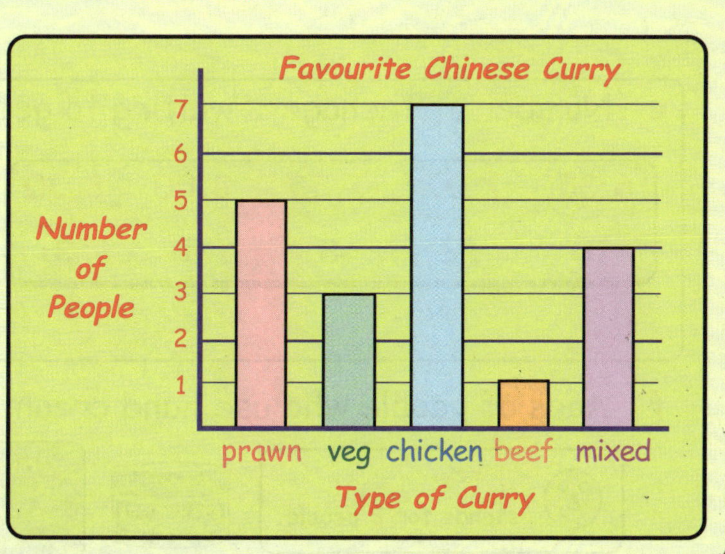

Exercise 1

Use the given **key** in each case to draw a **pictograph** to show the information given in the table.

1. **a** Kinds of fish for sale in a small market, late on in the day.

Cod	Haddock	Plaice	Bass	Sole
4	6	3	2	7

b Primary 4's favourite zoo animals.

Lion	Tiger	Giraffe	Seal	Panda
5	3	4	1	6

c Primary 7's favourite TV channels.

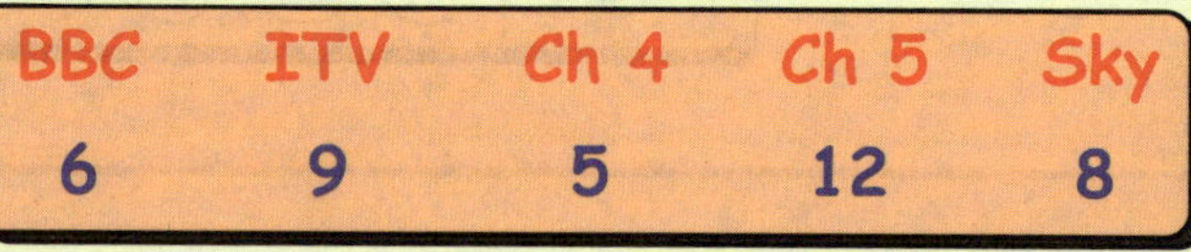

BBC	ITV	Ch 4	Ch 5	Sky
6	9	5	12	8

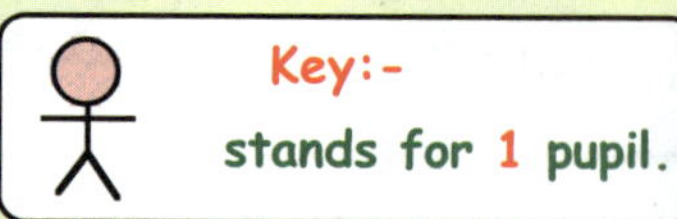

d Number of robins seen in my front garden over 5 days.

Mon	Tues	Wed	Thurs	Fri
4	10	6	8	2

e Number of teenagers waiting to get into a gig one night.

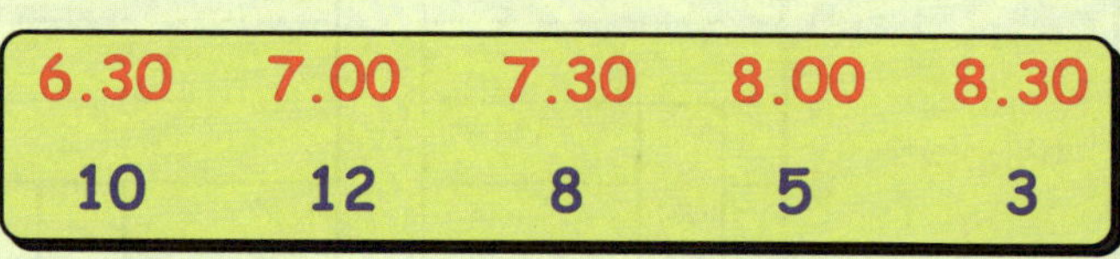

6.30	7.00	7.30	8.00	8.30
10	12	8	5	3

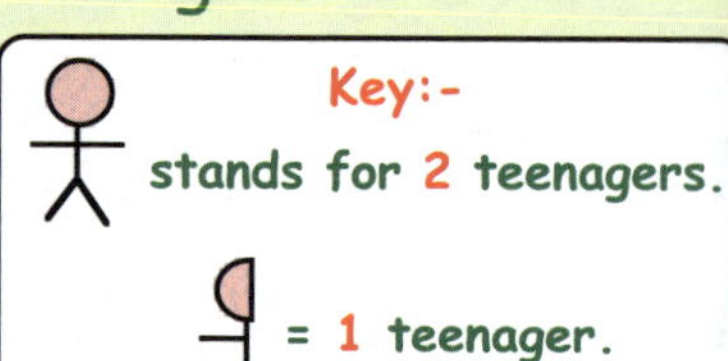

f Ages of people who use hand cream to protect their hands.

20's	30's	40's	50's	60's
4	6	10	5	8

Copy the bar graph in each question and use the information given in the table to complete it.

2. a The hair colour of a group of pupils was recorded.

Colour	No.
Brown	7
Black	2
Blond	4
Red	1

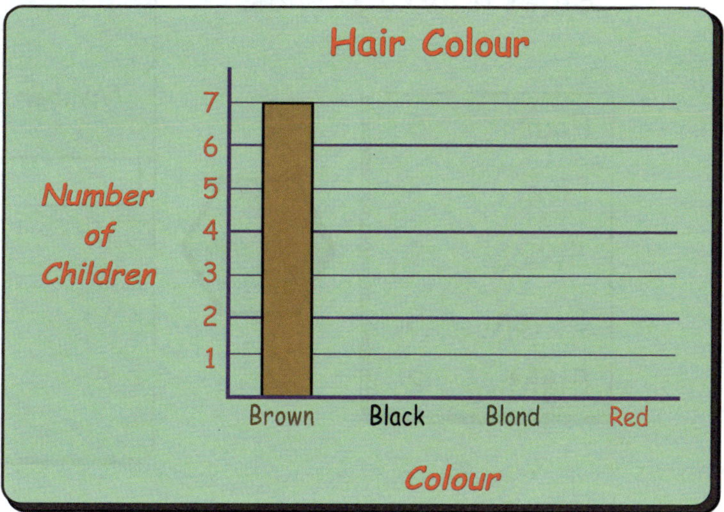

b Twenty children are asked to name their favourite drink.

Drink	No.
Orange	4
Lemon	3
Apple	1
Cola	7
Lime	5

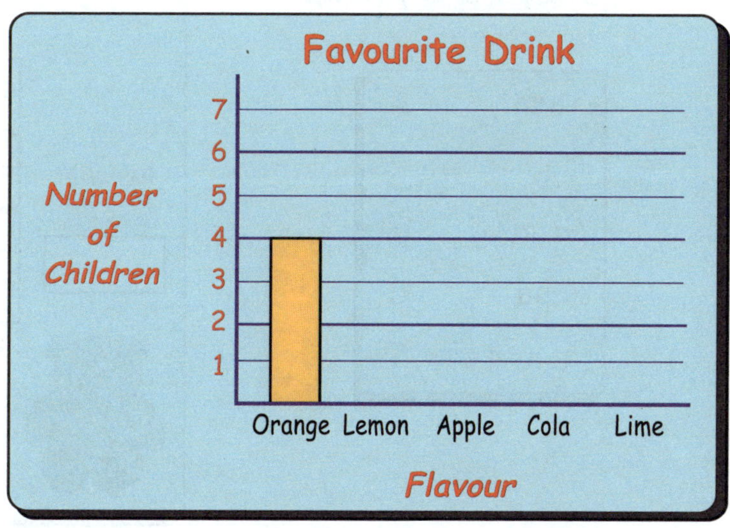

c A Primary 3 class were asked to name their favourite colours.

Colour	No.
Green	6
Blue	7
Red	5
Pink	2
Yellow	4

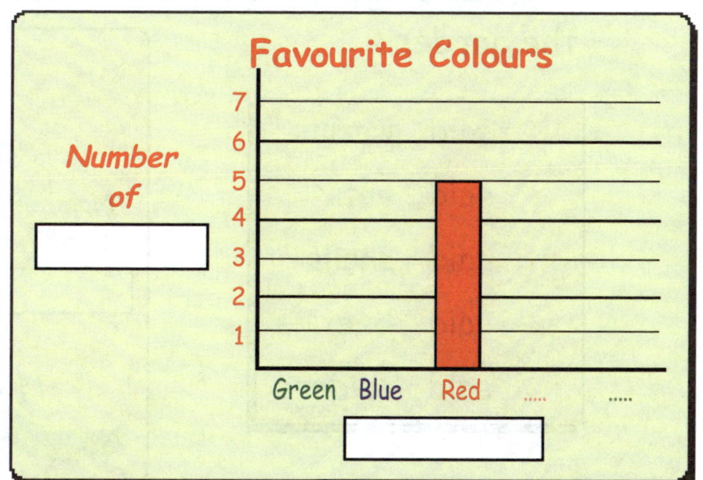

2. **d** Children in a maths class were asked how many sides a **hexagon** has.

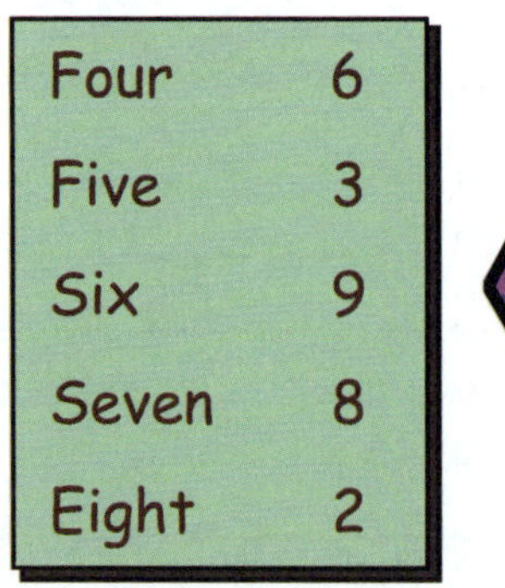

Four	6
Five	3
Six	9
Seven	8
Eight	2

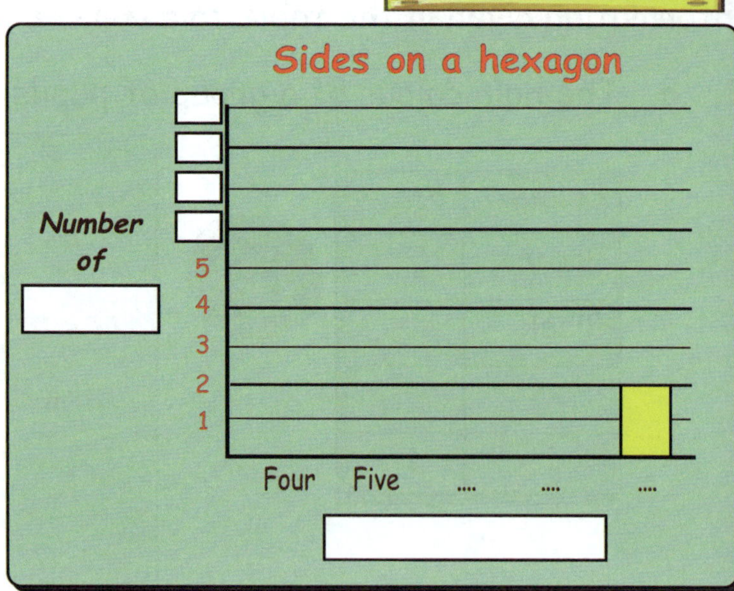

e Josie's family were asked how many teddy bears they owned when they were younger.

Mum	4
Dad	2
Gran	10
Papa	0
Aunt Isa	5

f A group of gardeners were asked what beasties they would find in the garden.

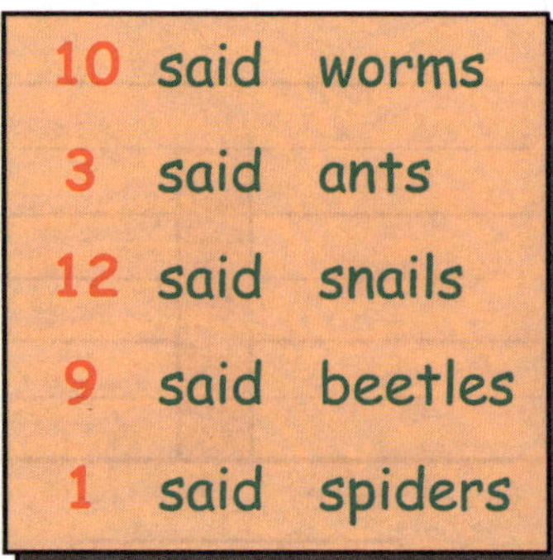

10	said	worms
3	said	ants
12	said	snails
9	said	beetles
1	said	spiders

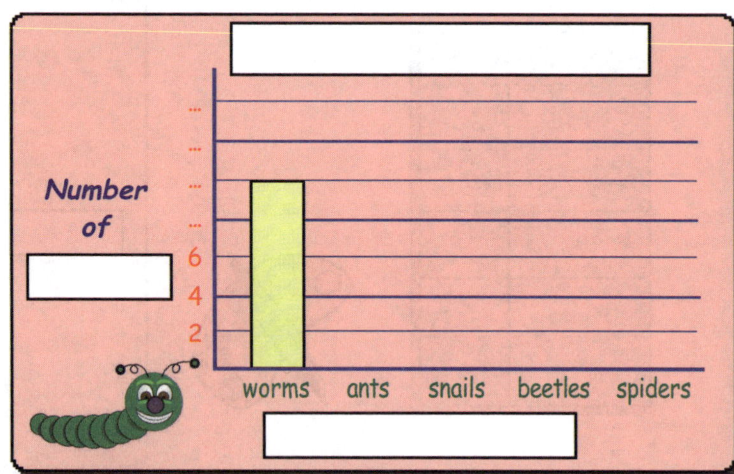

Be able to use tally marks to count and make up frequency tables.

Making a **tally table** (frequency table) makes it easier to understand lists of information.

Example

The colour of children's eyes can be shown in a list, ...

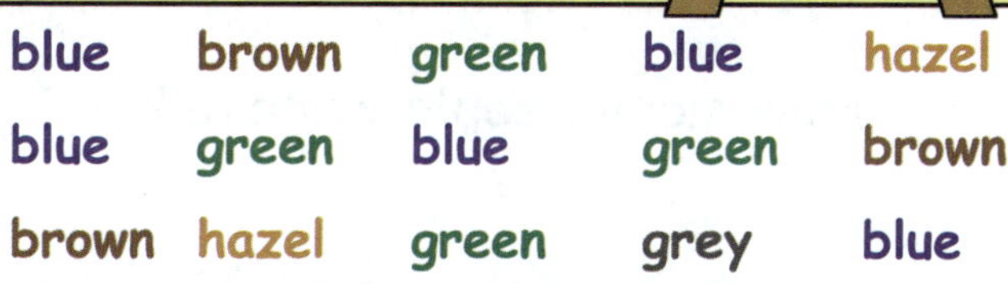

but isn't it easier to read the same information from a tally table ?

Eye Colour	Tally	Total
blue	I I I I I	5
brown	I I I	3
green	I I I I	4
grey	I	1
hazel	I I	2

3 children have brown eyes.

these are called **tally marks**

Exercise 2

1. From the tally table above :-

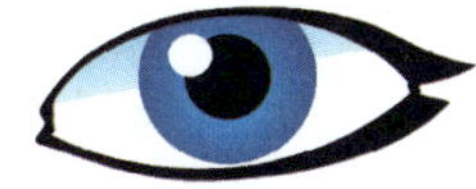

  a How many children have **green** eyes ?

  b How many children have **blue** eyes ?

  c How many children have **grey** eyes ?

  d What is the most **common** colour of eyes ?

  e How many **more** children have **green** eyes than **hazel** eyes ?

  f How many **fewer** children have **grey** eyes than **brown** eyes ?

  g What is the **total** number of children with **blue** or **brown** eyes ?

  h How many children **altogether** took part in the survey ?

2. People were asked to name any Scottish town starting with an A.

a **Copy** the table and complete the **total column**.

b How many people were asked ?

Town	Tally	Total
Ayr	I I I	3
Aberdeen	I I I I I I	...
Annan	I	...
Arbroath	I I	...
Airdrie	I I I I	...

3. People were asked to name all **6** cities of Scotland.

The table shows what they said :-

a **Copy** the table and fill in missing **tally marks** and **totals**.

b Find out which is **not** a city ?

c How many people gave a wrong answer ?

City	Tally	Total
Dundee	I I I I I	5
Inverness	I	...
Glasgow	....	8
Edinburgh	....	7
Stirling	I I	...
Perth	I I I I	...
Aberdeen	....	3

4. Here are the colours of the outfits some pupils wore to their school dance.

pink	black	blue	blue
red	black	black	black
orange	blue	red	red
blue	red	orange	red
black	orange	pink	black

Colour	Tally	Total
orange	...	...
Red	...	...
Black	...	...
Blue	...	...
Pink	...	...

a **Copy** the tally table and fill in all the **tally marks** and **totals**.

b Which colour of outfit did **most** pupils wear ?

c How many pupils were asked about the colour of their outfit ?

d How many pupils did **not** wear a **black** outfit ?

5. Use **tally marks** to show the number :-

a 3 (= |||) b 2 c 5 d 6

e 8 f 9 g 10 h 15.

Count these tally marks |||||||||||||||| . (15 or 16 ?)

It is too easy to lose count with bigger numbers !

It is better to put tally marks in groups of 5's.

~~||||~~	~~||||~~	~~||||~~	|
5	5	5	1

(**16** in total)

6. What **numbers** do these tally marks show ?

a ~~||||~~ |||

b ~~||||~~ ~~||||~~ ||

c ~~||||~~ ~~||||~~ ~~||||~~ ||||

d ~~||||~~ ~~||||~~ ~~||||~~ ~~||||~~ ~~||||~~ |

e ~~||||~~ ~~||||~~ ~~||||~~ ~~||||~~ ~~||||~~ ~~||||~~ ~~||||~~ ||

7. In the same way, use **tally marks** to show these numbers :-

a 5 b 7 c 10 d 15

e 17 f 20 g 26

8. Using tally marks in **groups of five**, make a **tally table** to show the responses to "what's your favourite flower ?"

Rose	Tulip	Pansy	Daffodil	Pansy
Pansy	Rose	Tulip	Pansy	Pansy
Tulip	Pansy	Tulip	Tulip	Daffodil
Marigold	Tulip	Rose	Daffodil	Marigold
Rose	Daffodil	Tulip	Tulip	Daffodil
Tulip	Pansy	Tulip	Rose	Daffodil

Flower	Tally	Total
Rose		
Pansy		

9. At a quiz night, one of the questions was to put a **word** before "................ ticket". The answers are shown in the table.

bus	train	plane	train	plane
plane	bus	train	plane	plane
train	train	plane	train	train
ferry	train	bus	train	train
bus	train	train	train	ferry
train	plane	train	bus	train

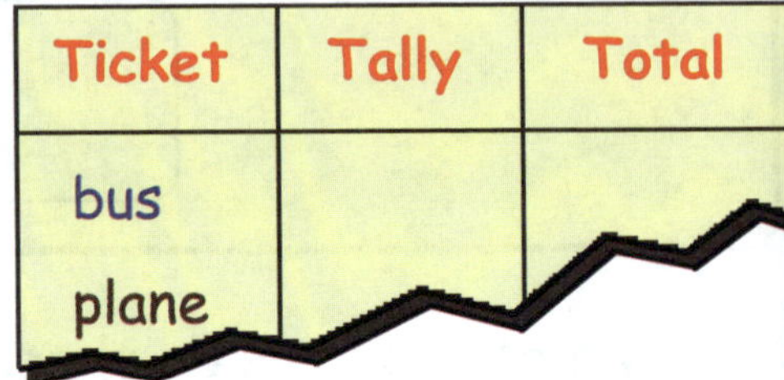

Ticket	Tally	Total
bus		
plane		

a **Copy** and **complete** the tally table.

b How many said "train ticket" ?

c How many **more** said plane than ferry ?

d How many people answered the question ?

10. Travelling business people were asked to name their favourite hotel.

Here are their answers :-

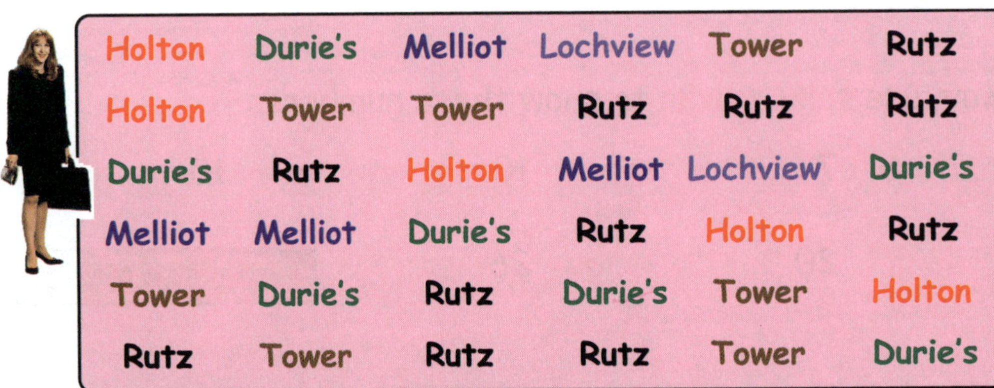

Holton	Durie's	Melliot	Lochview	Tower	Rutz
Holton	Tower	Tower	Rutz	Rutz	Rutz
Durie's	Rutz	Holton	Melliot	Lochview	Durie's
Melliot	Melliot	Durie's	Rutz	Holton	Rutz
Tower	Durie's	Rutz	Durie's	Tower	Holton
Rutz	Tower	Rutz	Rutz	Tower	Durie's

Ticket	Tally
Holton	
Durie's	

a **Copy** and **complete** the tally table.

b Which hotel was the **most** popular ?

c How many people voted for Holton Hotel ?

d How many took part in the survey ?

e Draw a **bar graph** to show the information.

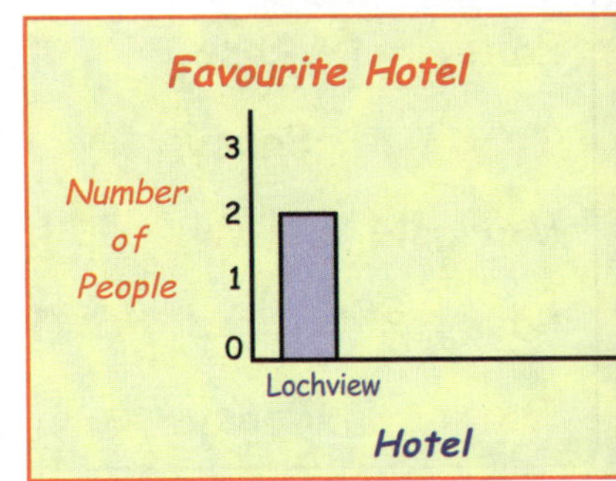

The 3 R's

Revisit - Review - Revise

1. 𝍸 represents the number **5**. Use tally marks to show :-

   a 8 b 12 c 21 d 33.

2. Use the given **key** to draw a **pictograph** showing the information which is in the table.

   Primary 3 pupils' favourite colour of socks.

Red	Blue	Green	Yellow	Pink
8	12	10	2	1

Key: (face) stands for **2** pupils.

3. Some people were asked which sauce they thought should go with lamb.

   Their answers are in the table.

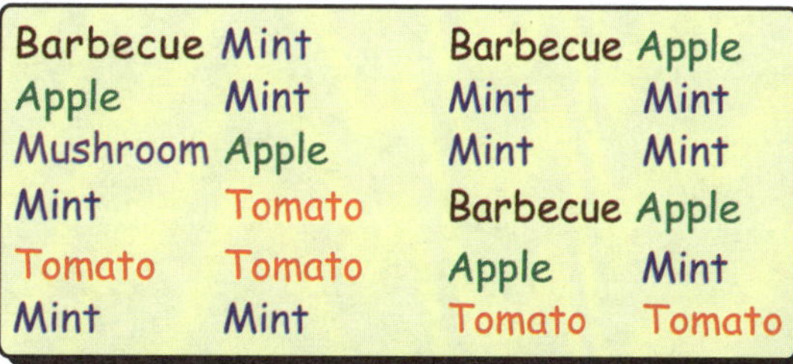

Barbecue	Mint	Barbecue	Apple
Apple	Mint	Mint	Mint
Mushroom	Apple	Mint	Mint
Mint	Tomato	Barbecue	Apple
Tomato	Tomato	Apple	Mint
Mint	Mint	Tomato	Tomato

   a Copy and complete the **tally table** to show these results.

Sauce	Tally	Total
Barbecue		
Apple		
Mint		
Mushroom		
Tomato		

   b How many people gave the answer "tomato" ?

   c How many people were asked ?

   d How many people gave the correct answer ?

Worksheet 25·7

   e Draw a **bar chart** from the table. (remember the scale; title; headings; labels and bars)

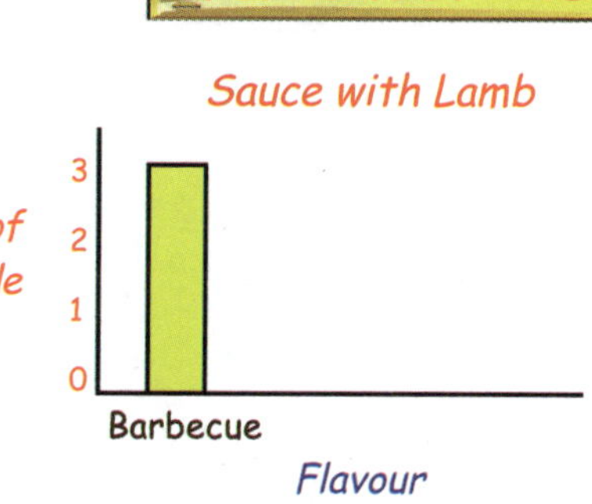

* There were some errors with the first printing of the answers to this book. These have been corrected and are now shown in red and are underlined.

answers to BOOK 1A

Answers to Ch 0 (page 1)

a
a
b
b
Lara
pen
basin
a 5 b 10 c 13 d 17
a 5 b 4
. a 15 b 7
4 7 10 13 17 20
. a 15 b 19
. a 9 b 6 c 10
d 7 e 9 f 8
. a 1 b 5 c 4
d 4 e 3 f 0
. a 10 b 5
. a 15 b 5
. a yes b no c no d yes
. a 7p b 9p c 13p d 18p
. a 5p, 2p, 2p b 10p, 5p, 1p
. a 5 b 5 c 4
. a 3p b 4p
. a 4 o`clock b 8 o`clock
c 11 o`clock
. a Tuesday b Sunday
. a 9 o'clock b 12 o'clock
c 3 o'clock d 6 o'clock
. 5
. a b

. a square b rectangle
c circle d triangle
. a cube b cone
c pyramid d cylinder
. a apple b banana
c melon
. a cone b cylinder
c cuboid

31. a goat b horse
c sheep d cow
32. a yes b no c yes
33. a 3 b 6
34. a 9 b 4 c 3
35. a 4 b 5 c 18 d 3
36. a 5 b 3 c 4
37. a 100m b 2.00 c noon
38. a Superstore b Toyshop
39. a (i) Kid Zone (ii) Cartoons
b (i) Quiz (ii) Weather
c BBC2 at 4.00
d Quiz

Answers to Ch 1 (page 10)

Ch 1 Exercise 1 (page 10)

1. a 4 units b 1 ten and 9 units
   c 1 ten and 2 units
2. a 4 6 10 b 12 15 18 19
   c 4 5 7 9 10 12 d 10 11 12 14 16
   e 8 5 4 f 5 7 9
   g 8 5 4 h 18 16 13 12
   i 8 6 j 14 13 12
   k 18 17 16 l 12 11 8

Ch 1 Exercise 2 (page 11)

1. a 13 b 16 c 18
   d 12 e 11 f 15
2. See drawings of jars
3. a 3 units b 2 tens and 6 units
   c 2 tens and 4 units
4. a 22 25 28 b 14 15 17 20
   c 20 21 22 23 25 27
   d 28 25 24
   e 22 20 17 16 f 17 19 20 21

Ch 1 Exercise 3 (page 13)

1. a 38 b 50 c 65 d 83
2. See drawings of jars
3. a 4 units b 6 tens and 8 units
   c 9 tens and 1 unit
4. a 33 35 37 38 40
   b 62 63 65 66 68
   c 86 88 89
   d 49 50 52 54 56
   e 80 82 f 39 41
   g 58 60 61 h 96 98 100
5. a 55 b 38 35
   c 89 87 d 66 63 62
6. a 38 b 57 c 80 d 91
7. a 47 b 22 c 80 d 59
8. Number grid 1 - 100
9. 100
10. a 14 b 17 c 24 d 41
    e 60 f 75
11. a 6 b 15 c 15 d 20

Ch 1 Exercise 4 (page 16)

1. Alex is 64
2. Joe has 62p
3. Kayley is 89cm
4. John is 43 kilograms
5. Jameela has £33
6. Dave is 47
7. Lynn has 29 dresses
8. The cat is 42cm

Ch 1 Exercise 5 (page 17)

1. 47
2. a 33 b 79 c 66 d 94
3. a 13 b 89 c 56 d 89

Ch 1 Exercise 6 (page 18)

1. 48 49 51
2. a 44 46 b 67 69 c 49 51 d 98 100
3. 64 68
4. a 34 38 b 82 86 c 20 24 d 89 93
5. 95 98 100
6. 80
7. 48 52 56 58 64 66 68
8. 49
9. 71 53
10. 97 42

Answers to Ch 2 (page 22)

Ch 2 Exercise 1 (page 22)

1. a yes b no c yes
   d yes e yes f no
2. a no b yes c yes
   d no e yes f yes
3. a 2 b 2 c 2
   d 4 e 6 f lots
4. a yes b yes c no
   d yes e yes f yes
   g no h no i yes

Ch 2 Exercise 2 (page 25)

2. a, c, f, g, i, j, l
3. a yes b yes c no
   d yes e yes f no
4. various
5. a one way traffic lights
   no right turn no entry
   max 30 mph roundabout
   b various
6. poster collection
7. C 8. G 9. Q

Answers to Ch 3 (page 29)

Ch 3 Exercise 1 (page 29)

1. 1 ten and 6 units
2. a 1 ten and 3 units
   b 2 ten and 7 units
   c 3 ten and 4 units
   d 4 ten and 1 unit
   e 6 ten and 8 units
   f 7 ten and 0 units
   g 0 ten and 9 units
   h 9 ten and 9 units
3. a 5 b 7
4. a 8 b 3
5. 2 hundreds 3 tens and 7 units
6. a 4 hundreds 1 tens and 8 units
   b 6 hundreds 5 tens and 7 units
   c 9 hundreds 0 tens and 2 units
   d 8 hundreds 9 tens and 2 units
   e 7 hundreds 6 tens and 0 units
7. a 3 hundreds 0 tens and 0 units
   b 7 hundreds 2 tens and 7 units
   c 6 hundreds 0 tens and 2 units
   d 9 hundreds 3 tens and 0 units
   e 2 hundreds 7 tens and 5 units
   f 3 hundreds 8 tens and 4 units
   g 7 hundreds 1 tens and 7 units
   h 9 hundreds 8 tens and 9 units
   i 1 hundreds 7 tens and 2 units
   j 6 hundreds 5 tens and 8 units
   k 2 hundreds 8 tens and 4 units
   l 5 hundreds 4 tens and 7 units
8. a £3 and 4 tens b £6 and 3 tens
   c £9 and 6 tens d £4 and 5 tens
   e £8 and 8 tens f £5 and 7 tens
   g £5 and 0 tens h £7 and 0 tens
   i £10 and 0 tens
9. a 174p b 248p c 620p d 582p
   e 45p f 180p g 978p
11. £4·39 12. £6.75

Ch 3 Exercise 2 (page 32)

1. a 23 b 38 c 41
   d 75 e 62 f 90
   g 12 h 80 i 59
2. a 117 b 243 c 564 d 327
   e 855 f 714 g 970 h 666
   i 808 j 999
3. a fifty eight b thirty two
   c forty six d nineteen
   e seventy f eighty eight
   g one hundred and seventy eight
   h three hundred and nineteen
   i nine hundred and nineteen
   j five hundred and four
   k eight hundred
   l one thousand
4. one hundred and thirty seven
5. 209
6. a 46 b 64 c 81 d 90
   e 76 f 59 g 344 h 627
   i 950 j 639 k 789 l 799
7. a 28 b 78 c 20 d 40
   e 99 f 103 g 369 h 110
   i 877 j 699 k 621 l 1000
8. 420
9. a 58 46 23 19 b 81 75 55 49 46
   c 88 81 79 72 70
   d 179 173 168 161 158
   e 511 453 388 302 297
   f 452 428 301 234 175
   g 857 800 703 578 519
   h 625 562 526 265 256
10. a 12 19 21 33 b 41 50 55 57 62
    c 106 114 140 165 172
    d 259 295 499 501 581
    e 330 357 389 403 430
    f 567 576 657 675 756
11. a Grandpa Sim b Auntie Ida
    c Grannie Marshall
    d Uncle Frank
12. a 24 b 29 c 102 d 107
    e 181 f 189 g 629 h 642
    i 943 j 955 k 966
13. a 6 b 65 c 298
14. 726
15. six hundred and seven
16. 427 cm 17. 46 kg

Answers to Ch 4 (page 37)

Ch 4 Exercise 1 (page 37)

1. Monday Tuesday Wednesday
   Thursday Friday Saturday Sunday
2. a Monday Tuesday Wednesday
   Thursday Friday
   b Saturday Sunday
3. a Tuesday Friday
   b Tuesday Friday Saturday
   Sunday
4. a Friday b Friday
   c Thursday d Tuesday
   e Saturday
5. a Saturday b Tuesday
   c Wednesday d Thursday
   e Sunday f Monday
6. Wednesday
7. a Wednesday b Wednesday
   c Saturday d Sunday
   e Wednesday f Wednesday
   g Monday

Ch 4 Exercise 2 (page 39)

1. January, February, March, April
   May, June, July, August, September
   October, November, December
2. a April b August
   c December February
   d May July August
   e January March
   f September November December
   January
3. a April b June
   c October d November
   e May f October
   g March h December
4. a August b November
   c May d May
   e March f December
5. May
6. a March b June
   c December d November
7. Jan 31 Feb 28 (29) Mar 31
   Apr 30 May 31 Jun 30
   Jul 31 Aug 31 Sep 30
   Oct 31 Nov 30 Dec 31

4 Exercise 3 (page 41)

a 2 o'clock b 8 o'clock
c 1 o'clock d 3 o'clock
e 9 o'clock f 4 o'clock
g 11 o'clock h 5 o'clock
i 7 o'clock j 6 o'clock
k 10 o'clock l 12 o'clock
a 2 o'clock b 5 o'clock
c 8 o'clock d 3 o'clock
e 4 o'clock f 10 o'clock
draw clock face 8 o'clock
draw clock face 3 o'clock
a 11 o'clock b 6 o'clock
c 7 o'clock d 7 o'clock
a 2 o'clock b 11 o'clock

4 Exercise 4 (page 43)

a half past 4 b half past 9
c half past 12 d half past 1
e half past 8 f half past 2
g half past 7 h half past 5
i half past 6
a quarter past 1
b quarter past 5
c quarter past 4
d quarter past 2
e quarter to 7
f quarter to 10
g quarter to 1
h quarter to 4
i quarter to 9
j quarter past 3
k quarter to 11
l quarter past 11
a half past 3 b half past 11
c quarter past 5
d quarter to 12
e quarter past 9
f 2 o`clock
g half past 6
h quarter to 11
i quarter past 6
j half past 12
k quarter past 10
l 12 o`clock
m quarter to 9
n half past 2
o half past 5

Answers to Ch 5 (page 47)

5 Exercise 1 (page 47)

a 19 b 25 c 68 d 59
e 88 f 94 g 36 h 49
i 67 j 27 k 59 l 78

2. a 38 b 28 c 16 d 88
e 49 f 34 g 28 h 97
3. 38p 4. 69p
5. 49 6. 65
7. 17 8. 29

Ch 5 Exercise 2 (page 49)

1. a 28 b 38 c 28 d 59
e 76 f 88 g 79 h 78
i 99 j 59 k 69 l 95
2. a 29 b 47 c 58 d 79
e 95 f 98 g 79 h 78
i 99 j 55 k 98 l 79
3. 58
4. 78
5. 75
6. 89
7. 58
8. 69
9. 89

Ch 5 Exercise 3 (page 51)

1. a 227 b 689 c 449 d 598
e 897 f 797 g 749 h 898
i 978 j 979 k 987 l 689
2. a 587 b 679 c 498 d 689
e 500 f 779 g 793 h 699
i 688 j 887 k 948 l 987
m 886 n 998 o 903 p 958
3. £485 4. 388
5. 864
6. 699
7. a 235p b 442p c 677p
8. 769

Ch 5 Exercise 4 (page 53)

1. a 54 b 31 c 60 d 74
e 84 f 94 g 40 h 53
i 91 j 45 k 98 l 30
2. a 46 b 31 c 80 d 92
e 95 f 40 g 65 h 86
3. 34p
4. 55p
5. 32
6. 71
7. 41
8. 64

Ch 5 Exercise 5 (page 55)

1. a 81 b 63 c 83 d 76
e 84 f 80 g 98 h 82
i 60 j 113 k 124 l 100
2. a 83 b 94 c 80 d 97
e 62 f 82 g 65 h 90
i 93 j 41 k 94 l 102
3. 92p
4. 66
5. 43
6. 124
7. 102
8. £67
9. a 72p b 91p

Ch 5 Exercise 6 (page 57)

1. a 243 b 566 c 790 d 885
e 921 f 615 g 911 h 876
i 910 j 810 k 986 l 1000
2. a 580 b 564 c 795 d 568
e 600 f 810 g 665 h 545
i 976 j 277 k 930 l 911
3. £950
4. 410
5. £944
6. 951
7. a chairs b £517 c £616
8. Micky (483)

Ch 5 Exercise 7 (page 59)

1. a 29 b 45 c 97 d 130
e 227 f 771 g 482 h 845
2. a 146 b 498 c 910 d 1095
3. 316
4. 119
5. 28
6. 85

Ch 5 Exercise 8 (page 60)

1. a 92 b 647
2. a 56 b 106 c 189 d 838
e 410 f 710 g 963 h 822
i 1000 j 1200 k 1300 l 1110
3. 320
4. 304

Answers to Ch 6 (page 62)

Ch 6 Exercise 1 (page 62)

1. See drawings
2. a 4 b 3 c 5 d 6
e 0 f 3 g 8 h 6
i 4 j 1 k 5 l 4

Ch 6 Exercise 2 (page 64)

1/4. Finding right angles
5. a yes b yes c no
d no e yes f no
6. a 4 b 1 c 3
7. 16
8. Tracing shapes with right angles

9. a 2 b 2 c 2
10. Drawing angles

Answers to Ch 7 (page 68)

Ch 7 Exercise 1 (page 68)

1. a 32 b 23 c 75 d 56
e 84 f 40 g 31 h 40
2. a 21 b 36 c 44 d 54
e 64 f 72 g 80 h 91
i 11 j 43 k 50 l 72
3. 22
4. 31
5. 43p
6. 50
7. 72
8. 61

Ch 7 Exercise 2 (page 70)

1. a 31 b 44 c 61 d 32
e 24 f 62 g 24 h 26
i 13 j 52 k 38 l 70
2. a 7 b 45 c 22 d 45
e 41 f 68 g 61 h 6
i 22 j 66 k 82 l 0
3. 26
4. 25
5. 44
6. 71
7. 45
8. 35
9. 30

Ch 7 Exercise 3 (page 72)

1. a 121 b 242 c 180 d 203
e 302 f 151 g 375 h 174
i 532 j 347 k 500 l 76
2. a 111 b 751 c 1 d 163
e 204 f 304 g 142 h 200
i 312 j 21 k 351 l 315
m 272 n 614 o 200 p 333
3. 171
4. 310
5. £773
6. 161
7. 357
8. £104

Answers to Ch 8 (page 75)

Ch 8 Exercise 1 (page 75)

1. a 10 b 20 c 5
d 10 e 10 f 25
2. a 9 b 87
3. a 5 b 23
4. a 3 b 19
5. a 8 b 10
6. 2
7. a 5 b 10 c 20 d 50
8. a 20p 5p b 50p 20p 10p
c 50p 5p 2p d 50p 20p 5p 1p
e 20p 20p 5p 2p 1p
f 50p 20p 20p 5p 2p 2p
9. various

Ch 8 Exercise 2 (page 78)

1. a 65p
b 90p
2. a 98p
b 34p
3. a £1.00
b 90p
c 10p
4. 15p
5. no (only have 92p)
6. a 33p b 20p 10p 2p 1p

Answers to Ch 9 (page 81)

Ch 9 Exercise 1 (page 81)

1. a 39 b 23 c 59 d 37
e 19 f 69 g 83 h 49
i 39 j 76 k 49 l 81
2. a 39 b 78 c 58 d 28
e 68 f 44 g 68 h 85
3. 46
4. 67
5. 51
6. 17
7. 88
8. 73

Ch 9 Exercise 2 (page 83)

1. a 25 b 23 c 39 d 17
e 38 f 19 g 24 h 19
i 79 j 46 k 65 l 41
2. a 48 b 36 c 16 d 18
e 59 f 32 g 48 h 9
3. 8
4. 16
5. a Val b 24
6. 34
7. 47
8. £55

Ch 9 Exercise 3 (page 85)

1. a 179 b 273 c 435 d 464
e 469 f 79 g 144 h 336
i 313 j 297 k 798 l 734
2. a 287 b 264 c 326 d 115
e 198 f 66 g 84 h 48
i 436 j 392 k 844 l 766
3. £188
4. £456
5. 315 ml
6. 482
7. 445
8. 28

Ch 9 Exercise 4 (page 87)

1. a 77 b 116 c 46 d 612
e 45 f 565 g 356 h 485
2. a 47 b 46 c 275 d 577
3. 17
4. 28
5. £118
6. £156

Ch 9 Exercise 5 (page 88)

1. a 44 b 525
2. a 9 b 18 c 6 d 56
e 84 f 49 g 358 h 16
i 498 j 278 k 150 l 225
3. 36 4. 186

Answers to Ch 10 (page 90)

Ch 10 Exercise 1 (page 90)

1. a £0·95 b £0·36
c £0·20 d £0·13
e £0·99 f £0·10
g £0·80 h £1.00
2. a 45p b 72p c 80p d 21p
e 50p f 75p g 100p h 4p
3. a 71p, £0·71 b 22p, £0·22
c 60p, £0·60 d 30p, £0·30

Ch 10 Exercise 2 (page 91)

1. a £0·49 b £0·78 c £0·78
d £0·71 e £0·92 f £0·92
g £0·80 h £0·80 i £1·00
j £0·86 k £1·00 l £0·98
m £0·79 n £0·84 o £0·71
p £0·99 q £1·10 r £1·20
2. a £0·22 b £0·15 c £0·30
d £0·22 e £0·12 f £0·10
g £0·30 h £0·15 i £0·17
j £0·18 k £1·00 l £0·09
m £0·52 n £0·27 o £0·24
3. a £0·99 b £0·91
c £0·52 d £0·72

a £0·02 b £0·25 c £0·34
d £0·19 e £0·32 f £0·86
g yes h yes i £0·05
j £0·19 k 7 l £2·17

10 Exercise 3 (page 94)

a £4·60 b £4·46 c £4·71
d £3·08 e £5·01 f £3·34
a £3·46 b £2·97 c £5·00
d £2·22 e £1·12 f £0·09
g £3·30 h £2·15 i £4·73
j £0·18 k £5·54 l £4·09
m £3·52 n £6·63 o £2·24
a £4·51 b £4·30 c £0·92

10 Exercise 4 (page 96)

a £8·65 b £8·88
a £5·46 b £8·98 c £10·00
d £3·22 e £3·12 f £2·55
g £9·33 h £2·15 i £8·23
j £2·08 k £9·54 l £0·29
m £2·04 n £6·39 o £4·14
Total cost £5·14 + £2·20 = £7·34
He does NOT have enough money

Answers to Ch 11 (page 98)

11 Exercise 1 (page 99)

a Monday, Tuesday, Wednesday, Thursday, Friday, Saturday Sunday
b January, February, March, April, May, June, July, August, September, October, November, December
c Spring, Summer, Autumn, Winter,
a Tuesday, Wednesday Friday Saturday
b May, June, August, September
c Summer, Autumn, Spring Summer, Winter
a Friday b May
c Summer
a 7.45 b 2.30 c 12.15
a Sunday b August

11 Exercise 2 (page 100)

a 10 minutes past 4
b 5 minutes to 6
c quarter to 11
d 10 minutes past 11
e 5 minutes to 2
f 20 minutes past 7
g 25 minutes past 9
h 5 minutes past 7
i 20 minutes to 4
j 10 minutes to 8
k quarter past 10
l quarter to 12
m half past 3
n 25 minutes to 1
o 8 o'clock
p 20 minutes past 3
q 10 minutes to 5
r 10 minutes past 6

2. See pupils' work
3. a 7.25 or twenty five past seven
   b 10.05 or five past ten
   c 5.40 or twenty to six
   d 8.45 or quarter to nine
   e 9.40 or twenty to ten
   f 6.55 or five to seven
   g 6.05 or five past six
   h 5.25 or twenty five past five
   i 11.55 or five to twelve

Answers to Ch 12 (page 104)

Ch 12 Exercise 1 (page 105)

1. a 4 b 6 c 8
   d 10 e 12 f 14
   g 16 h 18 i 20
2. Learn 2 times table
3. a 2 b 4 c 6
   d 9 e 0 f 7
   g 8 h 5 i 10
4. a 8 b 14 c 16

Ch 12 Exercise 2 (page 106)

1. a 24 b 52 c 68
   d 112 e 150 f 174
   g 98 h 106 i 56
2. a 28 b 90 c 72
   d 108 e 160 f 134
   g 158 h 166 i 196
3. 86
4. 116 kg
5. £1·50
6. 72
7. 52
8. a 36 b 66 c 92
   d 130 e 156 f 194

Ch 12 Exercise 3 (page 109)

1. a 6 b 9 c 12
   d 15 e 18 f 21
   g 24 h 27 i 30
2. Learn 3 times table
3. a 3 b 6 c 7
   d 5 e 8 f 10
   g 9 h 4 i 0
4. a 15 b 27 c 21

Ch 12 Exercise 4 (page 110)

1. a 42 b 75 c 93
   d 276 e 219 f 138
   g 171 h 267 i 147
2. a 51 b 39 c 75
   d 117 e 174 f 201
   g 132 h 240 i 288
3. a 75 b 210p c 141
4. a 26 b 69 c 82
   d 126 e 172 f 135
   g 116 h 291 i 138
5. 138
6. 261
7. £234

Answers to Ch 13 (page 113)

Ch 13 Exercise 1 (page 113)

1. rectangle
2. triangle
3. square
4. circle
5. a 5 b 5 c 5
   d 5 + 1 e 3 f 2
6. a square b circle
   c triangle d rectangle
   e triangle f square
   g circle h rectangle
7. a 5 b 3 c 5
   d 4 e 2

Ch 13 Exercise 2 (page 115)

1. See drawing
2. See drawing
3. all 4 sides same length in square
4. See drawing
5. a 1 b 0 c 0
6. a 4 b 4 c 4
7. a 4 b 4 c 4
8. a 3 b 3 c 3
9. a 5 b 5 c 5
   d pentagon
10. a 6 b 6 c 6
    d hexagon
11. a 5 b 5 c 5
12. a 8 b 8 c 8
13. a B, C, E b A c F
    d H e D f G
    It is called a semicircle.

14.

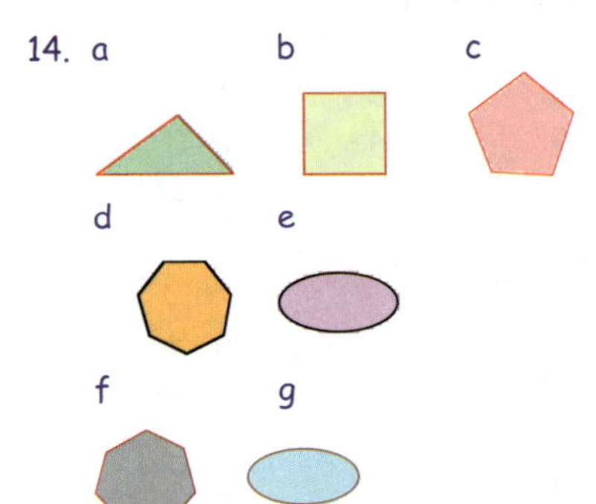

15. a octagon   b nonagon
c decagon   d dodecagon

Answers to Ch 14 (page 120)

Ch 14 Exercise 1 (page 120)

12. a/b practical work
c 4   d 8 divided by 2 = 4
2. a/b practical work
c 5   d 10 divided by 2 = 5
3. a/b practical work
c 6   d 12 divided by 2 = 6
4. a practical b 14 divided by 2 = 7
5. a practical b 8, 9, 10

Ch 14 Exercise 2 (page 122)

1. a 2   b 4   c 3
d   e 5   f 7
g 9   h 8   i
2. a 6   b 12   c 18
d 16   e 14   f 20
3. a 4   b 6   c 7
d 3   e 10

Ch 14 Exercise 3 (page 123)

1. a 13   b 23   c 11   d 22
e 31   f 34   g 42   h 41
i 32   j 44   k 21   l 14
2. a 23   b 40
3. a 13   b 14
4. a 21   b 32
5. a 15   b 20

Ch 14 Exercise 4 (page 126)

1. a/b practical work
c 4   d 12 divided by 3 = 4
2. a/b practical work
c 15 divided by 3 = 5
3. a/b practical work
c 18 divided by 3 = 6
4. a practical b 21 divided by 3 = 7
5. a practical b 8, 9, 10

Ch 14 Exercise 5 (page 127)

1. a 3   b   c 5
d 4   e 6   f 8
g 7   h 9   i 10
2. a 21   b 9   c 18
d 15   e 24   f 30
3. a 2   b 9   c 6
d 4   e 10
4. a 13   b 22   c 10
d 23   e 14   f 12
g 30   h 30   i 43
j 31   k 32   l 33
5. a 12   b 33   c 23
d 30 cm   e 13

Answers to Ch 15 (page 130)

Ch 15 Exercise 1 (page 130)

1. a 5   b 4   c 4
d 3   e 8   f 9
g 3   h 0   i 7
j 11   k 9   l 9
2. a 1   b 4   c 3
d 2   e 0   f 6
g 5   h 9   i 9
j 8   k 12   l 10
m 16   n 5   o 7

Ch 15 Exercise 2 (page 131)

1. a 5   b 5   c 9
d 3   e 6   f 7
g 4   h 12   i 9
j 12   k 14   l 15
m 14   n 16   o 20
2. a 5   b 10   c 8
d 5   e 7   f 3
g 12   h 8   i 7
j 6   k 19   l 9

Ch 15 Exercise 3 (page 132)

1. a 4   b 5   c 10
d 10   e 18   f 18
g 9   h 8   i 30
j 14   k 12   l 4
2. a 2   b 10   c 9
d 2   e 3   f 3
g 3   h 7   i 7
j 15   k 20   l 9

Ch 15 Exercise 4 (page 133)

1. a +   b -   c x
d ÷   e x   f -
g ÷   h +   i ÷
2. a -   b +   c x
d ÷   e -   f +
g x   h -   i ÷
j +   k x   l -

Answers to Ch 16 (page 135)

Ch 16 Exercise 1 (page 135)

1. See pupils' work
2. a yes   b yes   c no
3. a A yes   b B yes   c C yes
d D no   e E yes   f F no
4. a no   b 5   c 1
5. a no   b 2
6. a no   b 2
7. 6
8. 7
9. 8

Ch 16 Exercise 2 (page 138)

1. See pupils' work
2. yes
3. no
4. yes
5. A, B, C and D
6. $\frac{1}{4}$
7. a no   b Nick   c Wei
8. a no   b D   c C
9. a $\frac{1}{4}$ b $\frac{1}{2}$
10. a $\frac{1}{4}$ b $\frac{1}{2}$

Ch 16 Exercise 3 (page 141)

1. a 6   b 3
2. a 10   b 5
3. a 8   b 4
4. a 3   b 7
c 20   d 50
5. a 2   b 3
c 10   d 25

Answers to Ch 17 (page 143)

Ch 17 Exercise 1 (page 143)

1. a-f various
2. a various b inches, feet, yards, chains, furlongs,
3. Peoples' hands, paces and cubits vary in size.

Ch 17 Exercise 2 (page 144)

1. a 7 cm   b 12 cm   c 3 cm
d 9 cm   e 15 cm   f 14 cm

a 13 cm b 8 cm c 11 cm
d 4 cm e 15 cm f 6 cm
a 5 cm b 4 cm c 2 cm
d 8 cm e 10 cm f 14 cm
a 20 cm b 30 cm
c 5 cm d 50 cm (all approx)
See pupils' measurements
See pupils' drawings
a 3 cm by 3 cm
b 7 cm by 4 cm
c 16 cm by 2 cm
See pupils' drawings
See pupils' drawings
. a 2 b 1 c 2
d 1 e 2
. a yellow 10 cm, red 13 cm
green 11 cm, blue 9 cm
b red c blue

17 Exercise 3 (page 148)

various
See pupils' measurements
See pupils' measurements
practical
various
See pupils' measurements
a 100 cm b 500 cm c 800 cm
d 300 cm e 900 cm f 700 cm
g 600 cm h 1000 cm i 400 cm
j 50 cm k 25 cm l 150 cm
a 4 m b 8 m c 2 m
d 5 m e 7 m f 9 m
g 25 m h 10 m

nswers to Ch 18 (page 151)

18 Exercise 1 (page 151)

a 2 r 1 b 4 r 1 c 3 r 1
d 5 r 1 e 7 r 1 f 6 r 1
g 8 r 1 h 9 r 1
a 10 r 1 b 24 r 1 c 33 r1
d 42 r 1 e 13 r 1 f 30 r1
g 21 r 1 h 44 r 1
12 and 1 left over
20 and 1 left over
33 and 1 left over
41 and 1 left over
23 and 1 left over

18 Exercise 2 (page 153)

a 17 b 35 c 38
d 49 e 19 f 45
g 36 h 27
a 25 b 16

3. 37
4. 48
5. a 18 r 1 b 29 r 1 c 45 r 1
   d 36 r 1 e 8 r 1 f 16 r 1
   g 27 r 1 h 49 r 1
6. 19 and 1 left over
7. 28 and 1 left over
8. a 8 b 14 c 22 r 1
   d 48 r 1 e 25 r 1 f 42
   g 13 r 1 h 46 r 1
9. 43 with 1 left over
10. 11 with 1 on his own.

Ch 18 Exercise 3 (page 156)

1. a 3 r 2 b 5 r 1 c 6 r 2
   d 2 r 1 e 4 r 2 f 6 r 1
   g 7 r 1 h 8 r 1 i 9 r 2
2. a 10 r 2 b 11 r 1 c 20 r 1
   d 11 r 2 e 22 r 1 f 20 r 2
   g 31 r 1 h 15 r 2 i 24 r 1
   j 27 r 2 k 29 r 1 l 30 r 2
3. a 5 with 2 left over
   b 22 with 2 left over
   c £16 with 1 coin left over
   d 24 with 2 left over
4. a 9 b 12 c 14
   d 16 e 17 f 19
   g 24 h 26 i 28
   j 29 k 31 l 34
5. a 18 b 27
   c 6 d 24
6. a 14 r 1 b 17 r 2 c 6 r 2
   d 3 r 1 e 5 r 2 f 9 r 2
   g 15 r 1 h 24 r 1 i 25 r 1
   j 29 r 1 k 32 r 2 l 34 r 1
7. a 25 with 2 left over
   b 7 with 2 left over
   c 17 windows with 1 left over
   d 4 in each group with 1 extra
   e 12 bags with 2 spare
   f 28 fish with 2 left over
8. a 13 r 1 b 17 c 14
   d 10 r 1 e 22 r 1 f 12 r 2
   g 20 h 15 i 19 r 2
   j 26 k 20 r 1 l 31 r 1
   m 22 r 1 n 34 r 1 o 27
   p 38
9. 13 with 1 ml left over
10. 25 ropes with 1 metre left over
11. 20 minutes
12. a £39 b 33p

Answers to Ch 19 (page 161)

Ch 19 Exercise 1 (page 161)

1. a 4 b 7 c 5
   d 1 e 36
2. a 8·00 b 7·00 c half hr
3. a 19 b 21
   c Gerry - 62, Tanya - 61, 1 more
4. a £6 b £8
   c Tom saved £5 more
5. a £6 b £10 c £45
6. a Donna b Bhoona
   c Dave - Onion, Donna - Chapati
7. a 14 b 17, 22, 21
   c 31 d 80 (Sat/Sunday)
8. a 1.30 b Swimming Pool
   c Bingo
9. a Duty Call
   b B Team
   c Luv Me 2
   d Glasgow 9.00 or Aberdeen 5.00
10. a £70 b £300
    c Blackpool for 4 nights.

Ch 19 Exercise 2 (page 165)

1. a 10 b 7 c 25
   d Friday - no-one brings lunch
2. a 2 b 6 c 7
   d 9 e 10
3. a Nov 14, Dec 12, Jan 5
   Feb 11, Mar 13
   b Nov c Jan - Cold weather
   d 24
4. a 3 b 15
   c 22 d 13

Ch 19 Exercise 3 (page 167)

1. a 1 b 6 c 5
   d 4 e cinema f ice-rink
   g 5 h 19 i 13
2. a 5 b 3 c 7
   d 0 e Duty Calls f 19
3. a Bacon - 4, Cheese - 3, Plain - 7
   Vinegar - 2, Pickle - 6
   b Plain c Vinegar d 2
   e 5 f 22
4. a 6 b 5
   c Freezers - 14 d 4
5. a 4's b Cup Cake c 20
   d 6 e 12
   f 30 g 6
6. a 10 b 17
   c Holiday - 22 chose that
   d 4 e 57
7. a 4 b 22 c 7
   d 5 e 60

Answers to Ch 20 (page 173)

Ch 20 Exercise 1 (page 173)

1. red circle
2. yellow star
3. blue triangle
4. 9 5. 9
6. 3 7. 2
8. 7 9. the car
10. the bike 11. the bike
12. a the village b the ship

Ch 20 Exercise 2 (page 175)

1. move 5 slabs forward, turn left, move 3 slabs forward, turn right, move 4 slabs forward.
2. a move 2 slabs forward, turn left, move 1 slab forward, turn right, move 2 slabs forward, turn left, move 2 slabs forward, turn right, move 3 slabs forward
   b move 3 slabs forward, turn left, move 1 slab forward, turn right, move 2 slabs forward, turn left, move 1 slab forward, turn right, move 2 slabs forward
3. move 3 slabs forward, turn right, move 1 slab forward, turn left, move 4 slabs forward.
4. a move 3 slabs forward, turn right, move 1 slab forward, turn left, move 1 slab forward, turn right, move 2 slabs forward, turn left, move 3 slabs forwards
   b move 3 slabs forward, turn left, move 3 slabs forward, turn right, move 2 slabs forward, turn right, move 2 slabs foward turn left, move 2 slabs forwards
   c move 3 slabs forward, turn left, move 1 slab forward, turn right, move 2 slabs forward, turn right, move 3 slabs foward turn left, move 2 slabs forwards, turn left, move 1 slab forwards, turn right, move 1 slab forwards
   d move 3 slabs forward, turn left, move 4 slabs forward, turn right, move 2 slabs forward, turn right, move 2 slabs foward turn left, move 1 slab forward, turn right, move 2 slabs forwards, turn left, move 2 slabs forward, turn left, move 5 slabs forwards, turn right, move 2 slabs forwards.
5. Drive along Figgs Road. Take the 1st on the right onto Law Road. Law Farm at end of this road.
6. Drive along Figgs Road. Take the 2nd on the left and Lake Arta is at end of this road.
7. Drive along Figgs Road. Take the 1st left onto West Road. Drive along West road and take 2nd left. Creaf is on this road.
8. Drive along Figgs Road till you come to Heally. Turn left along North Way. Take the 1st on the left. Creely Airport is at end of this road.
9. Drive along Figgs Road. Take the 1st on the right onto Figgs Road. Take the 1st right and the Lighthouse is at end of this road.
10. Drive along Bradds road to the end. Turn right onto Figgs Road. Drive along Figgs Road to Heally. Turn right onto North Way. Take 1st left. Chury is at end of this road.
11. a Come out of Rab's house. Turn right. Take the 2nd right onto Dye Avenue. The post office is the 3rd block on the left .
    b Come out of Gill's house and turn right. Take the 2nd on the left onto Raw Road. Then take the 3rd right into Millar Street. Fire Station is on her right.
    c Come out of Police Station. Turn left. Take the 2nd on the left onto Cawley Road. Take 1st on the right onto Raw Road. Park is 1st on the left.
    d Come out school and turn right. Take the 2nd left to Cawley Road. Sweet shop is 2nd block on the right.

Answers to Ch 21 (page 180)

Ch 21 Exercise 1 (page 180)

1. yes
2. a yes b no c yes d no
   e no f yes g no h no
3. yes - 6 each
4. a no b £5
5. a a third b 8

Ch 21 Exercise 2 (page 182)

1. $\frac{1}{6}$
2. a $\frac{1}{2}$ b $\frac{1}{3}$ c $\frac{1}{4}$ d $\frac{1}{5}$
   d $\frac{1}{6}$ e $\frac{1}{7}$ f $\frac{1}{8}$ g $\frac{1}{9}$
3. a $\frac{1}{3}$ b $\frac{1}{6}$ c $\frac{1}{8}$ d $\frac{1}{10}$
   e $\frac{1}{4}$ f $\frac{1}{9}$ g $\frac{1}{3}$ h $\frac{1}{8}$
   i $\frac{1}{6}$ j $\frac{1}{7}$ k $\frac{1}{5}$ l $\frac{1}{14}$
4. a 100 b $\frac{1}{100}$
5. a $\frac{1}{6}$
6. £5
7. a 10 b 10
8. a 4 b 8
9. Jake. $\frac{1}{3}$ bigger than $\frac{1}{4}$ or $\frac{1}{5}$
10. 18

Answers to Ch 22 (page 186)

Ch 22 Exercise 1 (page 186)

1. a bush b dog c chair
   d balloon e chair f shed
   g pillow h car i chip
   j carrot
2. a football b cat c trolley
   d bowling e train f street
   g bath h bag i boots
   j calculator
3. Frog, Dog, Goat, Bull
4. Desk, Chair, Book, Pencil
5. a pineapple b lemon
   c grapes d watermelon
6. a mushroom b red apple
7. left side
8. They weigh the same

Ch 22 Exercise 2 (page 189)

1. a teapot b pram
   c girl d motorbike
2. a 8 kg, 4kg, 3kg,
   b 14kg, 11kg, 10kg, 9kg,
   c 20kg, 8kg, 6kg, 1kg
   d 31kg, 30kg, 27kg, 23kg
   e 211kg, 147kg, 131kg
   f 1000kg, 201kg, 130kg, 99kg
3. a various

b various

various

2

a 2 kg b 3 kg c $1\frac{1}{2}$ kg d 4 kg

various

22 Exercise 3 (page 191)

a 5 kg	b 3 kg	c 6 kg
d 53 kg	e 14 kg	f 41 kg
a 19 kg	b 67 kg	c 9 kg
d 80 kg	e 44 kg	f 61 kg
g 50 kg	h 33 kg	i $23\frac{1}{2}$ kg
a 2 kg	b 8 kg	c $1\frac{1}{2}$ kg
d 25 kg	e 17 kg	f 77 kg

nswers to Ch 23 (page 194)

23 Exercise 1 (page 194)

a b

c d

a b

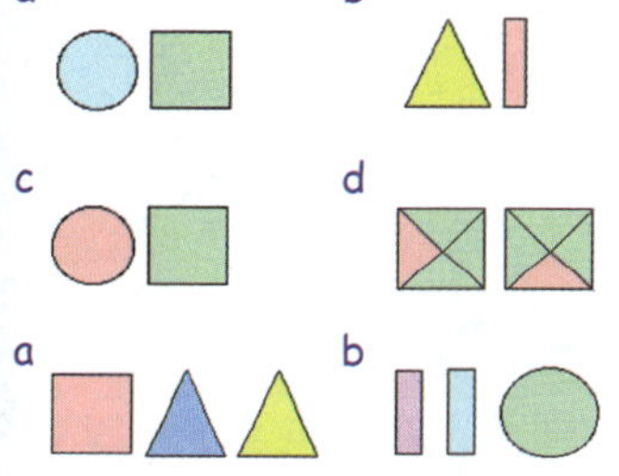

c 4 squares then 5 then 6.

d

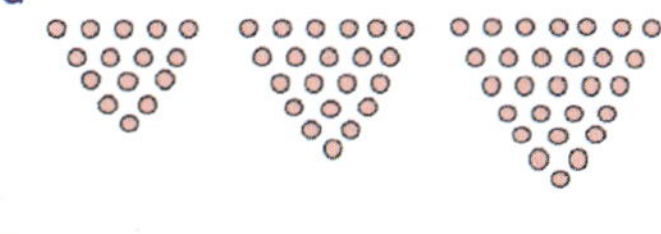

e

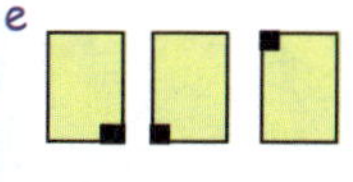

f

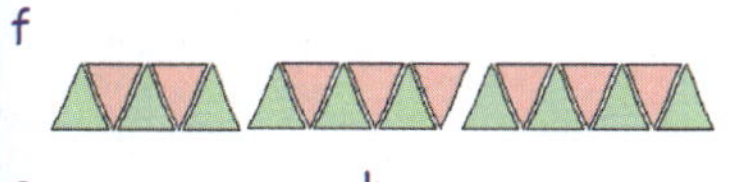

g h

23 Exercise 2 (page 196)

a b c d e f g h i j k l m n o p q
r s t u v w x y z

a s, t b I, J c G, F d n, p
e m, l f T, W g kl, mn h ev, fu
a P, Q, R, S, T, U
b q, p, o, n, m, l, k
c J, K, L, M, N, O, P
d L, N, P, R, T, V, X
various

Ch 23 Exercise 3 (page 197)

1. a 8, 9 b 22, 23
   c 23, 22 d 12, 14
   e 24, 28 f 20, 15
   g 40, 30 h 12, 9
2. a 10, 15, 20, 25, 30, 35
   b 5, 7, 9, 11, 13, 15, 17
   c 90, 80, 70, 60, 50, 40
   d 6, 9, 12, 15, 18, 21, 24
   e 28, 24, 20, 16, 12, 8
   f 11, 22, 33, 44, 55, 66
   g 31, 29, 27, 25, 23, 21
   h 42, 47, 52, 57, 62, 67
   i 12, 23, 45, 56, 67
   j 0, 50, 100, 150, 200, 250, 300

Answers to Ch 24 (page 199)

Ch 24 Exercise 1 (page 199)

1. a cube b cylinder c sphere
   d cuboid e cone f prism
3. square pyramid
4. a pyramid b cube c cone
   d cuboid e sphere f cylinder
   g cone h prism
4. a cuboid and triangular prism
   b cone and hemisphere
   c cone and cylinder
   d cylinder, cone and hemisphere
   e cuboid, cube and cylinder
   f pyramid and cube
   g cuboid, cube, cone and pyramid
   h 3 cylinders and a sphere
   i cylinder with cylinder hole cut out along with 4 small spheres
   j 4 cylinders, cuboid and prism

Ch 24 Exercise 2 (page 202)

1. 6 rectangles
2. 4 rectangles and 2 squares
3. a 4 triangles and a square
   b 3 rectangles and two triangles
4. a cube b cuboid
   c prism d pyramid
   e cone f cylinder
5. a 12 b 8
6. a 12 b 8
7. a 8 b 5
8. a 9 b 6
9. 2 circles and a rectangle

Answers to Ch 25 (page 205)

Ch 25 Exercise 1 (page 205)

1. a 1 cod, 1 haddock, 1 place less

c

d

e

6.30
7.00
7.30
8.00
8.30

f

20's
30's
40's
50's
60's

2. See Worksheets

Ch 25 Exercise 2 (page 209)

1. a 4 b 5 c 1
   d blue e 2 f 2
   g 8 h 15
2. a 3, 6, 1, 2, 4 b 16
3. a

IIIII	5
I	1
IIIIIIII	8
IIIIIII	7
IIII	4
III	3

   b Perth* c 4*
4. a

Yellow	I I I	3
Red	I I I I I	5
Black	I I I I I I	6
Blue	I I I I	4
Pink	I I	2

   b black c 20 d 14
5. a III b II c IIIII d IIIIII
   e IIIIIIII f IIIIIIIII g IIIIIIIIIII h IIIIIIIIIIIIIII
6. a 8 b 12 c 19
   d 26 e 37
7. a 𝍸 b 𝍸 II
   c 𝍸 𝍸 d 𝍸 𝍸 𝍸
   e 𝍸 𝍸 𝍸 II f 𝍸 𝍸 𝍸 𝍸
   g 𝍸 𝍸 𝍸 𝍸 𝍸 I
8.

Rose	𝍸	5
Pansy	𝍸 II	7
Tulip	𝍸 𝍸	10
Marigold	II	2
Daffodil	𝍸 I	6

9. a

Bus	𝍸	5
Plane	𝍸 II	7
Train	𝍸 𝍸 𝍸 I	16
Ferry	II	2

   b 16 c 5 d 30
10. a

Holton	𝍸	5
Durie's	𝍸 II	7
Melliot	IIII	4
Tower	𝍸 II	7
Rutz	𝍸 𝍸 I	11
Lochview	II	2

   b Rutz c 5 d 36
   e See pupils' drawings

* As of mid-2012, her majesty, the Queen, granted Perth city status !!!!